Sustainable Supply Chains 2.0

Blanka Tundys • Grażyna Kędzia
Tomasz Wiśniewski • Magdalena Zioło

Sustainable Supply Chains 2.0

Towards Environmental, Social, and Economic Resilience

palgrave
macmillan

Blanka Tundys
Institute of of Management
University of Szczecin
Szczecin, Poland

Grażyna Kędzia
Faculty of Management
University of Łódź
Łódź, Poland

Tomasz Wiśniewski
Institute of Management
University of Szczecin
Szczecin, Poland

Magdalena Zioło
Institute of Economics and Finance
University of Szczecin
Szczecin, Poland

ISBN 978-3-031-50336-8 ISBN 978-3-031-50337-5 (eBook)
https://doi.org/10.1007/978-3-031-50337-5

This Palgrave Macmillan imprint is published by the registered company Springer Nature Switzerland AG.
The registered company address is: Gewerbestrasse 11, 6330 Cham, Switzerland

Paper in this product is recyclable.

Introduction

In contemporary business it is important not only to create and implement a sustainable supply chain strategy but to create such models and solutions that will use mechanisms that build the resilience of the chain in the context of environmental, social, and economic risks and will respond to unknown (the COVID-19 pandemic) or unexpected (the war in Ukraine) threats. New categories of threats and risks are forcing managers to undertake new and innovative activities and actions in implementing supply chain management concepts. Many studies present the idea of the supply chain, sustainable chain, and its strategy in the context of risk mitigation, but no study provides guidance on how to build resilient supply chains that implement the principles of sustainable development. The scientific considerations lack an approach that includes modelling aspects in this area. Thus, the aim of the considerations in this publication is to describe the new concept together with the design of the basis for building new sustainable supply chains 2.0. For the mentioned strategies they have a different meaning and different impact, but at the same time, they are a common element that constitutes the basis for the development of a new generation of supply chains. This book aims to present a methodological approach to configuring sustainable and at the same time resilient supply chains, considering: environmental, social, and economic aspects. Building resilience in the context of 3BL while preserving the assumptions and principles of building sustainable chains is not simple. The main contribution of the book is to establish the priorities and constituent determinants of resilience in the process of building a sustainable supply chain strategy, which influences decision-making relating to the choice or reconfiguration of supply chain strategies. Building environmental, social, and economic resilience in light of sustainable supply chain goals and objectives is still little recognized in the literature.

In this book we've identified environmental, social, and economic issues not only as the basis for configuring a sustainable supply chain but also as important determinants of supply chain resilience. Resilience is therefore becoming part of a sustainable supply chain strategy. Feedback is identified between achieving integrated sustainability goals and enhancing supply chain resilience to disruptions originating from environmental and social sources as well as economic sectors. Risk and resilience capabilities, which hitherto modern business has not had to deal with, play a major role in this respect. Business was aware of them as a potential, but not present threat (we are talking about the COVID-19 pandemic and the war in Ukraine—both situations have had a significant impact on the creation and management of supply chains, also in the context of balancing them and building as much resilience as possible in the face of challenges related to on the one hand—business continuity costs and on the other hand—sustainability costs).

This triad of factors are bonding elements, influencing and determining the implementation of a sustainable supply chain strategy as well as a resilient supply chain strategy.

This book covers key topics related to supply chains (especially in the context of challenges faced by currently operating chains), which may include the aspects of sustainable development, resilience, and supply chain risk; resilient practices; and strategies supporting a sustainable supply chain: green, socially responsible, R-strategies, closed-loop supply chain). The discussion is enriched by the financial aspect (the role of financial markets in strengthening the resilience of sustainable supply chains) and the results of empirical research. Based on considerations and empirical research, the authors created a model of a sustainable and resilient supply chain, whose basic determinants are ecological, social, and economic aspects, addressing contemporary challenges and risks and interacting and striving to build the highest possible resilience to threats and the greatest possible sustainability of processes in the chain.

The research aim was to explore the dependencies, relationships* and determinants that contribute to the resilience of sustainable supply chains, as well as to identify factors that reduce it and increase vulnerability to risk. The outcome is the presentation of a new paradigm for supply chain strategy that has not been operating in this way to date, namely the resilient and sustainable supply chain model. The uncertain environment, and the impact of hitherto unknown risk factors on the activities of chains, on the one hand, and economic and developmental trends related to sustainable development, on the other, require new solutions to be proposed in order to more effectively implement and manage chain strategies at the same time. We need to develop a theoretical basis and create a new paradigm for the management of sustainable supply chains, considering the different types of risks present in this field. To date, researchers have only addressed the sub-individual aspects and elements of risk affecting the resilience of chains (especially sustainable chains). The authors' approach is novel and innovative, as it addresses both triple bottom line (3BL) and environmental, social, and governance (ESG) aspects, combining knowledge on risks that have so far not influenced business strategies (COVID-19 and the war in Ukraine). The book proposes solutions and mechanisms to make sustainable supply chains more resilient to identified threats and risks. We base our considerations not only on the literature and theory, but also on the research carried out and dedicated to the specific topic indicated. Building SSC 2.0 is not an easy challenge, as the literature and empirical studies have shown, and there are still many areas and activities to be investigated in order to make sustainable and resilient supply chains the dominant chain strategy in today's world.

The authors dedicate the considerations to supply chain managers, economic practitioners, business people in general, academics, students, and researchers in management, economics, and logistics, but also in environmental management or sustainable development. The project is financed within the framework of the program of the Minister of Science and Higher Education under the name "Regional Excellence Initiative" in the years 2019–2022; project number 001/RID/2018/19; the amount of financing PLN 10,684,000.00

The author, July 2023

Contents

1	**Environmental, Social, and Governance (ESG) Risk as a Challenge for Business**	1
	1.1 EU Taxonomy and ESG Risk: The Typology, Definitions, Discussion	1
	1.2 Influence of ESG Risk on the Business and Supply Chain Strategy	12
	1.3 Role and Challenges of Transport and Logistic Sectors in the Context of Dealing with ESG Risk	17
	References	20
2	**Sustainable Supply Chain: A New Paradigm for Supply Chain Strategy**	25
	2.1 Triple Bottom Line (3BL) as a Component of a Sustainable Supply Chain	25
	2.2 Environmental, Economic, Social, and Institutional–Political Governance as a Factor Supporting the Implementation of the Sustainable Supply Chain Concept	35

2.3 Construction and Framework of a Sustainable Supply Chain: Supporting Strategies 40
2.3.1 Green Supply Chain 42
2.3.2 Social Supply Chains 43
2.3.3 R-Strategies 46
2.3.4 Closed-Loop Supply Chains 47
2.4 Sustainable Supply Chains 49
2.4.1 Barriers 54
2.4.2 Drivers 56
2.4.3 Benefits 58
2.4.4 Challenges 59
2.4.5 Principles and Paradigms 59
2.4.6 Strategies and Concepts 60
2.4.7 Elements 61
2.4.8 Practices 62
References 63

3 Challenges for Resilient and Sustainable Supply Chains 85
3.1 Environmental, Social, and Economic Factors as Sources of Risk to Supply Chains 85
3.2 COVID-19 and War in Ukraine as a Part of Supply Chain Risk 101
3.3 Supply Chain Resilience 113
References 121

4 Modeling of Sustainable Supply Chain 2.0. (Framework) 137
4.1 Environmental, Social and Economic Resilience in Sustainable Supply Chain 137
4.2 The Role of Financial, Social and Governance Aspects in Strengthening a Sustainable Resilient Supply Chain 144
4.3 Analysis of the Research Data 147
4.3.1 Data Collection 152
4.3.2 Confirmatory Factor Analysis 157
4.3.3 Reliability Analysis 158

4.3.4 Structural Equation Modeling (SEM) 162
4.3.5 Model Evaluation 166
4.3.6 Structural Equation Modeling (SEM) with Groups (Company Size) 168
4.3.7 Conclusions and Futures Directions 171
References 172

Index 183

List of Figures

Fig. 1.1	ESG risk in supply chain. Source: own elaboration based on *Why ESG factors in the supply chain matter*, https://www.unpri.org/private-equity/managing-esg-risk-in-the-supply-chains-of-private-companies-and-assets/615.article (accessed: 22.06.2023)	13
Fig. 2.1	Sustainability links. Source: own elaborations	33
Fig. 2.2	PPP/Environment, Economy, Social (EES) in connection with supply chain organizations and customers. Source: own elaboration based on Sodhi and Tang (2021)	34
Fig. 2.3	Implementation of various concepts reflecting sustainability into the supply chain. Source: own elaborations	41
Fig. 2.4	Quantitative methods used in a sustainable supply chain—an analysis from the literature. Source: own elaborations	42
Fig. 2.5	Qualitative methods used in a sustainable supply chain—an analysis from the literature. Source: own elaborations	43
Fig. 2.6	Sustainable supply chain—concept. Source: own elaborations	53
Fig. 2.7	Sustainable supply chain—elements and concepts	53
Fig. 2.8	Sustainable supply chain—elements (part 2)	54
Fig. 2.9	Sustainable supply chain framework	55
Fig. 2.10	Framework of SSC on the basis of the literature. Source: own elaborations	56
Fig. 3.1	Various aspects of sustainable risk to supply chains. Source: own study	88

Fig. 3.2 Risk matrix. Source: own study 93
Fig. 3.3 Sustainable risk management process in the supply chain. Source: own study 96
Fig. 3.4 Externally driven supply chain disruptive factors in a volatility, uncertainty, complexity, ambiguity (VUCA) world. Source: own study 102
Fig. 3.5 COVID-19 pandemic uncertainty, increased risk and pressure on supply chains. Source: own study 104
Fig. 3.6 The ripple effect of war on the Ukraine on the global economy and supply chains. Source: own study 109
Fig. 3.7 Comprehensive understanding of SCRES in the literature. Source: own study 114
Fig. 4.1 Sustainable supply chain in the context of 3BL/ESG resilience. Source: own elaborations 139
Fig. 4.2 Diagram of an example structural equation model 149
Fig. 4.3 Theoretical research model 163
Fig. 4.4 The impact of sustainability supply chain on supply chain resilience—SEM model 167

List of Tables

Table 1.1	Environmental, social, and governance risk definitions	2
Table 1.2	Environmental risk in risk ranking (Top 5 risks Global Risks Report)	3
Table 1.3	Physical and transition environmental risk	4
Table 1.4	The most severe and impactful environmental and social risks in 2022	5
Table 1.5	ESG risk factors	6
Table 1.6	ESG regulations in selected countries/regions	7
Table 1.7	ESG risk factors	12
Table 1.8	Supply chains' impact on environment compared to direct operations	15
Table 2.1	3BL and PPP: A brief overview of the initiatives undertaken	29
Table 2.2	Social and environmental performance in supply chain	52
Table 4.1	Variables and parameters of the structural equation model	149
Table 4.2	Company profiles	153
Table 4.3	The set of variables included in the study	154
Table 4.4	Outer loadings with reliability indicators	159
Table 4.5	Values of Cronbach's alpha and AVE coefficients	161
Table 4.6	Values of squares of correlation coefficients (CS) between latent constructs	162

Table 4.7 Structural parameters of the analyzed structural model 165
Table 4.8 Fit statistics of the measurement model 167
Table 4.9 Structural parameters (only hypothesis) of the analyzed structural models 169

1

Environmental, Social, and Governance (ESG) Risk as a Challenge for Business

1.1 EU Taxonomy and ESG Risk: The Typology, Definitions, Discussion

ESG (environmental, social, and governance) risks affect businesses, which must take a number of adjustment measures to reduce the impacts of these risks. In response to the impacts of ESG risks, a number of companies take measures to adapt to ongoing changes determined by ESG factors. The activities undertaken are dominated by those that develop methods of including ESG risks in risk management systems and decision-making processes, as well as collecting and disclosing information on non-financial risks. Exposure to ESG risks is also taken into account in ratings and scoring systems (Table 1.1).

According to the European Environmental Agency (EEA), environmental risk is defined as the "likelihood, or probability, of injury, disease, or death resulting from exposure to a potential environmental hazard" (EEA, 2023). Environmental risks, which are worth emphasizing in the context of the interlinked nature of ESG risks, are types of risks related to health and property. The literature points out that environmental risks are understood not only as natural but also social problems and are related to social risks, especially health risks (Braubach & Fairburn, 2010). Social

B. Tundys et al., *Sustainable Supply Chains 2.0*,
https://doi.org/10.1007/978-3-031-50337-5_1

Table 1.1 Environmental, social, and governance risk definitions

Environmental risk	Social risk	Governance risk
The risks of any negative financial impact on the institution stemming from the current or prospective impacts of social factors on its counterparties or invested assets		
Environmental risks should be understood as the financial risks posed by an institution's exposures to counterparties or invested assets that may potentially be affected by or contribute to the negative impacts of environmental factors, such as climate change and other forms of environmental degradation (e.g., air pollution, water pollution, scarcity of fresh water, land contamination, biodiversity loss and deforestation), in addition to corrective policy actions aimed at addressing such factors	The risks of any negative financial impact on the institution stemming from the current or prospective impacts of social factors on its counterparties or invested assets	The risks of any negative financial impact on the institution stemming from the current or prospective impacts of governance factors on its counterparties or invested assets

Source: European Banking Authority (EBA), 2021, EBA Report on ESG risk management and supervision, https://www.eba.europa.eu/eba-publishes-its-report-management-and-supervision-esg-risks-credit-institutions-and-investment (accessed: 6.04.2023), pp. 3, 34, 47, 49

risks within the economy are defined in different ways, but a commonly used definition explains these phenomena as "the possibility for some potential threats to emerge and as a threat to the possibility of maintaining social relations and social cohesion as a result of negative events" (Lupu, 2019; Míka, 2009). Finally, "risk governance applies the

Table 1.2 Environmental risk in risk ranking (Top 5 risks Global Risks Report)

2010	2011	2012	2013	2014	2015	2016	2017	2018	2019	2020	2021	2022
E	En	E	E	S	G	S	En	En	En	En	En	En
E	En	E	E	En	En	En	S	En	En	En	En	En
S	G	En	En	E	G	En	En	T	En	En	En	En
E	En	T	S	En	G	G	G	T	T	En	S	S
G	En	S	S	T	E	En	T	En	T	En	En	S

Source: own elaboration based on https://www.statista.com/chart/20567/global-risks-considered-most-likely-wef/ (accessed: 30.12.2022) and *Global Risks Reports 2010–2022* (WEF) https://www.weforum.org/reports/global-risks-report-2022/digest (accessed: 30.12.2022)

aTypes of risks—E-economic (seven types of risks); S-social (ten types of risks); G-geopolitical (eight types of risks); T-technological (six types of risks); En-environmental (six types of risks)

principles of good governance to the identification, assessment, management and communication of risks[1]" (IRGC, 2023).

Currently, the problem of the impact of climate change on the economy has become more important due to the scale of the adverse phenomena determined by climate change.[2] Environmental risks dominate the top 10 risk rankings in terms of strength and impact on the contemporary economy (Global Risks Report, 2022) (Table 1.2.).

These types of risks affect almost all industries across the economy, and the five most threatened sectors are the fuel, metallurgy and mining, coal, refining and marketing, and chemical sectors (ESG risk 2021). The impacts of ESG risks on the economy manifest as two types of risk: so-called physical risks and transition (transformation) risks. According to Bua et al. (2022), physical risks include financial losses and occur in the form of increased costs from the impacts of chronic and acute physical events. Transition risks arise from costly adjustments toward a low-carbon economy. Some examples of physical and transition risks within the environmental scope are presented in Table 1.3.

[1] Risk governance is not included in the Global Risks Report rankings, which are dedicated to economic risks, environmental risks, geopolitical risks, societal risks, and technological risks.

[2] There are several examples of extreme phenomena, such as heat, droughts, floods, fires, and the extinction of plant and animal species, which have been confirmed by statistics, for example the extreme heat in Madrid in 2020 or the temperatures of -19C in Dallas, which had not been recorded for 72 years. See also The Global Risks Report, 2022, s. 8 https://www.weforum.org/reports/global-risks-report-2022 (accessed: 7.04.2023).

Table 1.3 Physical and transition environmental risk

Physical risk	*Types, examples*
Extreme weather events	Tropical cyclones/typhoons, floods, storms, heat waves, droughts, wildfires, hailstorms
Contamination of ecosystems	Soil pollution and degradation, air pollution, water pollution, marine pollution, accidents resulting in environmental pollution
Raising the water level	Prolonged sea level rise or sea wave action
Water shortage	Drought or insufficient water supply
Deforestation/ desertification	Deforestation leading to species extinction, climate change, desertification, and population displacement
Transition risk	*Types, examples*
Changing public policies	Energy transition policy, pollution control regulations, resource protection regulations
Technological changes	Raw material processing policy, drug control regulations, resource protection regulations
Changes in behavior and moods	Changes in consumer preferences for certain products, changes in investor sentiment for certain asset classes.
New business model	New ways of doing business (e.g., meetings that significantly reduce business travel; vertical farming (vertical farms) that challenges traditional farming)

Source: own elaboration based on *Overview of Environmental Risk Analysis by Financial Institutions*. Network for Greening the Financial System Technical document, Central Banks and Supervisors, September 2020, p. 5

According to the Global Risks Report, 2022, the 10 most severe risks on a global scale over the next 10 years are as follows:

- Five environmental risks (climate action, extreme weather, biodiversity loss, human environmental damage, and natural resource crises)
- Three social risks (social cohesion erosion, livelihood crises, and infectious diseases)
- One economic risk (debt crises)
- One geopolitical risk (geoeconomic confrontation) (Global Risks Report, 2022, p.14)

Table 1.4 presents a list of the environmental and social risks included in the 2022 Global Risks Report and Table 1.5 presents the key drivers of ESG risks.

Table 1.4 The most severe and impactful environmental and social risks in 2022

Environmental risk	Societal risk
Biodiversity loss and ecosystem collapse	Collapse or lack of social security systems
Climate action failure	Employment and livelihood crises
Extreme weather events	Erosion of social cohesion
Human-made environmental damage	Failure of public infrastructure
Major geophysical disasters	Infectious diseases
Natural resource crises	Large-scale involuntary migration
	Pervasive backlash against science
	Pollution-driven harms to human health
	Severe mental health deterioration
	Widespread youth disillusionment

Source: Global Risks Report, 2022 https://www.weforum.org/reports/global-risks-report-2022/ (accessed: 7.04.2023)

When discussing the concept of ESG risks, it is necessary to point out the differences between sustainable development risks and non-financial risks, which are sometimes indicated in the literature as synonyms of ESG risks. Regulation (EU) 2019/2088 of the European Parliament and of the Council of 27 November 2019 on sustainability-related disclosures in the financial services sector (Sustainable Finance Disclosure Regulation, SFDR) defines a sustainability risk (position 14 on the definitions list) as an "environmental, social or governance event or condition that, if it occurs, could cause a negative material impact on the value of the investment." Due to the similarities between the definitions of ESG risks and sustainability risks, some studies have pointed out that the term ESG risks refers to and is used by investors while sustainability risks apply to enterprises (GPW, 2021). In addition to ESG and sustainability risks, it is also worth paying attention to non-financial risks. Delegado pointed out that a "non-financial risk, whether related to misconduct, non-compliance, IT, reputational, cybersecurity or operational challenges, is not linked directly to financial decisions and has only a downside." In response to ESG risks and the need to reduce their negative impacts on the environment, many countries/regions (Table 1.6) have enacted ESG regulations.

Table 1.5 ESG risk factors

Risk	Risk factor
Environmental	Carbon intensity emissions, climate change, control of environmental impacts, eco-design (financial green products and services), eco efficiency, emissions, energy consumptions, environmental policy management, environmental reporting, environmental risk management, hazardous waste, materials recycled and reused, packaging, pollution management/ recourses, protection of biodiversity, raw material sourcing, renewable energy consumption, travel and transport impact, waste management reduction, water use and management, industry-specific criteria
Social	Business behavior, community relations, corporate citizenship/ philanthropy, customer relationship management, customer and product responsibility, diversity human capital development and training, human rights criteria, labor management, local suppliers, market ethics, non-discrimination, promotion equality, privacy and data security, protection of children, exclusion of child labor, quality of working condition, respect of trade unions, responsible investing, rights of indigenous people, social reporting, stakeholders engagement, supply chain management, talent attraction/retention, work—life balance, industry-specific criteria
Governance	Anti-takeover policy, audit and control system, board diversity, board structure, brand management, business ethics and fraud, codes of conduct/compliance, corporate government functions and commitments, prevention of corruption and bribery, remuneration of members of the executive team, respect of shareholders rights, risk and crisis management, transparency, vision and strategy, antitrust policy, industry-specific criteria

Source: M. Zioło, B. Z. Filipiak, B. Tundys: *Sustainability in Bank and Corporate Business.* Palgrave 2021; Escrig-Olmedo, E., Ángeles; Fernández-Izquierdo, M.; Ferrero-Ferrero, I.; Rivera-Lirio, J.M.; Muñoz-Torres M.J. (2019). Rating the Raters: Evaluating how ESG Rating Agencies Integrate Sustainability Principles, Sustainability, 11, 915, Ziolo, M.; Filipiak, B.Z.; Bąk, I.; Cheba, K. How to Design More Sustainable Financial Systems: The Roles of Environmental, Social, and Governance Factors in the Decision-Making Process. Sustainability 2019, 11, 5604

Table 1.6 ESG regulations in selected countries/regions

Country/region	Type of regulation
Europe	
European Union	Sustainable Finance Disclosure Regulation (SFDR); EU taxonomy Article 8; Corporate Sustainability Reporting Directive (CSRD);
United Kingdom	
	Sustainability Disclosure Requirements (SDR) and investment labels; diversity and inclusion on company boards and executive committees; climate-related disclosure requirements
America	
USA	Climate disclosure for public companies; climate—related financial risks and insurers;
Canada	
Chile	ESG—related investment disclosure for funds; climate-related disclosure for listed issuers;
Brazil	
	sustainability and corporate governance requirements in annual reports; management and disclosure of social, environmental, and climate risks
Asia-Pacific	
Australia	Prudential practice guidance on climate change financial risks
China	ESG-related amendments to the disclosure rules applicable to listed companies
Japan	
Hong Kong	Revisions of corporate governance code
New Zeeland	Green and sustainable finance strategy (climate-related disclosures)
Singapore	
South Korea	Mandatory task force for climate-related financial disclosures (TCFD) reporting
	Environmental risk management for assets managers, banks, insurers
	Mandatory ESG report disclosure

Source: own elaboration based on *Regulation at a Crossroads: Convergence or Fragmentation?* MSCI, https://www.msci.com/research-and-insights/2022-esg-trends-to-watch/regulation-at-crossroads-convergence-or-fragmentation (accessed: 10.10.2023)

The European Union (EU) enacted Regulation (EU) 2020/852 of the European Parliament and of the Council of 18 June 2020 on the establishment of a framework to facilitate sustainable investment and amended Regulation (EU) 2019/2088. The main goals of the EU taxonomy are as follows (EU Taxonomy Overview, 2023):

- The redirection of capital flows with a focus on sustainable investment
- The incorporation of sustainability as a component of risk management
- The support of long-term investment and economic activity

The taxonomy regulation also defines the three following groups of taxonomy users:

- Financial market participants offering financial products in the EU, including providers of occupational pension schemes
- Large companies that are already required to provide non-financial statements under the Non-Financial Reporting Directive
- EU and Member States when setting public measures, standards, or labels for green financial products or green (corporate) bonds

The EU taxonomy aims to increase environmental protection and reduce the negative impacts of economic activity on the environment by redirecting investment streams from those that are harmful to the environment to those that are environmentally friendly. The environmental objectives of the EU taxonomy are as follows (EU taxonomy, 2020):

- Climate change mitigation
- Climate change adaptations
- The sustainable use and protection of water and marine resources
- The transition to a circular economy
- Pollution prevention and control
- The protection and restoration of biodiversity and ecosystems

It should be noted, however, that the literature indicates that the EU taxonomy may not bring about the expected effects in the form of greenhouse gas reductions and, on the contrary, may even increase emissions due to the removal of high-emission activities to outside the EU. In turn, the promotion of green finance could lead to the loss of income due to differences in productivity (Fuest & Meier, 2022).

Therefore, financial institutions that control the flow of financial capital by financing investment and making decisions regarding the financing of companies play important roles in the EU taxonomy. The EU taxonomy remains consistent with the assumptions of the European Green Deal and is conducive to achieving its goals, particularly achieving climate neutrality by 2050. The EU taxonomy also intends to reduce the phenomenon of greenwashing by standardizing the classification of enterprises according to the degree of their business's impact on the environment.

The EU taxonomy has a direct impact on businesses as it defines how companies should conduct sustainable business and proposes a classification for companies according to their environmentally sustainable economic activities (EU taxonomy, 2020). The classification of an economic activity in terms of sustainability is based on the following criteria (EU taxonomy, 2023):

- Its contribution to one of the EU taxonomy environmental objectives;
- It does "no significant harm" (DNSH) to any of the taxonomy's environmental objectives;
- It meets "minimum safeguards," such as the UN Guiding Principles on Business and Human Rights, so as not to have any negative social impacts;
- It complies with the technical screening criteria developed by the EU Technical Expert Group (technical solutions for emission reduction).

For an economic activity that meets one or more of the six environmental objectives of the taxonomy to qualify as sustainable, it must not cause significant harm to any of the other objectives of the taxonomy. The technical screening criteria (TSC) set thresholds for compliance with the principle of no significant harm for each activity. The TSC define specific requirements and thresholds that economic activities must meet to be considered as contributing significantly to sustainable development (Doyle, 2021).

For each environmental objective, the taxonomy regulation recognizes two distinct types of significant contributions that can be considered as being aligned with the taxonomy (Final Report, 2020):

- Economic activities, which are activities that make significant contributions based on their own performance (e.g.,, environmentally sustainable economic activities)
- Enabling activities, which are economic activities that make it possible to make a significant contribution to other activities by providing products or services (e.g., economic activities that produce elements that improve the environmental performance of other activities)

The taxonomy is divided into two parts: sectors that make significant contributions to climate change mitigation (including an indication of whether the technical screening criteria are related to the conduct of the economic activity or whether it is an enabling activity) and activities that contribute significantly to climate change adaptations.

The EU taxonomy focuses on economic activities that contribute the most to greenhouse gas (GHG) emissions. These activities were ranked according to their contributions to greenhouse gas emissions in 2017. More activities could be added to the EU green taxonomy in the future (e.g., educational activities). To date, the regulation covers various industries, which have been classified in accordance with Nomenclature of Economic Activities (NACE).

According to the EU taxonomy directive, around 90% of industries are responsible for the greenhouse gas emissions in continental Europe. The taxonomy addresses the following sectors (Renewable, 2023):

- Electricity, gas, and steam
- Manufacturing
- Transportation and storage
- Agriculture, forestry, and fishing
- Water supply
- Mining and quarrying
- Information and communication
- Other

While the taxonomy is primarily a classification tool, it also has other functions. For example, it requires certain entities to disclose information about the extent to which their activities comply with the taxonomy. This is achieved by amending the disclosure requirements of the EU's Non-Financial Reporting Directive (NFRD) and the Sustainable Finance Disclosure Regulation (SFDR) (Doyle, 2021).

Each company subjected to the NFRD must disclose how and to what extent its activities are related to activities that are considered to be environmentally sustainable. Within this group, non-financial companies have to disclose the following information (Doyle, 2021):

- The percentage of turnover derived from taxonomic activities
- The proportion of capital and operating expenditures related to taxonomy activities

Entities within the scope of the SFDR are required to disclose information on any taxonomy adaptations made to their products. This disclosure covers products that aim toward sustainable investment (i.e., products covered by Article 9 of the SFDR) and products with environmental or social characteristics (i.e., products covered by Article 8 of the SFDR). These are known as Article 5 and Article 6 taxonomy disclosures, respectively (Doyle, 2021).

The information disclosed covers how and to what extent the investment underlying the financial product is invested in an economic activity that qualifies as environmentally sustainable under the taxonomy regulation. For financial products that do not take into account the EU criteria for environmentally sustainable economic activities, the entity must make such a statement in its disclosure. This is known as a taxonomy disclosure under Art. 7 (Doyle, 2021).

The taxonomy integrates financial and non-financial entities within activities for sustainable development. Enterprises are encouraged to make sustainable adaptations, while markets and financial institutions are encouraged to create sustainable financial products and contribute to financing sustainable investment.

1.2 Influence of ESG Risk on the Business and Supply Chain Strategy

ESG risks affect all business sectors; for some they become opportunities, while for others, they are a threat. Table 1.7 shows the sectors with the highest average ESG rating scores and the sectors with the highest ESG risk disclosure scores.[3]

Actions aimed at reducing ESG risks are important because there is a documented relationship between ESG risks and financial performance. Additionally, it is worth noting that the impacts of ESG risks on financial performance can be positive, negative, or neutral (Friede et al., 2015). The literature indicates that incorporating ESG risks into businesses increases stakeholder confidence and leads to reductions in business financing costs, consequently improving corporate financial performance (Friede et al., 2015). Other studies have indicated the positive impacts of

Table 1.7 ESG risk factors

Industries with high average ESG rating scores*	ESG risk disclosure**
Industrial conglomerates	Energy and Mining
Steel	Industrial products
Diversified metals	Retail and consumer
Precious metals	Financial services
Oil and gas producers	Health industries
	Technology
	Pharmaceutical and life sciences
	Entertainment, media, and communications

Source: *M. Chase: High-Impact ESG Issues: What Your Company Needs to Know, 2022; https://www.sustainalytics.com/esg-research/resource/corporate-esg-blog/high-impact-esg-issues-what-your-company-needs-to-know(accessed: 10.04.2023); **L. Rozin: ESG Risks Trickle Into Financial Filings, 2019 https://blog.nacdonline.org/posts/esg-risks-trickle-into-financial-filings(accessed: 10.04.2023)

[3] ESG disclosures have become widespread since 2006, when the United Nations Principles for Responsible Investment (UNPRI) report first described the concept of ESG. For more, see Iazzolino, G., Bruni, M. E., Veltri, S., Morea, D., and Baldissarro, G. (Iazzolino et al., 2023), The impact of ESG factors on financial efficiency: An empirical analysis for the selection of sustainable firm portfolios. Corporate Social Responsibility and Environmental Management, 1–11. https://doi.org/10.1002/csr.2463.

ESG risks on employee productivity, market value, profits, and management capability (Branco & Rodrigues, 2006; Iazzolino et al., 2023). At the same time, Chen et al. (2021) drew attention to the relationship between incorporating ESG risks and minimizing reputation risks. The main issues discussed in the literature related to ESG risk impacts on business focus on the following problems (Ziolo et al., 2023):

- ESG risk management
- ESG risks in decision-making/investment processes
- Sustainable (green) supply chains
- ESG risks in business models
- Risk cultureCommunication with stakeholders

ESG factors impact supply chains; as a consequence, reputation, financial and investment performance, assets, and general business can be destroyed by the impacts of ESG risks (Fig. 1.1.).

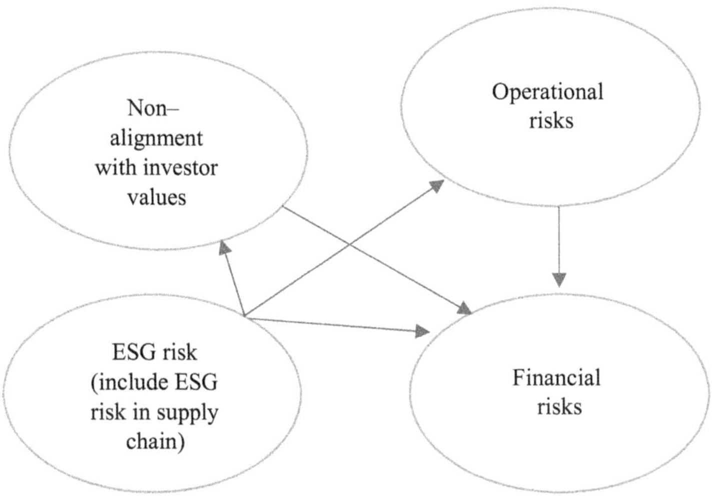

Fig. 1.1 ESG risk in supply chain. Source: own elaboration based on *Why ESG factors in the supply chain matter*, https://www.unpri.org/private-equity/managing-esg-risk-in-the-supply-chains-of-private-companies-and-assets/615.article (accessed: 22.06.2023)

The direct impacts of ESG risks on companies and supply chains can be expressed in many ways, including the following (United Nations Principles for Responsible Investment, UNPRI, 2017):

- Disturbances in the flow of materials, including raw materials and components
- Impacts on delivery times, with knock-on effects on customer satisfaction
- Poor financial management by suppliers, resulting in the inability to deliver goods on time
- The loss of the social acceptance of companies due to serious image problems related to environmental pollution, human rights violations, corruption, etc.
- Increases in material costs as companies are forced to switch suppliers at the last minute

Nearly two thirds (64%) of Canadian small and medium-sized businesses surveyed by KPMG said they are now integrating environmental, social, and corporate governance (ESG) principles, including climate change mitigation, into their supply chain management. Similarly, 63% said that they plan to hire "ethical sourcing managers" to ensure their suppliers meet their ESG performance requirements in policy and practice. This role also includes monitoring supplier non-compliance and helping suppliers to comply with regulations (KPMG, 2022). Trucost conducted a comparative study showing how supply chains affect the environment compared to direct operations (UNPRI, 2017) (Table 1.8).

Due to the financial and non-financial consequences related to the impacts of ESG risks on society and the economy, enterprises, governments, and regulators undertake actions that aim to reduce ESG risks systemically (Duque & Caracuel, 2021). Reducing ESG risks in companies also positively impacts environmental and social sustainability, which is crucial within the global context and ensures sustainable development. The consideration of ESG risks by companies implies their transition toward corporate sustainability and incorporating ESG risks into their business models, which is essential within the EU strategic context, for example, the European Green Deal or the taxonomy.

Table 1.8 Supply chains' impact on environment compared to direct operations

Sectors	Supply chain	Direct operations
Utilities	7%	93%
Oil and gas, chemicals, travel and leisure, basic resources	44–64%	36–56%
Construction and materials, insurance, industrial goods and services	70–72%	28–30%
Technology, health care, real estate	86–90%	10–14%
Telecommunications, retail, automotive, media, personal and household goods	96–95%	4–5%
Financial services, food and beverage, banking	98%	2%

Source: own elaboration based on *Why ESG factors in the supply chain matter*, https://www.unpri.org/private-equity/managing-esg-risk-in-the-supply-chains-of-private-companies-and-assets/615.article (accessed: 22.06.2023)

Wang et al. (2023) assumed that risks, information, and strategic perspectives reflect the key pathways through which ESG practices play a role in either directly or indirectly harming or creating value for companies. They also declared that macro-, meso-, and micro-factors modify the directions and ranges of the impacts. Additionally, the authors explained that considering the relationship between ESG performance and ESG disclosure is key to understanding the issue.

According to a study by Khalid et al. (2022), the governance structure of companies (i.e., board size, board independence, and cross-listing) plays an important role in their ESG disclosures. In addition, a low perception of corruption reflects higher ESG disclosures at target companies. Additional company characteristics, as well as liquidity indicators, point to better ESG reporting over the period. The study also confirmed that when considering ESG disclosures on a case-by-case basis, the productive roles of the board size, current liquidity ratio and the low level of corruption in relation to environmental matters. Finally, the results showed that board size and ESG disclosures contribute to better financial performance.

Research carried out by Kim et al. (2022) aimed to understand how environmental, social, and corporate governance (ESG) impacts business performance and the diversification effects of cross-border mergers and acquisitions (M&As) by examining 129 cross-border merger and acquisition events in the Korean Stock Price Index (KOSPI), representing emerging capital markets in 38 target countries over 2012–2018. The results indicated that better ESG engagement had positive impacts on the business outcomes of cross-border M&As, supporting stakeholder theory and confirming that ESG can be used as a strategy to increase business efficiency in cross-border M&As. The results also confirmed that diversification in cross-border M&As leads to reductions in business performance, which negatively impacts acquirers, whereas ESG involvement can mitigate these reductions as a friendly channel.

Gardiner and Endicott (2023) proposed the inclusion of sustainability risk management (SRM) as a critical component in Enterprise Risk Management (ERM). SRM is a process that addresses and manages a wide range of new and unknown threats arising from sustainability issues. The goal of this process is to deliver sustainable value for long-term survival. Due to the complexity of the risks organizations face, SRM should be covered by the ERM framework. The implementation of the ERM concept is a way to reduce the impacts of ESG risks on businesses and manage the risks comprehensively (Shad et al., 2019).

One of the important trends in ESG research is related to supply chains. ESG risks affect supply chains, which was particularly visible during the COVID-19 pandemic. The inclusion of ESG in supply chain management requires the assessment and recognition of the practices used by suppliers to determine how sustainable they are. To incorporate ESG into supply chain management, companies must first assess the ESG risks and opportunities within their supply chain. The tools that are useful in this assessment process include supplier audits, sustainability reports and stakeholder engagement. Companies should then set goals and metrics to monitor their progress and identify areas for improvement (ESG in supply chain, 2023).

Sustainable supply chain management (SSCM) is becoming a strategic requirement for companies (Song et al., 2017) as it is an important source of cost reductions and increases the long-term profitability of organizations (Wang & Sarkis, 2013). Supply chain management (SCM) is seen as a key factor in improving a company's efficiency and success (Mangla et al., 2015). Coqueret and Vu Le (2022) documented the impacts of ESG risks on supplier and customer returns to companies affected by

COVID-19. The authors suggested that these impacts depend not only on the sign and magnitude of the risk but also on the interaction between the risk and the magnitude of the ESG outcome.

Sardanelli et al. (2022) proposed integrated ESG, a financial model that evaluates both the financial and sustainability aspects of organizations based on the supply chains they belong to. The authors assumed that the model is particularly suitable for assessing the growth potential of small and medium-sized companies, which, unlike large corporations, are generally more opaque to financial markets and have less disclosure intensity. Therefore, this measurement system can be used both by financial institutions to assess potential borrowers and by individual companies to make internal assessments or evaluate the performance of partners at lower and higher levels.

Dai and Tang explained the value of ESG unification and end-to-end thinking in supply chains. The authors analyzed case studies of three supply chains that emerged during the COVID-19 pandemic, including online platforms, public health supply chains and the development, production, and distribution of vaccines. Based on these case studies, the authors highlighted gaps in research regarding the scopes of ESG and supply chain management.

1.3 Role and Challenges of Transport and Logistic Sectors in the Context of Dealing with ESG Risk

Research and reports have indicated that ESG risks, particularly after the COVID-19 pandemic, have radically changed approaches to conducting business. ESG engagement featured prominently among the 1200 industry professionals surveyed as part of the 2021 Agility Emerging Markets Logistics Index. Although one in five respondents reported lost sales and supply chain disruptions, 45.2% said their environmental sustainability plans were being implemented and another 26.9% said that they were more willing to invest in and enforce more green initiatives. The index was developed by transport intelligence analysts from the logistics industry (Thomas, 2021). Studies on Canadian companies have shown that they face many challenges in adapting to operating in ESG risk conditions. Almost six in ten (59%) SMEs said that they had "struggled to craft a compelling ESG story" and 61% had struggled to overcome stakeholder skepticism or perceptions of greenwashing. A similar proportion (61%) said that they expected to rely increasingly on third-party verification or validation of their ESG data (KPMG, 2022).

There are particular challenges in ESG risks related to the transport sector as this sector was responsible for approximately one quarter of the total CO^2 emissions in the EU in 2019, 71.7% of which was from road transport (European Environment Agency, 2023). The logistics industry produces around a quarter of global CO^2 emissions. According to the European Environment Agency, this share could increase to 40% by 2050 unless decisive action is taken (Applandeo, 2023). In addition to its impact on CO2 emissions, the logistics sector also affects water pollution. Ships are responsible for vast amounts of sewage and solid waste that enter the oceans and pollute ecosystems. The noise generated by shipping travels vast distances underwater, disorienting aquatic animals that have to attempt to move and communicate through the noise. Large marine mammals are also at risk of collisions with fast-moving vessels. Oil spills, which devastate ocean and coastal ecosystems, are also a threat. The logistics industry also uses many non-renewable resources, which is an environmental challenge in itself, mainly concerning fuel. Some improvements have been seen with the introduction of electric cars, but no such changes can be seen in the case of cargo planes or container ships. The shipping industry also uses large numbers of packages, pallets, and containers, many of which are disposable and create piles of garbage (Applandeo, 2023).

The carbon footprints of the transport and other air pollutants caused by road and air traffic not only contribute to the greenhouse effect and the rapid increase in global temperatures but they also directly affect people's health, causing lung and cardiovascular diseases and premature death. Transport was also one of the sectors that was particularly affected by the COVID-19 pandemic. The lockdowns directly affected transport services and, consequently, the budgets of transport sector entities. Passenger traffic was suspended or severely limited at that time, which also had financial consequences. In the post-pandemic period, some passengers still do not use (or have not returned to using) urban or regional transport, preferring alternative forms of communication, especially in the summer. Therefore, stabilizing the situation for public entities after the pandemic is still a challenge, for example, due to changes in taxes, high inflation, and rising interest rates, as well as the transitional period related to waiting for the availability of EU funds. The issues surrounding ESG risks and, above all, climate risks directly impact transport (i.e., the concept of sustainable transport) and the problems of transport inclusion, which determine financial outlays for adaptations to low-emission requirements.

Santhi and Muthuswamy (2022) diagnosed supply chain and logistics challenges, dividing them into traditional and contemporary challenges. The traditional challenges included those related to the following:

- Planning and forecasting
- Supplier relationship management
- Product quality
- Inventory management
- Competitiveness and customer service
- Risk identification and mitigation
- Data accessibility and management

In turn, the contemporary challenges were related to the following (Santhi & Muthuswamy, 2022):

- The scarcity of raw materials
- Increases in transportation costs
- Demand forecasting
- Logistical challenges (e.g., port congestion)
- Changes in consumer behavior
- Labor shortages

The transport and logistics sector actively deals with ESG risks and the accompanying changes in market and business models. Activities that aim to mitigate ESG risks in logistics and transport concern the following issues (Cello, 2023):

- Eco-friendly transportation
- The conversion of transportation modes
- The optimization of resource use
- Eco-friendly packaging, distribution, and processing
- Reverse logistics

In addition to the above, it has been noted that the negative impacts of logistics on the environment can be overcome via the following activities (Applandeo, 2023):

- Optimizing routes
- Tracking empty miles
- Increasing the efficiency of transportation
- Using more sustainable transportation options
- Warehouse management
- Implementing green logistics practices
- Collaborating with suppliers and customers

ESG risks affect every business sector. Many entrepreneurs are aware of the need to undertake risk-educating activities. A number of changes have already been introduced by many enterprises, as a result of both regulations and voluntary initiatives. However, the transport sector currently faces a number of low-carbon challenges.

References

Applandeo. (2023). https://applandeo.com/blog/the-environmental-impact-of-logistics-and-how-to-reduce-it/. Accessed 22 June 2023.

Branco, M., & Rodrigues, L. (2006). Corporate social responsibility and resource-based perspectives. *Journal of Business Ethics, 69*, 111–132.

Braubach, M., & Fairburn, J. (2010). Social inequities in environmental risks associated with housing and residential location—a review of evidence. *European Journal of Public Health, 20*(1), 36–42.

Bua, G., Knapp, D., Ramella, F., & Rognone, L. (2022, July). *Transition versus physical climate risk pricing in European financial markets: a text-based approach* (p. 3). Working Paper Series, European Central Bank, No 2677.

Cello. (2023). Will ESG management become the turning point in the logistics industry? https://www.cello-square.com/go-en/blog/view-559.do/. Accessed 22 June 2023.

Chen, I. J., Hasan, I., Lin, C. Y., & Nguyen, T. N. V. (2021). Do banks value borrowers' environmental record? Evidence from financial contracts. *Journal of Business Ethics, 174*, 687–713.

Coqueret, G., Vu Le, T. (2022, August 31). ESG news spillovers across the value chain. Available at SSRN: https://ssrn.com/abstract=4002705 or https://doi.org/10.2139/ssrn.4002705

Doyle, D. H. (2021). A short guide to the EU's taxonomy regulation. https://www.spglobal.com/esg/insights/a-short-guide-to-the-eu-s-taxonomy-regulation. Accessed 7 Apr 2023.

Duque, E., & Caracuel, J. (2021). Environmental, social and governance (ESG) scores and financial performance of multilatinas: Moderating effects of geographic international diversification and financial slack. *Journal of Business Ethics*, 168.

EBA. (2021). EBA Report on ESG risk management and supervision. https://www.eba.europa.eu/eba-publishes-its-report-management-and-supervision-esg-risks-credit-institutions-and-investment. Accessed 6 Apr 2023.

EEA. (2023). https://www.eea.europa.eu/help/glossary/eea-glossary/environmental-risk. Accessed 6 Apr 2023.

Escrig-Olmedo, E., Fernández-Izquierdo, M. A., Ferrero-Ferrero, I., Rivera-Lirio, J. M., & Muñoz-Torres, M. J. (2019). Rating the raters: Evaluating how ESG rating agencies integrate sustainability principles. *Sustainability, 11*, 915.

ESG in supply chain. (2023). https://www.tradecloud1.com/en/esg-in-supply-chain-management-the-future-of-corporate-responsibility/. Accessed 10 Apr 2023.

EU Taxonomy. (2020). https://finance.ec.europa.eu/sustainable-finance/tools-and-standards/eu-taxonomy-sustainable-activities_en. Accessed 7 Apr 2023.

EU taxonomy info. (2023). https://eu-taxonomy.info/info/eu-taxonomy-overview. Accessed 7 Apr 2023.

EU Taxonomy Overview. (2023). https://eu-taxonomy.info/info/eu-taxonomy-overview. Accessed 7 Apr 2023.

European Environment Agency. (2023). https://www.europarl.europa.eu/news/pl/headlines/society/20190313STO31218/emisje-co2-z-samochodow-fakty-i-liczby-infografiki. Accessed 22 June 2023.

Final report of the Technical Expert, Group on Sustainable Finance, March 2020 and Taxonomy report: technical annex, Updated methodology & Updated Technical Screening Criteria, March 2020.

Friede, G., Busch, T., & Bassen, A. (2015). ESG and financial performance: Aggregated evidence from more than 2000 empirical studies. *Journal of Sustainable Finance & Investment, 5*, 210–233.

Fuest, C., & Meier, V. (2022). Green finance and the EU-taxonomy for sustainable activities: Why using more direct environmental policy tools is preferable. *The Economists' Voice, 19*(2), 207–212.

Gardiner, T., & Endicott, M. (2023). ERM and sustainability: Beyond buzzwords. Available online: https://www.canadianunderwriter.ca/features/erm-and-sustainability-beyond-buzzwords/. Accessed 10 Apr 2023.

Global Risks Report. (2022). https://www.weforum.org/reports/global-risks-report-2022/. Accessed 6 Apr 2023.

Iazzolino, G., Bruni, M. E., Veltri, S., Morea, D., & Baldissarro, G. (2023). The impact of ESG factors on financial efficiency: An empirical analysis for the selection of sustainable firm portfolios. *Corporate Social Responsibility and Environmental Management*, 1–11. https://doi.org/10.1002/csr.2463

IRGC. (2023). What is risk governance? https://irgc.org/risk-governance/what-is-risk-governance/. Accessed 7 Apr 2023.

Khalid, F., Razzaq, A., Ming, J., et al. (2022). Firm characteristics, governance mechanisms, and ESG disclosure: How caring about sustainable concerns? *Environmental Science and Pollution Research, 29*, 82064–82077. https://doi.org/10.1007/s11356-022-21489-z

Kim, B.-j., Jung, J.-y., & Cho, S.-w. (2022). Can ESG mitigate the diversification discount in cross-border M&A? *Borsa Istanbul Review, 22*(3), 607–615. https://doi.org/10.1016/j.bir.2021.09.002. https://www.sciencedirect.com/science/article/pii/S2214845021000910

KPMG. (2022). ESG becomes a critical link in the supply chain for Canadian companies. https://www.newswire.ca/news-releases/esg-becomes-a-critical-link-in-the-supply-chain-for-canadian-companies-869872863.html. Accessed 22 June 2023.

Lupu, L. (2019). The concept of social risk: a geographical approach. *Quaestiones Geographicae, 38*(4), 6.

Mangla, S. K., Kumar, P., & Barua, M. K. (2015). Prioritizing the responses to manage risks in green supply chain: An Indian plastic manufacturer perspective. *Sustainable Production and Consumption, 1*, 67–86. https://doi.org/10.1016/j.spc.2015.05.002

Míka, V. (2009). Sociálne riziká ako problém krízového manažmentu. In *Proceedings of the international conference crises situations solution in specific environment* (pp. 173–194). FŠI ŽU.

Renewable. (2023). https://www.think-renewable.com/knowledge-hub/eu-taxonomy. Accessed 7 Apr 2023.

Santhi, R., & Muthuswamy, A. (2022). Pandemic, war, natural calamities, and sustainability: Industry 4.0 technologies to overcome traditional and contemporary supply chain challenges. *Logistics, 6*, 81. https://doi.org/10.3390/logistics6040081

Sardanelli, D., Bittucci, L., Mirone, F., & Marzioni, S. (2022). An integrative framework for supply chain rating: from financial-based to ESG-based rating models. *Total Quality Management & Business Excellence*, 1–20. https://doi.org/10.1080/14783363.2022.2069557

Shad, M. K., Lai, F.-W., Fatt, C. L., Klemeš, J. J., & Bokhari, A. (2019). Integrating sustainability reporting into enterprise risk management and its relationship with business performance: A conceptual framework. *Journal of Cleaner Production, 208*, 415–425. https://doi.org/10.1016/j.jclepro.2018.10.120

Song, W., Ming, X., & Liu, H.-C. (2017). Identifying critical risk factors of sustainable supply chain management: A rough strength-relation analysis method. *Journal of Cleaner Production, 143*, 100–115. https://doi.org/10.1016/j.jclepro.2016.12.145

Thomas. (2021). Survey: ESG a key concern for supply chain despite COVID-19. https://supplychaindigital.com/sustainability/survey-esg-key-concern-supply-chain-despite-covid-19. Accessed 22 June 2023.

UNPRI. (2017). Why ESG factors in the supply chain matter. https://www.unpri.org/private-equity/managing-esg-risk-in-the-supply-chains-of-private-companies-and-assets/615.article. Accessed 22 June 2023.

Wang, N., Pan, H., Feng, Y., & Du, S. (2023). How do ESG practices create value for businesses? Research review and prospects. *Sustainability Accounting, Management and Policy Journal*. https://doi.org/10.1108/SAMPJ-12-2021-0515

Wang, Z., & Sarkis, J. (2013). Investigating the relationship of sustainable supply chain management with corporate financial performance. *International Journal of Productivity and Performance Management, 62*, 871–888. https://doi.org/10.1108/IJPPM-03-2013-0033

Wytyczne do raportowania ESG Przewodnik dla spółek notowanych na GPW, EBRD, Maj 2021, p. 13.

Ziolo, M., Bak, I., & Spoz, A. (2023). Incorporating ESG risk in companies' business models: State of research and energy sector case studies. *Energies, 16*(4), 1–25.

Ziolo, M., Filipiak, B. Z., Bąk, I., & Cheba, K. (2019). How to design more sustainable financial systems: The roles of environmental, social, and governance factors in the decision-making process. *Sustainability, 11*, 5604.

Zioło, M., Filipiak, B. Z., & Tundys, B. (2021). *Sustainability in bank and corporate business.* Palgrave.

2

Sustainable Supply Chain: A New Paradigm for Supply Chain Strategy

2.1 Triple Bottom Line (3BL) as a Component of a Sustainable Supply Chain

The concept of sustainability, with all of its principles and assumptions, now underpins the actions taken by organizations and supply chains. In terms of definitions, there is currently no consensus on the interpretation of this concept or related phenomena, but it can be considered that sustainability is about processes and that sustainability is a state (Ahi & Searcy, 2015). Therefore, using resources to meet the needs of one's own generation in such a way that there is no loss of usable resources for future generations is the essence of sustainable development (Brundtland, 1987). This multidimensional process refers to processes that combine the needs to be efficient, solve problems, and meet social and environmental requirements, and this is becoming an increasingly important management concept, especially within supply chain management. One critical element, with defined standards, for the survival and competitiveness of global business and one of the basic concepts for operationalizing sustainability is the 3BL, whereby the results achieved and actions taken can be assessed within the environmental, economic, and social dimensions of sustainability (Elkington & Rowlands, 1999). There is no doubt

B. Tundys et al., *Sustainable Supply Chains 2.0*,
https://doi.org/10.1007/978-3-031-50337-5_2

that the concept is linked to the people, planet, and profit (PPP) approach, which reflects the main features of sustainable development (Żak, 2015). Resource depletion indicates that future companies will be judged not only on the economic benefits they achieve and offer to customers but also on how they implement sustainability principles. The growing importance of 3BL (Winter & Lasch, 2016) in the creation, operation, and management of supply chains indicates that environmental and social dimensions should be given special attention by business practitioners and treated on a par with the economic aspects of supply chains.

The application of sustainability principles, particularly including the triple bottom line (3BL), to the supply chain concept is becoming an integral component of new business strategies, which should be referred to as sustainable supply chains. The 3BL approach to this type of supply chain is often understood and interpreted in different ways, contributing to the fact that trade-offs between the three dimensions (economic, social, and environmental) are sought in solutions and process support. The desired direction for implementation is a synergistic approach, which can allow for simultaneous improvements in several dimensions without compromising the others. Such an approach does not lead to reductions in either the relevance or impact of individual elements on the overall strategy, but unifies the objectives of stakeholders, thus satisfying their different expectations. There is a wealth of empirical and theoretical evidence pointing to the need for increasing attention on the implementation of 3BL in order to promote sustainable supply chains (SCs) by simultaneously integrating social, economic, and environmental objectives (Ramanathan et al., 2017). Effective collaboration across sectors carries great potential for implementing 3BL within supply chains (He et al., 2019) and is not limited to sectors where such activities are able to be implemented quickly and with visible effects (e.g., the manufacturing sector).

The sustainability aspect is the drive to put into practice models of organizations and supply chains that are intelligent, create and transfer knowledge, modify their behavior to reflect new horizons, and allow them to adapt to ever-changing environments in order to achieve dominant positions within markets. It is also the exploitation of conditions created by the environment and the ability of organizations to continuously learn, adapt, grow, revitalize, reconstruct, and reorient. Business models based on the principles of sustainable development are undoubtedly capable of implementing ecological innovations, which, as a rule, involve technological and organizational innovations and manage organizations in such a way as to reduce their negative impacts on the environment. The measures taken are implied in the products, services, production processes, and other (non-production) parts of organizations' activities, infrastructures, and management, as well as supply chains. Today's actors need to be aware of the environmental implications of their supply chain logistics strategies. New solutions should be introduced in such a way that the environmental impacts of logistics processes and activities can be skillfully assessed. It is also important to point out appropriate directions for change. It is not only transport or storage processes that create negative environmental impacts. Product development itself, as well as the expansion of the level and scope of customer service and trends observed within supply chain strategies (including the increasing importance of reverse logistics and recycling), affects the creation of new strategies and business models, which must be based on the 3BL concept (Tundys, 2018).

There are a number of factors that can be identified as motivators for actions taken in supply chains in response to sustainability needs. These can include the following (Ahi & Searcy, 2015): the desire to reduce costs, skillful risk management, environmental certification, the desire to raise quality standards, greater employee involvement, increased value, investor pressure, customer demands, collaboration with suppliers, the integration of supply networks, the improved efficiency or productivity of processes, proactive approaches to preventing harmful activities, and the desire to be more competitive. The multidimensionality of sustainability is a feature that makes the search for appropriate measures to monitor sustainability performance very difficult (Bodini, 2012).

The unique characteristic of the 3BL approach, whether applied to a single organization or a whole supply chain, is its multidimensionality. The essence of the approach is not only to respect and protect the environment but also to meet multiple objectives simultaneously. This means that the environment must be protected while also respecting other aspects of human activity, such as human rights, local obligations and laws, public participation in decision-making, and seeking to eliminate exclusions. When treating the activities of economic actors in the environment, social sphere, and financial performance equally, the 3BL approach and the association of the concept with PPP explicitly means targeting performance in these spheres (Żak, 2015). This means that the 3BL method allows supply chains to not only look at the economic value of the organizations that they generate but also to consider, assess, and often multiply environmental and social values. Therefore, the use of 3BL in supply chains can serve as an element of monitoring, controlling, and verifying compliance with the implementation of the various components within individual organizations and supply chains. The concept can be considered holistically as the totality of values, issues, and processes that need to be addressed within supply chains to minimize the negative impacts of activities while generating social, economic, and environmental gains and value.

Global supply chains, global links, and links that operate in often diverse economic, political, and social environments must be aware of the need to implement 3BL, and must look at their performance through the lens of not only their immediate stakeholders but also the downstream environment, including local communities and governmental and non-governmental organizations, whose actions and requirements must be taken into account. A common supply chain strategy based on 3BL, an understanding of it, and the consistent monitoring of the activities being carried out can help in this effort.

The 3BL approach is an extremely difficult concept to implement because it forces organizations to be more committed and accountable. It is not just economic performance that counts here—social and environmental performance measures are equally important. Economic efficiency is equated with profit and products offered to customers according to their requirements, while environmental efficiency refers to the skillful use of natural resources, as well as the creation and disposal of byproducts and waste. The context of social efficiency refers to the impacts that supply chains have on communities. The implementation of the individual elements alone is difficult, so measurement systems that can reflect the effects of the actions being taken must be properly applied.

It is worth pointing out that the individual elements of the 3BL concept and the measurement of their effects on supply chains are not the simple sum of these activities. The concept is based on the use of three types of capital: social, economic, and environmental (Srivastava et al., 2022). The extent of capital possessed, both in terms of its scarcity and abundance, clearly determines the prospects for the development of organizations or supply chains from global, local, regional, and national perspectives (Elkington et al., 2004) (Table 2.1).

Table 2.1 3BL and PPP: A brief overview of the initiatives undertaken

Area		Characteristic/description
People	Society	– fair business practices toward people, employees, the local community, and the region in which the business is conducted – the welfare of employees, owners, shareholders, and other stakeholders is interdependent – fair relationships – the best possible working conditions – security – financial satisfaction – support for development – no child labor (including monitoring that all links in the chain comply with this requirement) – ethical behavior – activities to strengthen and develop the local community – employee health protection – support of the education system
Planet	Environment	– sustainable environmental practices – prevention of environmental pollution (water, soil, air) – recycling – waste segregation – reduction of waste, defective products – use of materials and substances which have no harmful effects on the environment – taking action to develop environmentally neutral products (including manufacturing processes) – use of renewable energy
Profit	Economy	– traditional economic profit plus environmental and social profit – inclusion of social and environmental impacts in addition to traditional accounting – reporting on the effectiveness of economic capital management – introduction of relevant ISO standards – shared responsibility for socioeconomic development

Source: own elaboration

The positive effects of 3BL implementation activities occur when there is harmonization and understanding not only of the goals but also of the initiatives taken by all links within the supply chains in order to implement 3BL in an appropriate way. Therefore, barriers and difficulties regarding goals, motivation, system priorities, institutionalization, beneficiaries, and the concept of responsibility itself must be overcome (Geissdoerfer et al., 2017). It is also important to remember that the objectives of the different areas are often contradictory. Therefore, there is a need to find common strategies so that the objectives not only become consistent but also have decisively positive effects, including win-win outcomes. This makes it possible, in the long run, to establish measurement systems and evaluate sustainable supply chains in an appropriate manner. There is no doubt that the environmental approach has dominated the global literature. However, the social aspects seem to be particularly neglected, and are only distinguished within the context of possible links to environmental aspects or as part of 3BL. It should be noted that the 3BL approach is present in the literature within the context of reviews covering a wide range of topics, most often referring to network designs or general supply chain management approaches. In this respect, the social dimension is included in the scope of consideration by assessing the impacts on regional development in terms of supply chain service, the number of jobs created, and reference to health or safety. The implementation of social approaches depends on the functions of the supply chains, as well as the specifics of the processes and their nature. Social functions can include coordination, people management, CSR implementation, collaboration, and supplier relations. In the vast majority of cases, the social aspect is non-quantitative, covering ethical supply chains, the fair treatment of stakeholders, education and training, social justice, and diversity (Martins & Pato, 2019). As already mentioned, the environmental perspective occupies the most space within sustainable supply chain research. In this respect, environmental performance, air emissions, soil and water pollution, the need to reduce the use of natural resources, and increasing the recovery of materials and products are the most commonly discussed topics in the context of 3BL. These areas can be considered on their own or integrated into the 3BL approach. The functions that play the most important roles here are transport, production or reverse logistics, and closed supply chains.

No longer so new, the concept of the triple bottom line, as it emerged in the 1990s, implies the need to consider environmental and social aspects in addition to the traction financial aspects of organizational management. The economic aspect of 3BL refers to making profits and maintaining competitive advantage through sustainability. The environmental dimension includes factors related to climate change, global warming, air, and the environment. The social aspect includes the issues of health and safety, community well-being, employment opportunities, charities, cultural sensitivities and demands, and organizational behavior. This approach indicates that the sustainability of supply chain processes is necessary. Additionally, climate change, resource depletion, and improving working conditions and the quality of life of societies require that business processes and economic standards that use available technology balance with supply chain processes because this can result in better, greater, and more beneficial added value for all of the chains (Gopalakrishnan et al., 2012).

The literature defines economic sustainability in terms of financial and non-financial aspects (Duong, 2022). Much more often, the former aspect is presented within the context of, for example, asset returns or equity returns (Orji & Wei, 2016; Wang & Sarkis, 2017); however, both approaches are relevant for exploring the relationship between economic and social development in supply chains (Nakamba et al., 2017).

Therefore, it can be concluded that the need to create shared value must produce positive (win-win) outcomes that benefit all parties. This means doing good (i.e., being socially responsible and environmentally friendly) and performing processes, operations, and activities well (i.e., cost-effectively) (Tang, 2018).

In the context of the social dimension, consideration should be given to maximizing the well-being of people, including both employees and external stakeholders (Gopalakrishnan et al., 2012). There is no doubt that important elements include ensuring the health and safety of employees, nurturing their development, and enhancing their competencies and continuous growth. In the context of external stakeholders, actions need to relate to customers, local communities, suppliers, and municipal authorities, and specific actions need to build positive relationships between these groups and ensure fair, honest, and ethical trade (Zhang et al., 2020). In the social context, there is certainly a lot of focus on relationships, community-oriented culture (Prokesch, 2010), and building good relationships with local and regional suppliers, manufacturers, and logistics companies that are part of local or regional communities serving the designated markets (Tate et al., 2010). In terms of the aspect of cooperation with government, long-term relationships based on cooperation and partnership should be built. The economic context focuses on generating and maintaining long-term profits while minimizing negative social and environmental impacts. In this respect, it is important to control costs, increase revenue, and increase market shares, which directly affect economic returns. It is also important to identify social sustainability within supply chains to avoid social maladjustment, which negatively affects local societies, the promotion of well-being, and the benefits that such solutions provide to workers and communities (Huq et al., 2016). At the same time, critical elements can be identified that can serve as a basis for assessing sustainable supply chains from a social perspective. In this respect, these elements include the safety, health, and well-being of workers (Castka & Corbett, 2016; Giannakis & Papadopoulos, 2016). In addition to these aspects, the following should also be added: diversity, philanthropy, and human rights (Duong & Ha, 2021; Duong & Quang-An, 2021). Additionally, depending on the economic situation of the country (including those with developing economies), security, exclusion, and equality should also be considered (Duong, 2022; Vachon & Klassen, 2008).

A reflection of the linkages and the identification of the 3BLs and 3Ps as included in the supply chain is shown in Fig. 2.1.

As shown in Fig. 2.1 and in the text, sustainability, in the sense of 3BL and PPP, is a necessity, which is why this element is so important for the construction of sustainable supply chains. People, planet, and profit make up not only the bottom line but also the entire sustainability effort.

Referring briefly to the aspects of PPP, the first category ("people") is a social one, encompassing relationships with stakeholders and

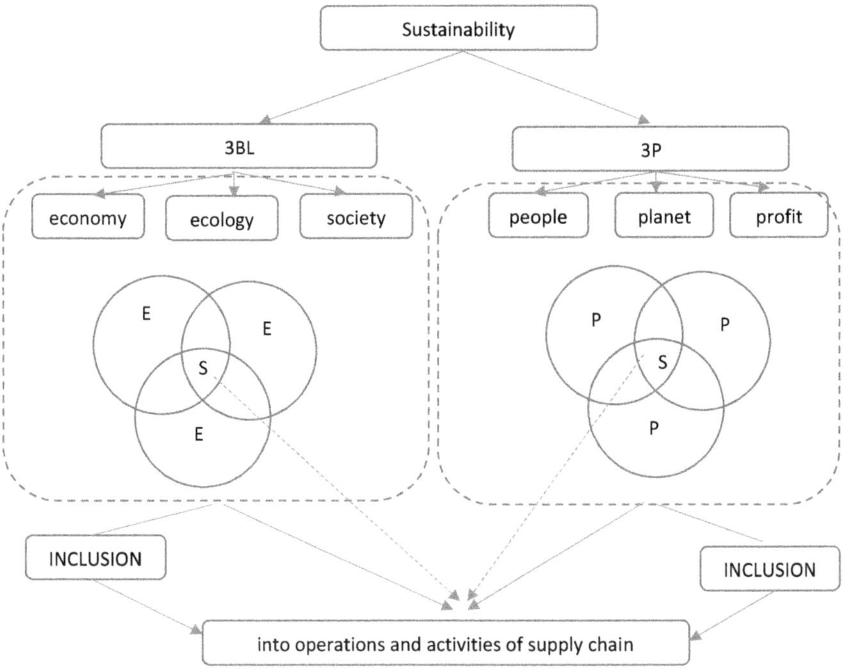

Fig. 2.1 Sustainability links. Source: own elaborations

beneficiaries, ranging from shareholders to local communities in small villages comprising farmers, workers, and consumers. The health and safety of stakeholders, both internal and external, are also captured within this category. Therefore, a broad understanding of this area and the actions taken can be seen. "Planet" refers to the category related to the environment, encompassing everything concerning the impacts of organizations and their supply chains on the Earth. In this area, the focus is on actions concerning energy conservation, sustainable sourcing, the greater use of renewable energy, reducing waste, and moving toward a circular economy. "Profit" is the financial category, and in this respect it refers to finding ways to reduce production costs and logistics but also enter new markets while building the net value of organizations and their supply chains.

Based on the current socioeconomic conditions, "AAA" (i.e., agility, adaptability and alignment (Lee, 2004)), in conjunction with PPP

(Elkington, 2013), should be included in considerations and solutions in order to gain supply chain competitive advantages (Sodhi & Tang, 2021).

Summarizing the considerations that characterize 3BL within the field of sustainable supply chains, it can be concluded that environmental and social aspects play relatively minor roles in the current literature compared to the use of operational and financial indicators for research and practical applications. Studies related to environmental aspects have often only covered one indicator and have not undertaken holistic or large-scale experiments. Toxic emissions have been most often studied in terms of the design and creation of sustainable supply chains. Few studies have emerged that have covered other areas, for example, the water footprint (Allaoui et al., 2018). The least explored area is the social aspect. In this respect, the most commonly detected indicators are job creation and its associated conditions (Chavez et al., 2020).

A reflection of the PPP and 3BL aspects of the supply chain is presented in Fig. 2.2.

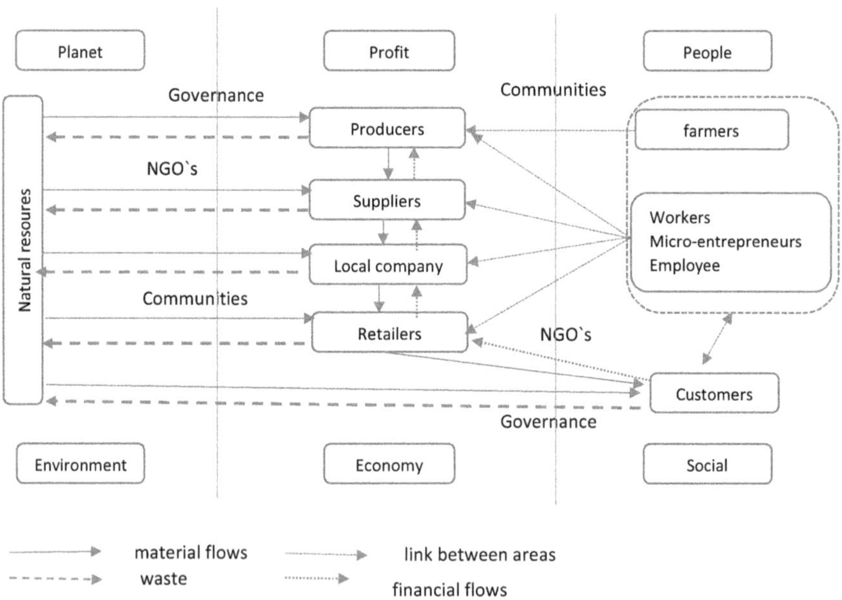

Fig. 2.2 PPP/Environment, Economy, Social (EES) in connection with supply chain organizations and customers. Source: own elaboration based on Sodhi and Tang (2021)

2.2 Environmental, Economic, Social, and Institutional–Political Governance as a Factor Supporting the Implementation of the Sustainable Supply Chain Concept

Before sustainability strategies can be fully integrated into supply chains, various actors, stakeholders, and beneficiaries need to consider specific factors that affect the success of the strategy implementation. These include the following (Walker & Brammer, 2012): understanding the concept itself, as well as government and social policies and legislation in this area; estimating financial capacity (as sustainability implementation is not cheap as it relies on innovations); and implementing the right organizational culture to avoid not only organizational and structural changes but also mental changes.

There is no doubt that among the key elements of supply chains that implement sustainable practices are the initiation and maintenance of appropriate relationships between the various links, particularly between suppliers and local business partners. Good, understandable relationships that are based on the same goals can result in adequate operational efficiency (both financial and environmental or social), positive environmental impacts, cost reductions and flexibility to adapt to changing business conditions, as well as greater opportunities to implement organizational, technological, and managerial innovations. The actions taken, especially in terms of increasing competence in sustainable practices, should be supported by appropriate training programs, adequate systems for monitoring, quality control and systematic auditing, and communication around how sustainable development is understood (Gavronski et al., 2011).

Increasingly, sustainable financing strategies that take into account environmental, social, and governance factors are being used within the context of sustainability, including supply chain issues (Friede et al.,

2015; Yoo et al., 2021). The financial aspect is important insofar as it is one of the pillars of sustainability, while at the same time, investors expecting profitability also receive assurances of sustainability and social responsibility. ESG aspects are increasingly taken into account when making business decisions (Tsang et al., 2023) as they are both challenging and integral to sustainable supply chain strategies. Corporate Social Responsibility (CSR) aspects (i.e., the social aspect) and Sustainability Development Goals (SDGs) should also be considered in the context of supply chain support through various initiatives. In the context of supply chains, it should be pointed out that CSR conceptually develops responsible organizations in terms of 3BL, while ESG is used to quantify the relevant concepts using measurement indicators (Gillan et al., 2021). Referring to the above concepts, it is certainly important to note that from an environmental point of view, the elimination, abuse, misuse, and destruction of natural resources in supply chain operations is significant. From the social perspective, a human-centered focus is encouraged for assessing the impacts of organizations and supply chains so that people-centered atmospheres can be created. From a governance perspective, ethical and resilient supply chain management policies should be developed to be fully compliant with ethical business standards and codes of conduct (Tsang et al., 2023).

Other very important elements supporting the construction and indication of sustainable supply chain frameworks are administrative, legal, and governance regulations. Establishing appropriate legal regulations, as well as adhering to certain governance (especially environmental and community governance but also economic), can effectively eliminate and control the impacts of organizations and supply chains within the indicated areas. There are a number of regulations that legally govern how companies can offset the negative impacts of their activities on the environment. Known and existing legislation aim to encourage companies to integrate sustainable processes and sustainability, while also indicating how to report and control individual harmful emissions. Proactive approaches to regulation and compliance (e.g., the EU taxonomy) are very beneficial from virtually every point of view (i.e., economically, environmentally, and socially). This is because strategies that aim to mitigate the negative impacts of organizations and supply chains on all three areas of sustainability can be more effectively introduced. The obligations that are contained in the regulations definitely influence greater care when implementing the individual elements of sustainability.

Another supportive element is stakeholder pressure. Stakeholder pressure can involve a great deal of knowledge, competence, and commitment on the part of organizations' employees and management. Embedding the principles of sustainability in organizational strategies or missions is extremely important. The involvement and satisfaction of employees also play large roles (i.e., the social aspects) in supporting the indicated principles. Employee satisfaction is directly proportional to the effectiveness and efficiency of any organizational change. At the same time, their resistance may result in the failure of companies to implement sustainability programs (Gopalakrishnan et al., 2012). Consumers should also not be forgotten. Their pressure depends on the organizations and their perceptions of the organizations within the markets. The sensitivity of organizations and their impacts are driven by consumers and this, in turn, translates into financial performance. Therefore, it is important to see organizations as components or links within supply chains; then, it is easier to translate customer pressure into positive effects and success not only for the organizations but also for all of the supply chains. Customers are clearly linked to competitors. Competitors set the norms and standards. Additionally, in recent years, society in general has played an increasing role in shaping and supporting sustainability principles and practices in supply chains. Society has become increasingly aware and, therefore, knows what socially, environmentally, and economically sustainable supply chain processes should be. This means that individual companies need to introduce new business practices that suit their target groups.

Another important element that serves as a supportive element in creating sustainable supply chains is environmental management. The environmental management systems set up in organizations are part of the organizations' overall management systems. However, in their scope and operation, they not only cover the organizational structures but also the planning and use of appropriate procedures, as well as the implementation of processes with adequate resources for the development, implementation, execution, review, and indication of rules of conduct and the maintenance of properly defined and executed environmental policies. These are some of the elements supporting the minimum environmental burden of organizational activities. Applied environmental management practices and regulations can contribute to the increased use of sustainable supply chain practices. Issues related to increasing environmental performance include the re-education of emissions, effluents, and waste, reducing the use of toxic substances, and the implementation of green practices, such as eco-design, green investment, and green purchasing. These issues all have in common that environmental management strategies use reuse, remanufacturing, recycling, repair, and renewal protocols, which contribute decisively to reducing negative environmental impacts (Özceylan & Paksoy, 2014). According to theoretical assumptions, internal environmental management contributes to improvements in environmental performance using environmental management programs that support themselves with ISO 14001, the whole environmental certification system, information technology, and by highlighting the importance of environmental quality (Zhu et al., 2013). Environmental management systems can simultaneously support the creation and achievement of economic benefits (Kirchoff et al., 2016). The elements of internal environmental management can include commitment to green and sustainable supply chain practices, cross-functional collaboration to improve environmental protection, achieving total quality environmental management, using compliance and environmental auditing programs to achieve better environmental performance, being ISO 14001 certified, and implementing environmental management systems (Namagembe et al., 2019). Internal environmental management is also important from the point of view of customers who expect green products that are produced using environmentally friendly raw materials and processes. It also integrates environmental objectives with long-term plans that are included in strategic management records (Do et al., 2020).

Environmental regulations are extremely important in the context of creating sustainable supply chain solutions as they can be based on law and cross-sectoral arrangements and apply to specific sectors and industries. The creation and enforcement of long-term policy regulations that are sustainable and avoid unintended side effects can strengthen the actions taken (Hombach et al., 2018). Political–economic decisions relating to environmental aspects unequivocally influence the development and implementation of sustainable strategies within the framework of supply chains, while being highly relevant for all long-term, irreversible decisions with high investment, such as network structures, technology choices, and capacities (Hombach & Walther, 2015).

Governance indicators, within which we can distinguish between economic, political, and institutional governance, influence the creation of new organizational structures, as well as the implementation of sustainability aspects within supply chain strategies. The literature points to governance indicators that are proxied by economic governance (Asongu & Odhiambo, 2020), institutional governance (Zhang & Kim, 2022), and political governance (Patterson et al., 2017). Furthermore, due to the limitations of global renewable energy resources, trade and economic growth have become key commodities for the development of supply chain strategies. It can certainly be pointed out that the financial development of economies can contribute to increasing pollution levels. Economic governance promotes environmental quality by reducing pollution through quality regulation. Furthermore, institutional governance induces pollution through weaker rules of law, while the control of corruption also exacerbates pollution levels. Accountability can have positive impacts on the environment, but this depends on the type of economy as initiatives and positive effects are mainly seen in developed countries (Ofori et al., 2023).

All of these elements concerning various governance, financial, economic, political, social, and environmental support solutions also support the creation of new business strategies, which can certainly be applied to sustainable supply chains. Various indicators, solutions, examples, and case studies can be used to support these strategies. Including at least some of the elements that are part of the ESG and 3BL approaches, the SDGs are intended to create a better foundation and element base to develop a broad framework for sustainable supply chains.

2.3 Construction and Framework of a Sustainable Supply Chain: Supporting Strategies

Not only organizations but also entire supply chains are increasingly integrating sustainability aspects into their operations and strategies. The motivations for these actions taken may vary, but the essential element is the desire to provide maximum value to all stakeholders (Weber, 2008). However, research on sustainable and green supply chains has focused on the context of organization performance (Ghosh, 2019; Singh et al., 2019).

One way to implement and achieve the 3BL goals is to create and use closed-loop supply chain (CLSC) strategies (Ramanathan et al., 2023). This type of supply chain strategy not only covers the entire life cycle of a product, that is, referring to standard supply chain processes, but also combines recycling processes and various types of reverse logistics (Simonetto et al., 2022). The economic value of recycled materials within such chains should also be taken into account in this respect so that this context is considered within a circular economy (Colucci & Vecchi, 2021; Lotfi et al., 2022). Reusing materials and linking forward chains with R-strategies support the 3BL approach in terms of the economic, social, and environmental aspects while pointing to the potential of closed supply chains. The context and components of CLSCs have been defined from different perspectives (Govindan et al., 2015; Tunn et al., 2021). CLSCs are defined as the design, control, and operation of systems that maximize value creation throughout product life cycles with dynamic value recovery from different types and magnitudes of returns over time (Guide & Van Wassenhove, 2009), as well as the need for concerted efforts from all links in the supply chains to identify and highlight economic, environmental, and social value (through cultural and social change) from each process, in both traditional and return processes. The creation of theoretical frameworks and practical applications in the context of forward and reverse supply chains (and consequently, CLSCs) share some characteristics in terms of material and information flows, which definitely differ in terms of inter-organizational collaboration due to the different reasons for creating reverse chains (Simonetto et al.,

2022). In such chains, it is more difficult to define the roles and responsibilities of supply chain members, and operations are also more fuzzy and more difficult to plan (Wilson & Goffnett, 2022), which may make it more difficult to manage and achieve the planned operational efficiency, as well as the strategic objectives of all of the chains and, thus, the efficiency of the CLSCs.

Referring to the sustainable supply chain research methods that have been used, it can be pointed out that they have included both qualitative (including descriptions and case studies) and mathematized methods (including model-based terms, life cycle-based models, the use of Analytic Hierarchy Process (AHP) and fuzzy AHP analyses, decision-making using Multiple-criteria decision-making (MCDM), models based on input–output analyses, best–worst analyses, and composite methodologies). An analysis of the recent literature on the subject, along with descriptions of the research methods, is indicated in Fig. 2.3. Many quantitative methods have been used in this field. Highly popular methods have included multi-criteria methods (Li & Mathiyazhagan, 2018; Luthra & Mangla, 2018; Padhi et al., 2018) to explore critical success factors or barriers to new business strategies, and social and environmental practices. The literature also provides reviews of different modeling approaches (Oliveira et al., 2016) that can inform decision-making by political decision-makers to assess trade-offs between the economic, energy, environmental, and social pillars of sustainability for sustainable supply chains. Models to help decision-makers deal with fuzzy information have also been developed (Lin et al., 2018).

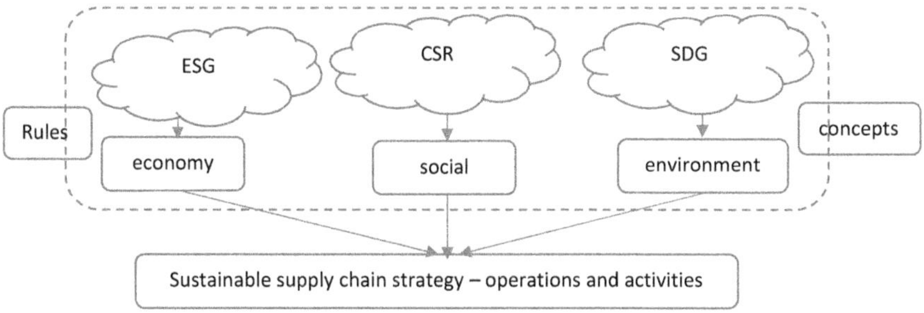

Fig. 2.3 Implementation of various concepts reflecting sustainability into the supply chain. Source: own elaborations

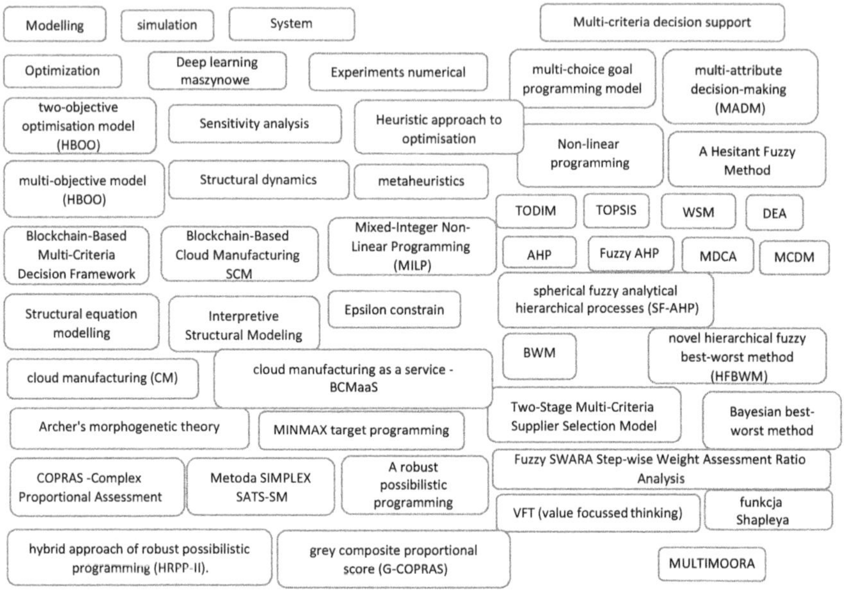

Fig. 2.4 Quantitative methods used in a sustainable supply chain—an analysis from the literature. Source: own elaborations

Data envelopment analysis (DEA) methodologies are also often used to assess green supply chain management practices, including green designs that use fuzzy data (Azadi et al., 2015).

A selection of the most common quantitative tools and methods in the literature is presented in Fig. 2.4.

The sustainable supply chain is also the subject of qualitative research, a selection of which, most frequently appearing in the literature, is shown in Fig. 2.5.

2.3.1 Green Supply Chain

Referring to the three areas of sustainability, it should be pointed out that the environmental dimension focuses on minimizing the negative environmental impacts of supply chain operations (Hassini et al., 2012) and is intrinsically linked to green supply chain management (de Sousa

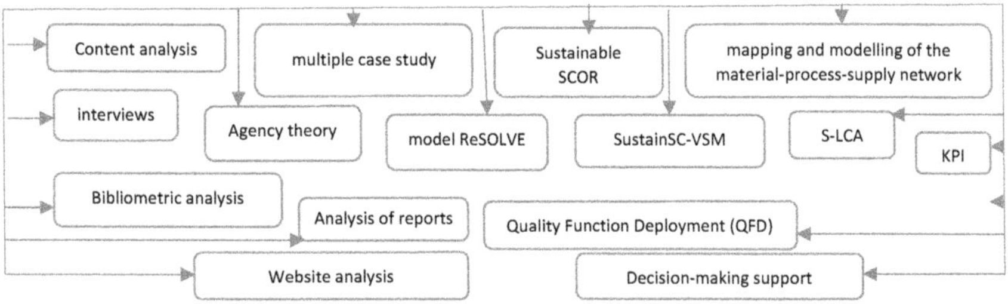

Fig. 2.5 Qualitative methods used in a sustainable supply chain—an analysis from the literature. Source: own elaborations

Jabbour, 2015; Luthra et al., 2014). Managing the environmental aspect requires a variety of elements, including environmental cooperation and monitoring (Xu & Gursoy, 2015).

Important elements included in the framework of environmental cooperation that involves pollution prevention and environmental protection are as follows:

1. Product redesign (Vachon, 2007)
2. Redesigning production processes in the context of green byproducts (Tsai et al., 2011)
3. Product management during use (Neto et al., 2013)
4. Product life extension (Matos & Hall, 2007)
5. End-of-life recovery processes (Linton et al., 2007)

The indicated elements are the main sources of practical representations of the green supply chain concept. Green processes occur along entire supply chains and this forms the basis for developing the theoretical and practical framework for this type of supply chain strategy.

2.3.2 Social Supply Chains

The creation of assumptions and their consistent observance within the area of social responsibility in supply chains relate primarily to ethical behaviors and environmental impacts, which are monitored and controlled by NGOs and human rights activists. Companies are assessed and perceived by the public through the lens of corporate social responsibility. At the same time, any negative practices or actions that are uncovered translate into negative implications for organizations and their supply chains, which can unequivocally contribute to reducing market shares and damaging corporate reputations (Ghasemy Yaghin & Sarlak, 2020). Responsible supply chains can be unequivocally identified using the integration of CSR activities into supply chain modalities, strategies, and management. In such chains, there is not only the autonomous responsibility of the organizations but of all of the chains, as well as the extended notion incorporating social sustainability, which is becoming increasingly important in the development of such strategies. Therefore, we can consider socially responsible purchasing (Johnsen et al., 2017; Schulze & Bals, 2020; Silva & Ruel, 2022), as well as socially responsible logistics (Miao et al., 2012; Sudarto et al., 2016, 2017; Uyar et al., 2020) and social responsibility in transportation and shipping (Yuen et al., 2017). Responsible supply chains can be part of virtually any supply chain, whether traditional, green, or agile. At the same time, they can form the basis and one of the main elements of creating sustainable supply chain frameworks. This concept implements CSR principles, although not only for individual links, activities, or processes. A great deal of importance is placed on the human–organization (supply chain) relationship. Certainly, in defining and distinguishing the characteristic parts of these chains, it is necessary to include atypical actors who play important roles in their functioning. In addition to consumers, trendsetters and influencers with prescriptive and regulatory tools are rulers (as consumers, as well as the regulators, coordinators, and transmitters of incentives), non-governmental organizations (NGOs, who transmit knowledge, have power, and are able to use the tools of pressure and coercion), and institutional investors (Tundys, 2016). In the context of the social aspects, it is important to mention that there is virtually no consensus on how to measure the social performance of companies. The constituent elements and determinants of this aspect are indicated as justice, ethics, human rights, philanthropy, safety, health, and welfare, which are broadly understood as the elements of CSR (Ayton et al., 2022).

The most important standards that underpin the implementation of this type of concept, either as a stand-alone strategy or as part of a more elaborate concept (e.g., sustainable supply chains), include meeting legal requirements regarding environmental aspects, labor laws, and the laws and regulations that are applicable in all countries where links in the supply chains are located. Particular importance is attributed to anti-corruption aspects concerning the conduct of business, among other areas. In addition, another important element is the implementation of effective environmental policies and support for environmental protection, the freedom and fairness of employment (i.e., no slave or forced labor), the avoidance of child labor, and compliance with the principles of non-discrimination, meaning equal opportunities and development opportunities for all employees, regardless of race, origin, gender, nationality, age, disability, sexual orientation, or religion. The standards on the payment of wages are in accordance with all applicable local practices, as is adherence to standardized and applicable working hours and the right of employees to freedom of association, humane treatment, and the provision of appropriate health and safety rules, as well as anti-corruption measures (Tundys, 2018). Incorporating responsible business standards into supply chain management achieves the following benefits: reducing business risks and increasing market shares, optimizing costs, increasing supplier and customer loyalty, increasing the quality of suppliers' products and services, and better access to business financing options (Chauhan et al., 2022; Yu et al., 2023).

The principles and determinants of corporate social responsibility are transforming and becoming elements of socially responsible supply chains, as linked to society's expectations (Pfajfar et al., 2022). Social responsibility in supply chains is voluntary, involves internalizing and managing externalities, is oriented toward stakeholders, aligns the aspects of social and economic responsibility, addresses both practical solutions and value systems, and goes beyond mere philanthropy (Yuen & Lim, 2016). The approaches to and elements of social responsibility have been transformed by the impact of the COVID-19 pandemic on all global economies (Sheehy & Farneti, 2021; Zhao, 2021). It is a broad concept, covering many areas and issues, far beyond classically understood philanthropy (Amaeshi et al., 2016). Responsible supply chains involve taking responsibility beyond the organizations and beyond the extended enterprises (Spence & Bourlakis, 2009). Four key features of supply chain responsibility have been outlined in the literature (Spence & Bourlakis, 2009): the commitment of chain participants to achieving social (and environmental) benefits; the ability of each link in supply chains to present its own position; a true partnership approach; and the acceptance of different approaches to ethical issues that are specific to the different organizational forms present in the supply chains. Such activities often require the use of advanced management tools as part of their management activities (Miemczyk et al., 2012); therefore, within such chains, it is important to move from traditional negotiations, cooperation, and close collaboration to partnerships with different stakeholders within the chains, who often have conflicting objectives for their actions and completely different perceptions of the markets (Dwivedi et al., 2022; Orji et al., 2020; Pfajfar et al., 2022).

2.3.3 R-Strategies

R-strategies, identified as parts of a circular economy and thus parts of closed supply chains, are an important element to be considered when creating sustainable supply chains. In this respect, the basis for consideration is the model developed by the Ellen MacArthur Foundation (Ellen MacArthur, 2015) that identifies technical and biological cycles that are related to linkages and processes that occur in all economies and creates assumptions for such concepts. Within the framework of the identified solutions, activities are promoted that can transform organizations and their supply chains, as well as entire economies, toward closed business cycles. These include, in classic terms, regenerating, sharing, optimizing, looping, virtualizing, and exchanging (Nowicka, 2021). Research and practical solutions have made it possible to decisively extend the indicated actions and create a catalogue of strategies, referred to in the literature as "R-strategies" (Morseletto, 2020; Potting et al., 2017; Reike et al., 2018). The most commonly discussed, researched, and identified R-strategies in the literature include the following (Ossio et al., 2023; Papamichael et al., 2023): refuse, rethink, reduce, redesign, return, reuse, repair, refurbish, remanufacture, repurpose, renovate, recycle, and recover. The assumptions of the circular economy are becoming the basis for new environmental models that are being implemented by organizations and their supply chains. The following practices should be used as much as possible as parts of new strategies: maintenance, repair, refurbishment, redistribution, upgrading, resale, and waste minimization (Fogarassy & Finger, 2020). Therefore, closed-loop economies are emerging as sustainability paradigms that are capable of decoupling economic growth from resource consumption and waste generation (Bressanelli et al., 2020), and R-strategies implemented in sustainable supply chains can add value to the individual processes. The value is in using each of the R-strategies as an additional element to support environmental sustainability and protection.

2.3.4 Closed-Loop Supply Chains

The concept of closing the loops within supply chains refers to integrating both forward and return activities into processes. It is considered as an option for increasing sustainability (Banasik et al., 2017). There are many publications that have indicated the current state-of-the-art practices within this field (Battini et al., 2017; Bressanelli et al., 2019a, 2019b). Many studies and scientific publications have been based on specific solutions and, unfortunately, cannot be generalized or applied as universal solutions (Bag et al., 2022; Bag & Pretorius, 2022; Kurniawan et al., 2022; Simonetto et al., 2022).

Analyzing the theoretical assumptions of closed-loop supply chains, forward flows are responsible for meeting demand for new products, while reverse flows are responsible for collecting and recovering returned products (Haddadsisakht & Ryan, 2018). The CLSC concept can offer many benefits, including savings, compared to traditional supply chains (Fleischmann et al., 2001). The implementation of the concept proposes the use of various methods and analysis tools from linear programming (Beamon & Fernandes, 2004; Özkır & Başlıgıl, 2012) to case study analysis and generalizable models (Salema et al., 2007), which use global factors to unify the models as much as possible (Amin & Baki, 2017). In the context of recent research and also extending this line of research, it is important to point to another strand of research on issues involving uncertainty that are related to changes in business environments. Optimization models that deal with uncertainty and are based on loop closure strategies have been presented (Ramezani et al., 2013). Fuzzy linear programming that optimizes solutions and builds resilient chains that also integrate different types of risks has also been presented (Jabbarzadeh, Fahimnia, & Sabouhi, 2018; Jindal & Sangwan, 2014; Subulan et al., 2015). The social aspect has also been covered in the research (Fathollahi-Fard et al., 2018). Another strand of research is the environmental aspect, incorporating environmental costs (Paksoy et al., 2011), facility location models (Das & Posinasetti, 2015), and environmental uncertainty (nodal footprint study) in studies and models (Mohajeri & Fallah, 2016). Optimization issues have also been explored, identifying opportunities to control supply chain uncertainties by integrating environmental approaches (Talaei et al., 2016). The literature is also rich in models that integrate 3BL approaches and cover the social, economic, and environmental aspects (Mota et al., 2018). In this respect, a great deal of work and solutions have been developed using quantitative methods to optimize closed-loop supply chains (Alegoz et al., 2020). In terms of closed-loop supply chains, the concept can be said to be successful when there is extensive collaboration and engagement between forward supply chains and reverse supply chains, as well as collaboration in decision-making and an understanding of the importance of sustainability in all processes and operations (Ramanathan et al., 2023). The scope, assumptions, and elements that are considered when attempting to create research frameworks for closed-loop supply chains are aligned with those for sustainable supply chains. Different perspectives and tools can be considered when developing the theoretical underpinnings and practical verifications of the models, and those assumptions then underpin sustainable supply chains. One analysis of the literature and practical solutions for CLSCs indicated an interest in designs from customer, product, and process perspectives (Simonetto et al., 2022), taking into account backward and forward processes (i.e., the environmental and economic contexts). Closed-loop supply chains focus on eliminating waste and using products and processes repeatedly without any unnecessary take-offs, taking into account the changes that take place in economies and societies (Bressanelli et al., 2019b).

2.4 Sustainable Supply Chains

Strong, innovative, and sustainable supply chains place appropriate emphasis on social development, ensuring income equality, workplace safety, social inclusion, ethical business practices, and fair working conditions (Gopalakrishnan et al., 2012). Holistically, integrating the areas of sustainability (social practices and environmental aspects) has been examined in terms of organizational performance (Das, 2018; Das & Jharkharia, 2018). However, other extremely important elements are the context of their design and the creation of frameworks that guide other organizations and supply chains on what activities they should integrate into their newly developed business strategies and how.

Sustainable chain issues can be considered from different perspectives. They relate to the development of conceptual frameworks, exploring the dependencies and linkages in the different areas of the chains or analyzing methods (managerial and quantitative) to address the management of the chains.

Therefore, it is necessary to start with the design of sustainable supply chains and the practices and methods that support this process, while taking into account 3BL indicators. There are several frameworks that can be used to classify the activities undertaken: presenting frameworks for performance (Chardine-Baumann & Botta-Genoulaz, 2014), bibliometric analyses, descriptive analyses of sustainable supply chain assumptions (Martins & Pato, 2019), and evaluating and measuring the sustainability performance of SCs and methods (Qorri et al., 2018).

Most of the models for sustainable supply chain designs presented in the literature are conceptual approaches. Solutions based on mathematical models can also be found in this field (Altmann, 2015; Brandenburg et al., 2014; Guo et al., 2021). Often, a selection of indicators has been used in the designs to reflect the individual areas of sustainability. These serve to support the assumptions and justifications of particular models, including elements related to energy management, the carbon footprints of demand functions, profits, emissions vs. costs, production allocation vs. energy mix size, and recycling technology alternatives. Individual indicators are often linked to other measures to provide coherent approaches and address the areas of 3BL. In addition, also included in the design is the scope of the closed-loop chains. As part of the solutions, socially responsible closed-loop models of supply chains have been developed, taking into account, for example, donations and the recycling of used products (Kazemi et al., 2019; Modak et al., 2019). In this aspect, much emphasis is placed on modular product development to facilitate faster manufacturing, disassembly, remanufacturing, refurbishment, and using new, reusable, and repairable components and modular assemblies (Das & Posinasetti, 2015), including aspects of reverse logistics (Haddadsisakht & Ryan, 2018; Sgarbossa & Russo, 2017).

The social aspect is collaborative planning (Allaoui et al., 2019). The moral and ethical values of managers and employees are important in terms of sustainable supply chain practices and are an important part of implementing new concepts (Paulraj et al., 2017). In this regard, the creation of new jobs can be discussed in conjunction with the economic aspect (Chavez et al., 2020).

The implementation of sustainability practices can be considered as initiatives of organizations themselves (Piyathanavong et al., 2019), which can be considered as elements of competitive advantage. This advantage can be seen as socially legitimate by stakeholders (Baliga et al., 2020). Various motivators for the actions taken can be distinguished; there are motivators of moral, instrumental, and relational nature, which affect the dimensions of sustainability practices within sustainable supply chains to different extents and in different ways (Aguilera et al., 2007).

It is worth pointing out that in many studies, the authors have justified the choice and necessity of implementing the concept of sustainability within supply chains and have referred to management theory, including the theory of stakeholders, who, through the pressure they exert, have been able to force changes in the strategies that have been carried out so far, including the elimination of the negative impacts of organizations and supply chains on the environment, the failure to respect the rights of employees, and the identification of negative impacts in terms of the social aspect (Touboulic & Walker, 2015). It is also not insignificant to refer to institutional theory (Paulraj et al., 2017). Organizations that strive for social sustainability are more reputable, respected, and less vulnerable to risks (Ajmal et al., 2018). It is worth pointing out that the scope of the research has included resilience and sustainability (Jabbarzadeh, Haughton, & Khosrojerdi, 2018) and the impact of sustainability practices on supply chain risks (Gouda & Saranga, 2018). There is also emerging research on sustainability in relation to innovation (Gupta et al., 2020; Kusi-Sarpong et al., 2019).

Another area of research that is quite popular in the literature is the problem of supplier selection, which includes both economic and environmental criteria (Azadnia et al., 2015; Hashemi et al., 2015; Yoon et al., 2018). 3BL can also be extended to supplier selection, as well as their evaluation (Dai & Blackhurst, 2012).

Many of the elements associated with sustainable supply chains are related to the problem of uncertainty, which has been studied using stochastic approaches (Lee et al., 2010) to design sustainable logistics networks. The extent of the operational and environmental trade-offs in the indicated processes and demand uncertainty have also been studied (Martí et al., 2015). Nonlinear programming models that assume demand uncertainty have also been used in this regard (Mirzapour Al-e-hashem et al., 2013).

To summarize, it should be pointed out that the literature defines a sustainable supply chain as the management of materials, information, and capital flows and cooperation between the companies along the supply chain while achieving the goals set within the three dimensions of sustainability (i.e., economic, social, and environmental), which are derived from the requirements of customers and stakeholders (Seuring & Müller, 2008). In terms of the theoretical construction of this type of strategy, there is a focus on the voluntary integration of social, economic, and environmental aspects in business systems, leading to the creation of coordinated supply chain concepts that can effectively manage the materials, information, and capital associated with logistics processes to improve the profitability of the flows. Supply chains that are built in this way are pro-environmental, as well as sources of profits in the long term (Hou et al., 2019; Taghipour & Beneteau-Piet, 2020).

There are many factors that can determine the functioning of sustainable supply chains. These include "green" warehousing, strategic cooperation with suppliers, environmental protection, continuous improvement, the use of information technology, the optimization of logistics processes, internal pressure, institutional pressure, social and ethical values, corporate strategies and commitments, economic stability, green product design, social pressure, increased customer expectations, organizational image, regulations, competitive pressure, the scarcity of natural resources, and sustainable partnerships. Holistic approaches are needed for the creation and management of these supply chains, which require the synergistic combination of corporate social responsibility, environmental management, and supply chain management (Calzolari et al., 2022; Hendiani et al., 2022; Saeed & Kersten, 2017; Tseng et al., 2022; Tundys & Fernando, 2019).

Characteristics and an indication of the importance of social and environmental performance are shown in Table 2.2.

In the simplest terms, the idea of sustainable supply chains can be understood as a coherent concept encompassing the assumptions and principles of efficient, that is, traditional, supply chains, which form the basis for building the new concept, then adding the principles of green, socially responsible chains (along with the need to take into account various atypical stakeholders). Undoubtedly, when considering the issues of sustainable supply chain strategies, it is additionally necessary to add

Table 2.2 Social and environmental performance in supply chain

Supply chain		Social performance: Low	Social performance: High
Environmental performance	Low	Efficient SC (linked to the old, traditional business paradigm, where decisions are made and based solely on financial performance)	Social SC (linked to incentives for decision-making based on social outcomes (often in addition to financial results)
	High	Green SC (linked to incentives for decision-making based on environmental performance (often in addition to financial performance)	Sustainable SC (linked to the new business paradigm, in which decisions are based on balancing economic, social, and environmental objectives)

Source: own elaborations on the basis of Silvestre (2016)

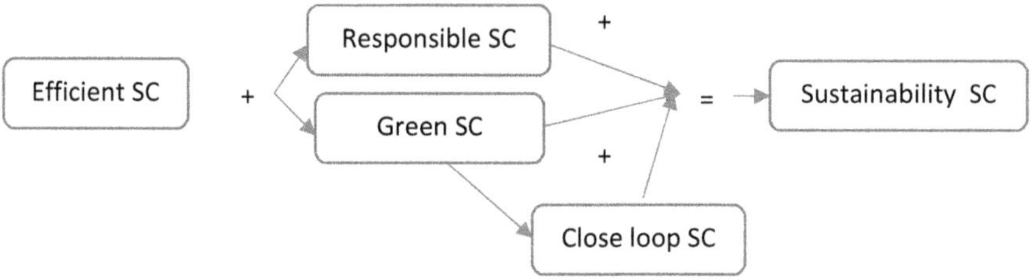

Fig. 2.6 Sustainable supply chain—concept. Source: own elaborations

$$SSC = ESC + GSC + SRSC + CLSC$$

SSC – sustainable supply chain, ESC – efficiency supply chain, GSC – green supply chain, SRSC – social responsible supply chain, CLSC – close loop supply chain

Fig. 2.7 Sustainable supply chain—elements and concepts

elements related to closed-loop supply chains. In this case, it is primarily a matter of including new solutions for the R-strategies and reverse logistics processes; then, a holistic and broadly understood basis for sustainable supply chains can emerge. A graphical reflection is presented in Fig. 2.6.

Thus, when considering the assumptions of a sustainable supply chain, it can be pointed out that it contains all the requirements and components of the concepts associated with a green, responsible, closed (especially reverse) supply chain (Fig. 2.7).

Expanding on the issues identified in Fig. 2.7, individual concepts can be considered in more depth (Fig. 2.8).

The framework of a sustainable supply chain is shown in Fig. 2.9.

Summarizing the considerations in general into the framework of a sustainable supply chain and its assumptions, it is possible to show the elements that can be found in Fig. 2.10.

Analyzing the data in Fig. 2.10, it is important to point out that there are a number of challenges and components facing the implementation of sustainability practices in current supply chain frameworks. The effectiveness, efficiency, and, above all, prevalence of such solutions can be influenced by global economic situations, crises, and challenges that are

$$SSC = C + Q + T + TBL + CSR + ESG + R`s$$

C- cost, Q-quality, T- time, TBL – triple bottom line, CSR – corporate social responsibility, ESG - Environmental, social, and governance, R`s- Strategy R

Fig. 2.8 Sustainable supply chain—elements (part 2)

associated with them (e.g., COVID-19, the war in Ukraine, demonetization), which is clearly associated with new regulations in the sense of administrative and governmental restrictions and regulations (Vishwakarma et al., 2022), as well as increases in customer demands for products and other external issues (Chowdhury et al., 2021). Nonetheless, environmental, economic, and social issues are extremely important and, at the same time, can provide competitive advantages (De Angelis et al., 2018). Therefore, it is important to identify the factors that motivate or compel companies to integrate sustainability into their operations (Alzubi & Akkerman, 2022).

2.4.1 Barriers

There are many barriers that can be identified when innovating sustainability practices (Gupta et al., 2020). Among the most important barriers, both in the context of creating a circular economy and for extending research to sustainable supply chains, are the following aspects (Galvão et al., 2018; Kayikci et al., 2021): technological, policy and regulatory, financial and economic, performance indicators, customers, and social. Other important elements that can be considered as barriers that have been mentioned in the literature include the following (Albloushy & Hiller Connell, 2019; Kitsis & Chen, 2023; Vishwakarma et al., 2022): communication gaps between stakeholders, the increased costs of adopting SSCM, the adoption of modern technologies for cleaner production, barriers that effect performance, government policies and regulations, the lack of training and education about sustainability, consumer-related barriers (lack of awareness about purchasing eco-friendly apparel), the lack of eco-literacy among supply chain partners, capacity constraints, and the lack of reverse logistics practices. From another perspective, barriers can also include information and knowledge

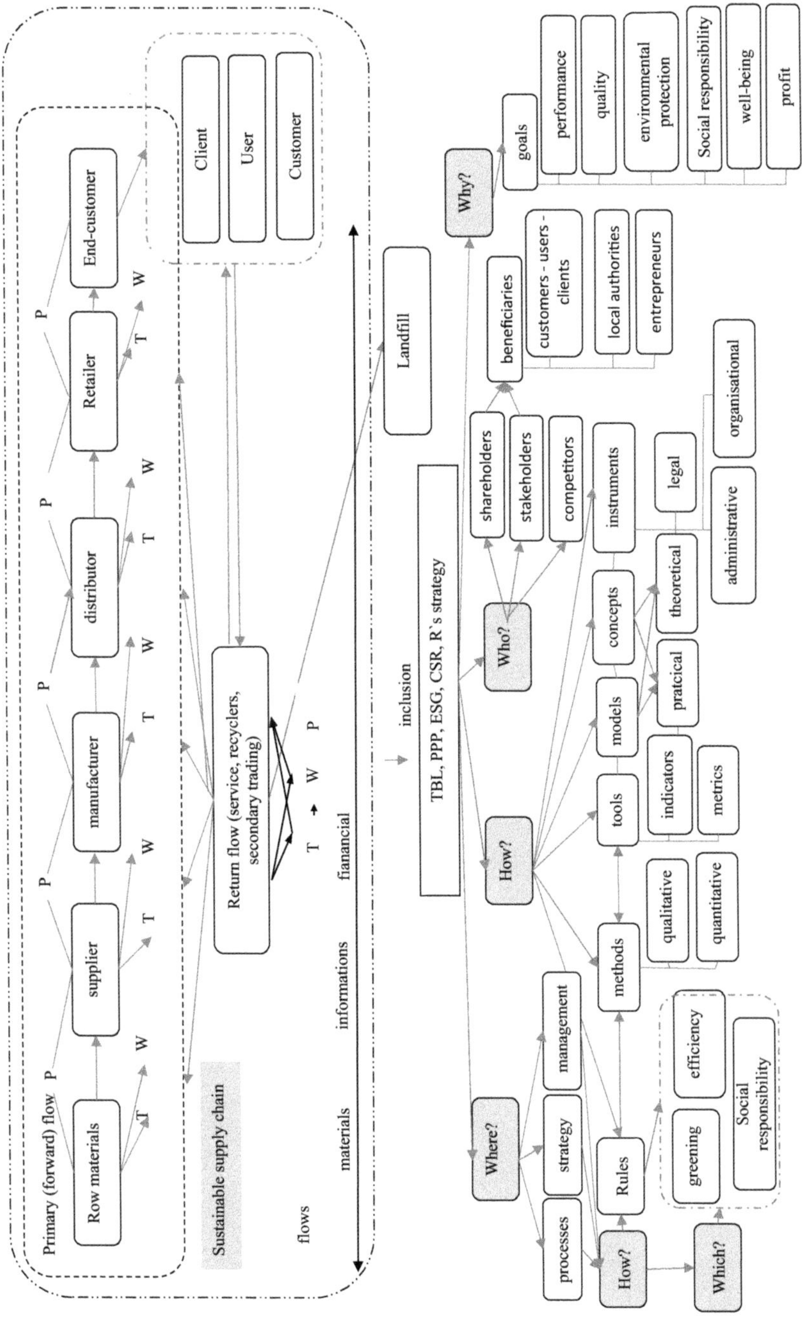

Fig. 2.9 Sustainable supply chain framework

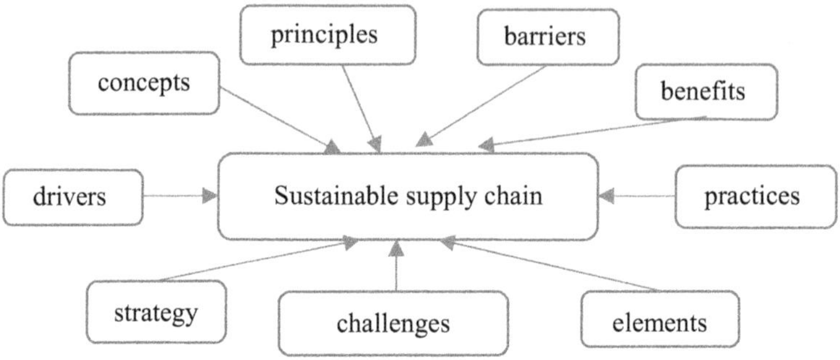

Fig. 2.10 Framework of SSC on the basis of the literature. Source: own elaborations

gaps, communication, compliance or implementation gaps regarding guidelines, and power gaps related to relationships between supply chain actors (Boström et al., 2015). The recent literature has cited the following as the most important barriers to implementing sustainable supply chains: the lack of sustainable outsourcing, the lack of sustainable manufacturing and distribution, fear of and resistance to sustainable competitiveness and innovation, trust deficits in sustainable buyer–supplier relationships, the lack of buyer–supplier relationships, the lack of sustainable marketing and organizational culture, difficulties in sustainable knowledge sharing, the complexity of adopting sustainable technology practices, the risk of misguided investments, insufficient legislation and controls, the lack of government and management support, organizational cultures that are inhibitive to sustainability/CSR, the lack of regulations and the enforcement of environmental standards, the lack of green purchasing, the lack of performance metrics/evaluation standards for sustainability, and resistance to change and adopting innovations in sustainability (Govindan & Hasanagic, 2018; Kumar et al., 2021; Majumdar & Sinha, 2019; Menon & Ravi, 2021; Nazam et al., 2020).

2.4.2 Drivers

There are many reasons and incentives for organizations to adopt sustainability principles as part of their supply chain strategies. In the literature, the main drivers have been defined as external (outside the organizations) or internal (inside the organizations) factors (Saeed & Kersten, 2019). The external elements have been further divided into regulatory pressures (certifications, government legislation, regional or international regulatory bodies, and trade associations), social pressures (social welfare, consumer organizations, and media and public pressures), and market pressures (globalization, customer pressure, reputational image, supplier pressure, competitive advantage, competitive pressure, shareholder pressure, and institutional pressure). The external factors also include corporate strategies (organizations' operational/economic performance, cost pressures, and top management commitment), organizational culture (sociocultural responsibility, innovations, codes of business conduct, information dissemination, and health and safety), organizational resources (resource depletion, human capital, employee pressure/engagement, technology and equipment, and training and development), and organizational characteristics (position in supply chains, industry sector, size, geographic location, the degree of internationalization, and the current level of sustainability efforts). The internal elements also include economic optimization, business risk management, brand image, and top management support to achieve commitment to the implementation of environmental regulations (Guimarães et al., 2022; Sajjad et al., 2015). Certainly, drivers for SSC implementation can include management commitments, organizational commitments, supportive cultures, improved productivity, eliminating waste, and being able to compete and gain better competitive positions, greater social commitments, and corporate social responsibility, as well as meeting environmental regulatory requirements and increasing the involvement of various stakeholders (including consumers), as well as regulatory pressure, institutional pressure, international environmental regulations, competition, environmental regulations, and reputation. From another perspective, it can be said that the motivating factors offer opportunities to enter new markets, obtain new business opportunities, reduce costs, intensify regulations, improve consumer awareness and supply chain cooperation (i.e., helping to manage risks and integrate sustainable practices into production processes), and manage corporate images of damage, competitive risk, social responsibility (Olatunji et al., 2019), and collaboration and transparency among supply chain members (Yadav et al., 2020). Other motivators include financial stability, flexible and green product design, organizational culture, strategic supplier collaboration, enabling technologies and information, logistics optimization, and corporate commitment on the topic (Shibin et al., 2016). Barriers to implementing sustainable supply chains can be divided into internal and external barriers (Sajjad et al., 2015). Internal barriers include the lack of interest from top and middle management, financial constraints or high costs, legal and administrative complexities, risk aversion, the lack of awareness, negative perceptions of environmental procurement, and the lack of management skills, experience, and necessary tools. External factors include the lack of ability to measure sustainable supply chain performance, inadequate regulations, substandard performance metrics, the lack of cooperation among supply chain partners, the lack of standardized approaches to environmental principles, and the necessary outcomes to reduce the negative environmental impacts of logistics processes (Olatunji et al., 2019). Additionally, the lack of awareness and understanding of the benefits that flow from and can be obtained by implementing sustainability principles is of great importance, as well as uncertainty about processes and market acceptance of sustainable innovations (Gupta et al., 2020).

2.4.3 Benefits

Adopting and implementing SSC principles provides many benefits and profits for companies and their supply chains, including reduced product costs, better customer–supplier relationships, and achieving a circular economy (De Angelis et al., 2018; Unger & Landis, 2016). In terms of benefits, the most straightforward aspects of PPP can be pointed out as follows: "people" = job quality, workforce capability, and societal conditions (Caiado et al., 2022; Yadav et al., 2020), "planet" = energy savings, resource savings, and design; "profit" = flexibility, time for market cycles, quality, and cost/profit relations; as well as better working conditions, improved product quality, and reduced health and safety costs (Ahmed et al., 2019; Qin & Chen, 2022; Schoenherr et al., 2014; Wang et al., 2023).

2.4.4 Challenges

The main challenges of implementing sustainable supply chains are overcoming problems with inadequate communication between suppliers, including information distortion, low environmental awareness, and inaccessibility of the latest technologies, as well as financial barriers, the lack of perfectly educated managers who can ensure strategic cooperation, and the good integration of SSC principles (Shibin et al., 2016). Nowadays, in addition to the aspects previously indicated, there are also disruptions related to increased risks that did not exist before, such as those concerning the ripple effect (Dolgui & Ivanov, 2021), COVID-19 (Sajjad, 2021; Sharma et al., 2022) and the war in Ukraine, as well as the threat of other armed conflicts, which can affect not only the effective functioning of supply chains but also the implementation of innovative solutions, such as the principles of sustainable development (Allam et al., 2022; Krykavskyy et al., 2023; Nurpribadi & Rulianti, 2022).

2.4.5 Principles and Paradigms

In terms of principles, there are all kinds of assumptions and principles that are involved in the frameworks of components, including those of 3BL and PPP (i.e., the environmental, economic, and social aspects), CSR (i.e., the assumptions of the most socially responsible approach to be implemented within the frameworks of individual processes, activities, and operations in supply chains), and ESG (based on the assumptions of environmental, social, and financial governance). These principles and paradigms also include the implementation of the new EU taxonomy in activities and fundraising for supply chain operations, the assumptions of the R-strategies concerning agile processes in supply chains, and the general principles of a circular economy. There are also elements related to extending the life cycles of products, waste-free designs, and the use of regenerative resources (Giudice et al., 2020). These elements also support the creation of closed-loop supply chains (Fogarassy & Finger, 2020; Wuyts et al., 2020). The implementation of the principles identified in the earlier concepts could provide long-term opportunities for building economic resilience, while contributing to the achievement of 3BL in terms of social, economic, and societal development (Ferrari et al., 2023; Nandi et al., 2021). There is no doubt that the paradigm of sustainability, with its ties to economic, social, and environmental aspects, is the most important element in creating sustainable supply chains (Joshi, 2022).

2.4.6 Strategies and Concepts

Innovative solutions that are based on sustainability issues form the basis of new supply chain strategies. These strategies include appropriately redefined management and the process of controlling and managing the flow of information, materials, and capital, as well as cooperation between companies along the supply chains, taking into account the triple bottom line (i.e., the economic, social, and environmental dimensions) of sustainability, as well as the requirements of customers and stakeholders (Reefke & Sundaram, 2018; Seuring & Müller, 2008). In this regard, new sustainable supply chain strategies and concepts are characterized by the integration and implementation of supply chain structures and the linkages of economic, social, and environmental aspects that relate to the processes of the planning, execution, disposal, and return of products, as well as the processes, actions, and decisions taken along the chains (Esfahbodi et al., 2016; Kusi-Sarpong et al., 2019). These strategies mean that resources, information, and finances within supply chains are managed so as to maximize profits and social well-being while minimizing environmental concerns, taking into account as much as possible the principles and actions adopted in the circular economy and the implementation of the R-strategies. This means that the scope of the strategies helps to reduce the negative impacts of supply chain operations on the environment while taking care of social welfare and improving the performance of organizations from social, economic, and environmental perspectives (Feng et al., 2018; Tachizawa & Yew Wong, 2014). Sustainable supply chain strategies achieve "win-win-win" situations (Danese et al., 2019) by achieving conflicting goals, as maximizing profits means reducing operating costs, minimizing environmental impacts, and maximizing social well-being, which may require additional costs

(Hassini et al., 2012). These strategies must have the tools to solve standard problems, deal with multiple actors along the supply chains, and also evaluate the decisions made from the point of view of social benefits and environmental impacts, while being linked to other strategies in the supply chains related to inventory management, product planning, distribution, warehousing or appropriate packaging, transportation mode selection, recovery, green design energy, waste management, and emissions reduction.

In terms of concepts, there are universal solutions that are based on models (quantitative (optimization) or qualitative (management decisions)). Concepts associated with models are often verified in practice so that their assumptions can be reflected in business practices. Based on the assumptions in the literature, it can be pointed out that sustainable supply chain concepts include concepts related to value creation, as well as social, environmental, and economic aspects (Stindt, 2017), supply chain planning matrices, supply chain operations reference (SCOR) models (Ntabe et al., 2015), and reverse supply chain planning matrices, in which all phases along which SSC practices should be considered, including raw material extraction, procurement, supply chain coordination, manufacturing, distribution, utilization, and returns. These concepts also include the research fields of sustainable product design, sustainable supply chain design, sustainable procurement, sustainable manufacturing, sustainable warehousing and inventory management, industrial symbiosis, product stewardship, sustainable logistics, eco-efficient manufacturing, and human-oriented manufacturing.

2.4.7 Elements

The elements included in sustainable supply chain frameworks are presented in Figs. 2.2 and 2.9. One of the most important elements of sustainable supply chains is the implementation of sustainability principles within the scope of each element of the chains, including feedback processes. In addition, certain concepts, such as CSR, ESG, and the R-strategies, should also be considered.

2.4.8 Practices

Practices not only refer to improving environmental impacts and reducing negative impacts but also to improving performance. The practice parts of the solutions refer to the correlations between the elements of the chains, as well as the activities included in the strategies, such as trust and reciprocity (Dias & Silva, 2022) and supply chain performance, which is related to, for example, information sharing and resource sharing (Dias et al., 2023). Various studies have shown the positive correlations and performance impacts of information sharing, resource sharing, trust, and reciprocity (Najjar et al., 2019). Sustainable supply chain practices can be internal or external and can affect sustainable performance and quality assurance (Kuwornu et al., 2023).

Another practical reflection is taking actions that are expected to result in increased quality. These practices include activities that concern the environment (environmental protection) and society (minimum security, equity, philanthropy, and human rights). There are not only many factors that prompt chain balancing efforts but there are also many different types of practices. These identified factors determine the scope and type of sustainable supply chain practices (León-Bravo et al., 2019).

Sustainable supply chain practices can be divided into internal and external practices (Alzubi & Akkerman, 2022). Internal SSCM practices include redesigning products using biodegradable materials and designing more energy-efficient manufacturing and distribution processes (Carter et al., 2020; Wu et al., 2018). In addition, these practices include waste reduction, the use of clean energy, process redesigns to reduce pollution, energy use, water use, and the implementation of ISO 14001, which can have a significant impact on environmental performance and overall competitiveness (De Giovanni, 2012; De Giovanni & Vinzi, 2012; Ikram et al., 2020). Companies' responsibility for the environment should also not be forgotten, such as the use of recyclable materials for product and packaging redesign (Rehman et al., 2021). External practices include those outside organizational boundaries that are related to supplier selection, working with stakeholders, and auditing organizations based on their environmental performance, which can lead to improved product quality and increased market shares by attracting new customers (Rao & Holt, 2005; Tseng et al., 2018).

Within the context of sustainable supply chain practices, there are two strategies that firms can apply: compliance, in which companies follow rules and regulations, or voluntary strategies, in which companies voluntarily adopt SSCM practices to gain a competitive advantage (Peters et al., 2011). Organizations can be proactive or reactive in applying SSCM practices within their operations (Rehman et al., 2021). There are many reasons why organizations undertake sustainability-related activities and adopt such practices in their operations, such as improving their image, better competitive position, improving environmental quality, reducing costs (including energy costs), improving the quality of their products, services, and processes, or simply increasing the awareness of managers (Bloemhof & Soysal, 2017). The adoption of these practices is helped or required by government regulations, stakeholder pressures, efficiency, safety, market forces, social issues, and global warming (León Bravo et al., 2021). Supply chain activities become complex and social footprints and demand flows require better attention (Davis-Sramek et al., 2022; Fernando et al., 2022), so steps must be taken to make supply chains as sustainable as possible.

References

Aguilera, R. V., Rupp, D. E., Williams, C. A., & Ganapathi, J. (2007). Putting the S back in corporate social responsibility: A multilevel theory of social change in organizations. *Academy of Management Review, 32*(3), 836–863.

Ahi, P., & Searcy, C. (2015). Assessing sustainability in the supply chain: A triple bottom line approach. *Applied Mathematical Modelling, 39*(10–11), 2882–2896.

Ahmed, M. U., Gölgeci, I., Bayraktar, E., & Tatoglu, E. (2019). Environmental practices and firm performance in emerging markets: The mediating role of product quality. *Production Planning & Control, 30*(4), 315–328.

Ajmal, M. M., Khan, M., Hussain, M., & Helo, P. (2018). Conceptualizing and incorporating social sustainability in the business world. *International Journal of Sustainable Development & World Ecology, 25*(4), 327–339.

Albloushy, H., & Hiller Connell, K. Y. (2019). Purchasing environmentally sustainable apparel: The attitudes and intentions of female Kuwaiti consumers. *International Journal of Consumer Studies, 43*(4), 390–401.

Alegoz, M., Kaya, O., & Bayindir, Z. P. (2020). Closing the loop in supply chains: Economic and environmental effects. *Computers & Industrial Engineering, 142*, 106366.

Allam, Z., Bibri, S. E., & Sharpe, S. A. (2022). The rising impacts of the COVID-19 pandemic and the Russia–Ukraine war: Energy transition, climate justice, global inequality, and supply chain disruption. *Resources, 11*(11), 99.

Allaoui, H., Guo, Y., Choudhary, A., & Bloemhof, J. (2018). Sustainable agro-food supply chain design using two-stage hybrid multi-objective decision-making approach. *Computers & Operations Research, 89*, 369–384.

Allaoui, H., Guo, Y., & Sarkis, J. (2019). Decision support for collaboration planning in sustainable supply chains. *Journal of Cleaner Production, 229*, 761–774.

Altmann, M. (2015). A supply chain design approach considering environmentally sensitive customers: The case of a German manufacturing SME. *International Journal of Production Research, 53*(21), 6534–6550.

Alzubi, E., & Akkerman, R. (2022). Sustainable supply chain management practices in developing countries: An empirical study of Jordanian manufacturing companies. *Cleaner Production Letters, 2*, 100005.

Amaeshi, K., Adegbite, E., Ogbechie, C., Idemudia, U., Kan, K. A. S., Issa, M., & Anakwue, O. I. (2016). Corporate social responsibility in SMEs: A shift from philanthropy to institutional works? *Journal of Business Ethics, 138*, 385–400.

Amin, S. H., & Baki, F. (2017). A facility location model for global closed-loop supply chain network design. *Applied Mathematical Modelling, 41*, 316–330.

Asongu, S. A., & Odhiambo, N. M. (2020). Foreign direct investment, information technology and economic growth dynamics in Sub-Saharan Africa. *Telecommunications Policy, 44*(1), 101838.

Ayton, J., Krasnikova, N., & Malki, I. (2022). Corporate social performance and financial risk: Further empirical evidence using higher frequency data. *International Review of Financial Analysis, 80*, 102030.

Azadi, M., Jafarian, M., Saen, R. F., & Mirhedayatian, S. M. (2015). A new fuzzy DEA model for evaluation of efficiency and effectiveness of suppliers in sustainable supply chain management context. *Computers & Operations Research, 54*, 274–285.

Azadnia, A. H., Saman, M. Z. M., & Wong, K. Y. (2015). Sustainable supplier selection and order lot-sizing: An integrated multi-objective decision-making process. *International Journal of Production Research, 53*(2), 383–408.

Bag, S., Dhamija, P., Bryde, D. J., & Singh, R. K. (2022). Effect of eco-innovation on green supply chain management, circular economy capability, and performance of small and medium enterprises. *Journal of Business Research, 141*, 60–72.

Bag, S., & Pretorius, J. H. C. (2022). Relationships between industry 4.0, sustainable manufacturing and circular economy: Proposal of a research framework. *International Journal of Organizational Analysis, 30*(4), 864–898.

Baliga, R., Raut, R. D., & Kamble, S. S. (2020). Sustainable supply chain management practices and performance: An integrated perspective from a developing economy. *Management of Environmental Quality: An International Journal, 31*(5), 1147–1182.

Banasik, A., Kanellopoulos, A., Claassen, G. D. H., Bloemhof-Ruwaard, J. M., & van der Vorst, J. G. (2017). Closing loops in agricultural supply chains using multi-objective optimization: A case study of an industrial mushroom supply chain. *International Journal of Production Economics, 183*, 409–420.

Battini, D., Bogataj, M., & Choudhary, A. (2017). Closed loop supply chain (CLSC): Economics, modelling, management and control. *International Journal of Production Economics, 183*, 319–321.

Beamon, B. M., & Fernandes, C. (2004). Supply-chain network configuration for product recovery. *Production Planning & Control, 15*(3), 270–281.

Bloemhof, J. M., & Soysal, M. (2017). Sustainable food supply chain design. In *Sustainable supply chains: A research-based textbook on operations and strategy* (pp. 395–412).

Bodini, A. (2012). Building a systemic environmental monitoring and indicators for sustainability: What has the ecological network approach to offer? *Ecological Indicators, 15*(1), 140–148.

Boström, M., Jönsson, A. M., Lockie, S., Mol, A. P., & Oosterveer, P. (2015). Sustainable and responsible supply chain governance: Challenges and opportunities. *Journal of Cleaner Production, 107*, 1–7.

Brandenburg, M., Govindan, K., Sarkis, J., & Seuring, S. (2014). Quantitative models for sustainable supply chain management: Developments and directions. *European Journal of Operational Research, 233*(2), 299–312.

Bressanelli, G., Perona, M., & Saccani, N. (2019a). Assessing the impacts of circular economy: A framework and an application to the washing machine

industry. *International Journal of Management and Decision Making, 18*(3), 282–308.
Bressanelli, G., Perona, M., & Saccani, N. (2019b). Challenges in supply chain redesign for the Circular Economy: A literature review and a multiple case study. *International Journal of Production Research, 57*(23), 7395–7422.
Bressanelli, G., Saccani, N., Pigosso, D. C., & Perona, M. (2020). Circular economy in the WEEE industry: A systematic literature review and a research agenda. *Sustainable Production and Consumption, 23*, 174–188.
Brundtland, G. H. (1987). Our common future—Call for action. *Environmental Conservation, 14*(4), 291–294.
Caiado, R. G. G., Scavarda, L. F., Azevedo, B. D., de Mattos Nascimento, D. L., & Quelhas, O. L. G. (2022). Challenges and benefits of sustainable industry 4.0 for operations and supply chain management—A framework headed toward the 2030 agenda. *Sustainability, 14*(2), 830.
Calzolari, T., Genovese, A., & Brint, A. (2022). Circular economy indicators for supply chains: A systematic literature review. *Environmental and Sustainability Indicators, 13*, 100160.
Carter, C. R., Hatton, M. R., Wu, C., & Chen, X. (2020). Sustainable supply chain management: Continuing evolution and future directions. *International Journal of Physical Distribution & Logistics Management, 50*(1), 122–146.
Castka, P., & Corbett, C. (2016). Adoption and diffusion of environmental and social standards: The effect of stringency, governance, and media coverage. *International Journal of Operations & Production Management, 36*(11), 1504–1529.
Chardine-Baumann, E., & Botta-Genoulaz, V. (2014). A framework for sustainable performance assessment of supply chain management practices. *Computers & Industrial Engineering, 76*, 138–147.
Chauhan, C., Kaur, P., Arrawatia, R., Ractham, P., & Dhir, A. (2022). Supply chain collaboration and sustainable development goals (SDGs). Teamwork makes achieving SDGs dream work. *Journal of Business Research, 147*, 290–307.
Chavez, M. M. M., Sarache, W., Costa, Y., & Soto, J. (2020). Multiobjective stochastic scheduling of upstream operations in a sustainable sugarcane supply chain. *Journal of Cleaner Production, 276*, 123305.
Chowdhury, P., Paul, S. K., Kaisar, S., & Moktadir, M. A. (2021). COVID-19 pandemic related supply chain studies: A systematic review. *Transportation Research Part E: Logistics and Transportation Review, 148*, 102271.

Colucci, M., & Vecchi, A. (2021). Close the loop: Evidence on the implementation of the circular economy from the Italian fashion industry. *Business Strategy and the Environment, 30*(2), 856–873.

Dai, J., & Blackhurst, J. (2012). A four-phase AHP–QFD approach for supplier assessment: A sustainability perspective. *International Journal of Production Research, 50*(19), 5474–5490.

Danese, P., Lion, A., & Vinelli, A. (2019). Drivers and enablers of supplier sustainability practices: A survey-based analysis. *International Journal of Production Research, 57*(7), 2034–2056.

Das, D. (2018). The impact of sustainable supply chain management practices on firm performance: Lessons from Indian organizations. *Journal of Cleaner Production, 203*, 179–196.

Das, C., & Jharkharia, S. (2018). Low carbon supply chain: A state-of-the-art literature review. *Journal of Manufacturing Technology Management, 29*(2), 398–428.

Das, K., & Posinasetti, N. R. (2015). Addressing environmental concerns in closed loop supply chain design and planning. *International Journal of Production Economics, 163*, 34–47.

Davis-Sramek, B., Hopkins, C. D., Richey, R. G., & Morgan, T. R. (2022). Leveraging supplier relationships for sustainable supply chain management: Insights from social exchange theory. *International Journal of Logistics Research and Applications, 25*(1), 101–118.

De Angelis, R., Howard, M., & Miemczyk, J. (2018). Supply chain management and the circular economy: Towards the circular supply chain. *Production Planning & Control, 29*(6), 425–437.

De Giovanni, P. (2012). Do internal and external environmental management contribute to the triple bottom line? *International Journal of Operations & Production Management., 32*(3), 265–290.

De Giovanni, P., & Vinzi, V. E. (2012). Covariance versus component-based estimations of performance in green supply chain management. *International Journal of Production Economics, 135*(2), 907–916.

de Sousa Jabbour, A. B. L. (2015). Understanding the genesis of green supply chain management: Lessons from leading Brazilian companies. *Journal of Cleaner Production, 87*, 385–390.

Dias, G. P., & Silva, M. (2022). Revealing performance factors for supply chain sustainability: A systematic literature review from a social capital perspective. *Brazilian Journal of Operations & Production Management, 19*(1), 1–18.

Dias, G. P., Silva, M. E., & Gold, S. (2023). Microfoundations of supply chain sustainability practices: A social capital perspective. *International Journal of Production Economics*, 108947.
Do, A., Nguyen, Q., Nguyen, D., Le, Q., & Trinh, D. (2020). Green supply chain management practices and destination image: Evidence from Vietnam tourism industry. *Uncertain Supply Chain Management, 8*(2), 371–378.
Dolgui, A., & Ivanov, D. (2021). Ripple effect and supply chain disruption management: New trends and research directions. *International Journal of Production Research, 59*(1), 102–109.
Duong, N. H. (2022). Relationship of social sustainability, operational performance and economic performance in sustainable supply chain management. *Global Business & Finance Review, 27*(4), 46.
Duong, N. H., & Ha, Q. A. (2021). The links between supply chain risk management practices, supply chain integration and supply chain performance in Southern Vietnam: A moderation effect of supply chain social sustainability. *Cogent Business & Management, 8*(1), 1999556.
Duong, N. H., & Quang-An, H. A. (2021). The impacts of social sustainability practices on supply chain performance: Mediating role of supply chain integration. *Journal of Distribution Science (JDS), 19*, 37–48.
Dwivedi, Y. K., Hughes, L., Baabdullah, A. M., Ribeiro-Navarrete, S., Giannakis, M., Al-Debei, M. M., et al. (2022). Metaverse beyond the hype: Multidisciplinary perspectives on emerging challenges, opportunities, and agenda for research, practice and policy. *International Journal of Information Management, 66*, 102542.
Elkington, J. (2013). Enter the triple bottom line. In *The triple bottom line: Does it all add up?* (pp. 1–16). Routledge.
Elkington, J., Henriques, A., & Richardson, J. (2004). The triple bottom line: Does it all add up. In *Adressing the sustainability of business and CSR*. Earthscan.
Elkington, J., & Rowlands, I. H. (1999). Cannibals with forks: The triple bottom line of 21st century business. *Alternatives Journal, 25*(4), 42.
Ellen MacArthur. (2015). *Within: A circular economy vision for a competitive Europe*. McKinsey Center for Business and Environment.
Esfahbodi, A., Zhang, Y., & Watson, G. (2016). Sustainable supply chain management in emerging economies: Trade-offs between environmental and cost performance. *International Journal of Production Economics, 181*, 350–366.
Fathollahi-Fard, A. M., Hajiaghaei-Keshteli, M., & Mirjalili, S. (2018). Multi-objective stochastic closed-loop supply chain network design with social considerations. *Applied Soft Computing, 71*, 505–525.

Feng, M., Yu, W., Wang, X., Wong, C. Y., Xu, M., & Xiao, Z. (2018). Green supply chain management and financial performance: The mediating roles of operational and environmental performance. *Business Strategy and the Environment, 27*(7), 811–824.

Fernando, Y., Halili, M., Tseng, M. L., Tseng, J. W., & Lim, M. K. (2022). Sustainable social supply chain practices and firm social performance: Framework and empirical evidence. *Sustainable Production and Consumption, 32*, 160–172.

Ferrari, A. A., Bogner, K., Palacio, V., Crisostomo, D., Seeber, N., & Ebersberger, B. (2023). The COVID-19 pandemic as a window of opportunity for more sustainable and circular supply chains. *Cleaner Logistics and Supply Chain, 7*, 100101.

Fleischmann, M., Beullens, P., Bloemhof-Ruwaard, J. M., & Van Wassenhove, L. N. (2001). The impact of product recovery on logistics network design. *Production and Operations Management, 10*(2), 156–173.

Fogarassy, C., & Finger, D. (2020). Theoretical and practical approaches of circular economy for business models and technological solutions. *Resources, 9*(6), 76.

Friede, G., Busch, T., & Bassen, A. (2015). ESG and financial performance: Aggregated evidence from more than 2000 empirical studies. *Journal of Sustainable Finance & Investment, 5*(4), 210–233.

Galvão, G. D. A., de Nadae, J., Clemente, D. H., Chinen, G., & de Carvalho, M. M. (2018). Circular economy: Overview of barriers. *Procedia CIRP, 73*, 79–85.

Gavronski, I., Klassen, R. D., Vachon, S., & do Nascimento, L. F. M. (2011). A resource-based view of green supply management. *Transportation Research Part E: Logistics and Transportation Review, 47*(6), 872–885.

Geissdoerfer, M., Savaget, P., Bocken, N. M., & Hultink, E. J. (2017). The circular economy–A new sustainability paradigm? *Journal of Cleaner Production, 143*, 757–768.

Ghasemy Yaghin, R., & Sarlak, P. (2020). Joint order allocation and transportation planning under uncertainty within a socially responsible supply chain. *Journal of Modelling in Management, 15*(2), 531–565.

Ghosh, M. (2019). Determinants of green procurement implementation and its impact on firm performance. *Journal of Manufacturing Technology Management, 30*(2), 462–482.

Giannakis, M., & Papadopoulos, T. (2016). Supply chain sustainability: A risk management approach. *International Journal of Production Economics, 171*, 455–470.

Gillan, S. L., Koch, A., & Starks, L. T. (2021). Firms and social responsibility: A review of ESG and CSR research in corporate finance. *Journal of Corporate Finance, 66*, 101889.

Giudice, F., Caferra, R., & Morone, P. (2020). COVID-19, the food system and the circular economy: Challenges and opportunities. *Sustainability, 12*(19), 7939.

Gopalakrishnan, K., Yusuf, Y. Y., Musa, A., Abubakar, T., & Ambursa, H. M. (2012). Sustainable supply chain management: A case study of British aerospace (BAe) systems. *International Journal of Production Economics, 140*(1), 193–203.

Gouda, S. K., & Saranga, H. (2018). Sustainable supply chains for supply chain sustainability: Impact of sustainability efforts on supply chain risk. *International Journal of Production Research, 56*(17), 5820–5835.

Govindan, K., & Hasanagic, M. (2018). A systematic review on drivers, barriers, and practices towards circular economy: A supply chain perspective. *International Journal of Production Research, 56*(1–2), 278–311.

Govindan, K., Soleimani, H., & Kannan, D. (2015). Reverse logistics and closed-loop supply chain: A comprehensive review to explore the future. *European Journal of Operational Research, 240*(3), 603–626.

Guide, V. D. R., Jr., & Van Wassenhove, L. N. (2009). OR FORUM—The evolution of closed-loop supply chain research. *Operations Research, 57*(1), 10–18.

Guimarães, Y. M., Eustachio, J. H. P. P., Leal Filho, W., Martinez, L. F., do Valle, M. R., & Caldana, A. C. F. (2022). Drivers and barriers in sustainable supply chains: The case of the Brazilian coffee industry. *Sustainable Production and Consumption, 34*, 42–54.

Guo, Y., Yu, J., Boulaksil, Y., Allaoui, H., & Hu, F. (2021). Solving the sustainable supply chain network design problem by the multi-neighborhoods descent traversal algorithm. *Computers & Industrial Engineering, 154*, 107098.

Gupta, H., Kusi-Sarpong, S., & Rezaei, J. (2020). Barriers and overcoming strategies to supply chain sustainability innovation. *Resources, Conservation and Recycling, 161*, 104819.

Haddadsisakht, A., & Ryan, S. M. (2018). Closed-loop supply chain network design with multiple transportation modes under stochastic demand and uncertain carbon tax. *International Journal of Production Economics, 195*, 118–131.

Hashemi, S. H., Karimi, A., & Tavana, M. (2015). An integrated green supplier selection approach with analytic network process and improved Grey relational analysis. *International Journal of Production Economics, 159*, 178–191.
Hassini, E., Surti, C., & Searcy, C. (2012). A literature review and a case study of sustainable supply chains with a focus on metrics. *International Journal of Production Economics, 140*(1), 69–82.
He, Q., Gallear, D., Ghobadian, A., & Ramanathan, R. (2019). Managing knowledge in supply chains: A catalyst to triple bottom line sustainability. *Production Planning & Control, 30*(5–6), 448–463.
Hendiani, S., Liao, H., & Jabbour, C. J. C. (2022). A new sustainability indicator for supply chains: Theoretical and practical contribution towards sustainable operations. *International Journal of Logistics Research and Applications, 25*(4–5), 384–409.
Hombach, L. E., Büsing, C., & Walther, G. (2018). Robust and sustainable supply chains under market uncertainties and different risk attitudes–A case study of the German biodiesel market. *European Journal of Operational Research, 269*(1), 302–312.
Hombach, L. E., & Walther, G. (2015). Pareto-efficient legal regulation of the (bio) fuel market using a bi-objective optimization model. *European Journal of Operational Research, 245*(1), 286–295.
Hou, G., Wang, Y., & Xin, B. (2019). A coordinated strategy for sustainable supply chain management with product sustainability, environmental effect and social reputation. *Journal of Cleaner Production, 228*, 1143–1156.
Huq, F. A., Chowdhury, I. N., & Klassen, R. D. (2016). Social management capabilities of multinational buying firms and their emerging market suppliers: An exploratory study of the clothing industry. *Journal of Operations Management, 46*, 19–37.
Ikram, M., Zhang, Q., Sroufe, R., & Shah, S. Z. A. (2020). Towards a sustainable environment: The nexus between ISO 14001, renewable energy consumption, access to electricity, agriculture and CO2 emissions in SAARC countries. *Sustainable Production and Consumption, 22*, 218–230.
Jabbarzadeh, A., Fahimnia, B., & Sabouhi, F. (2018). Resilient and sustainable supply chain design: Sustainability analysis under disruption risks. *International Journal of Production Research, 56*(17), 5945–5968.
Jabbarzadeh, A., Haughton, M., & Khosrojerdi, A. (2018). Closed-loop supply chain network design under disruption risks: A robust approach with real world application. *Computers & Industrial Engineering, 116*, 178–191.

Jindal, A., & Sangwan, K. S. (2014). Closed loop supply chain network design and optimisation using fuzzy mixed integer linear programming model. *International Journal of Production Research, 52*(14), 4156–4173.

Johnsen, T. E., Miemczyk, J., & Howard, M. (2017). A systematic literature review of sustainable purchasing and supply research: Theoretical perspectives and opportunities for IMP-based research. *Industrial Marketing Management, 61*, 130–143.

Joshi, S. (2022). A review on sustainable supply chain network design: Dimensions, paradigms, concepts, framework and future directions. *Sustainable Operations and Computers, 3*, 136–148.

Kayikci, Y., Kazancoglu, Y., Lafci, C., & Gozacan, N. (2021). Exploring barriers to smart and sustainable circular economy: The case of an automotive eco-cluster. *Journal of Cleaner Production, 314*, 127920.

Kazemi, N., Modak, N. M., & Govindan, K. (2019). A review of reverse logistics and closed loop supply chain management studies published in IJPR: A bibliometric and content analysis. *International Journal of Production Research, 57*(15–16), 4937–4960.

Kirchoff, J. F., Tate, W. L., & Mollenkopf, D. A. (2016). The impact of strategic organizational orientations on green supply chain management and firm performance. *International Journal of Physical Distribution & Logistics Management, 46*(3), 269–292.

Kitsis, A. M., & Chen, I. J. (2023). Does environmental proactivity make a difference? The critical roles of green operations and collaboration in GSCM. *Supply Chain Management: An International Journal, 28*(2), 209–224.

Krykavskyy, Y., Chornopyska, N., Dovhun, O., Hayvanovych, N., & Leonova, S. (2023). Defining supply chain resilience during wartime. *Eastern-European Journal of Enterprise Technologies, 1*(13), 121.

Kumar, P., Singh, R. K., & Kumar, V. (2021). Managing supply chains for sustainable operations in the era of industry 4.0 and circular economy: Analysis of barriers. *Resources, Conservation and Recycling, 164*, 105215.

Kurniawan, T. A., Othman, M. H. D., Hwang, G. H., & Gikas, P. (2022). Unlocking digital technologies for waste recycling in industry 4.0 era: A transformation towards a digitalization-based circular economy in Indonesia. *Journal of Cleaner Production, 357*, 131911.

Kusi-Sarpong, S., Gupta, H., & Sarkis, J. (2019). A supply chain sustainability innovation framework and evaluation methodology. *International Journal of Production Research, 57*(7), 1990–2008.

Kuwornu, J. K., Khaipetch, J., Gunawan, E., Bannor, R. K., & Ho, T. D. (2023). The adoption of sustainable supply chain management practices on perfor-

mance and quality assurance of food companies. *Sustainable Futures, 5*, 100103.
Lee, H. L. (2004). The triple-A supply chain. *Harvard Business Review, 82*(10), 102–113.
Lee, D. H., Dong, M., & Bian, W. (2010). The design of sustainable logistics network under uncertainty. *International Journal of Production Economics, 128*(1), 159–166.
León Bravo, V., Moretto, A., & Caniato, F. (2021). A roadmap for sustainability assessment in the food supply chain. *British Food Journal, 123*(13), 199–220.
León-Bravo, V., Caniato, F., & Caridi, M. (2019). Sustainability in multiple stages of the food supply chain in Italy: Practices, performance and reputation. *Operations Management Research, 12*, 40–61.
Li, Y., & Mathiyazhagan, K. (2018). Application of DEMATEL approach to identify the influential indicators towards sustainable supply chain adoption in the auto components manufacturing sector. *Journal of Cleaner Production, 172*, 2931–2941.
Lin, K. P., Tseng, M. L., & Pai, P. F. (2018). Sustainable supply chain management using approximate fuzzy DEMATEL method. *Resources, Conservation and Recycling, 128*, 134–142.
Linton, J. D., Klassen, R., & Jayaraman, V. (2007). Sustainable supply chains: An introduction. *Journal of Operations Management, 25*(6), 1075–1082.
Lotfi, R., Nazarpour, H., Gharehbaghi, A., Sarkhosh, S. M. H., & Khanbaba, A. (2022). Viable closed-loop supply chain network by considering robustness and risk as a circular economy. *Environmental Science and Pollution Research, 29*(46), 70285–70304.
Luthra, S., Garg, D., & Haleem, A. (2014). Green supply chain management: Implementation and performance–a literature review and some issues. *Journal of Advances in Management Research, 11*(1), 20–46.
Luthra, S., & Mangla, S. K. (2018). When strategies matter: Adoption of sustainable supply chain management practices in an emerging economy's context. *Resources, Conservation and Recycling, 138*, 194–206.
Majumdar, A., & Sinha, S. K. (2019). Analyzing the barriers of green textile supply chain management in Southeast Asia using interpretive structural modeling. *Sustainable Production and Consumption, 17*, 176–187.
Martí, J. M. C., Tancrez, J. S., & Seifert, R. W. (2015). Carbon footprint and responsiveness trade-offs in supply chain network design. *International Journal of Production Economics, 166*, 129–142.
Martins, C. L., & Pato, M. V. (2019). Supply chain sustainability: A tertiary literature review. *Journal of Cleaner Production, 225*, 995–1016.

Matos, S., & Hall, J. (2007). Integrating sustainable development in the supply chain: The case of life cycle assessment in oil and gas and agricultural biotechnology. *Journal of Operations Management, 25*(6), 1083–1102.

Menon, R. R., & Ravi, V. (2021). Analysis of barriers of sustainable supply chain management in electronics industry: An interpretive structural modelling approach. *Cleaner and Responsible Consumption, 3*, 100026.

Miao, Z., Cai, S., & Xu, D. (2012). Exploring the antecedents of logistics social responsibility: A focus on Chinese firms. *International Journal of Production Economics, 140*(1), 18–27.

Miemczyk, J., Johnsen, T. E., & Macquet, M. (2012). Sustainable purchasing and supply management: A structured literature review of definitions and measures at the dyad, chain and network levels. *Supply Chain Management: An International Journal, 17*(5), 478–496.

Mirzapour Al-e-hashem, S. M. J., Baboli, A., & Sazvar, Z. (2013). A stochastic aggregate production planning model in a green supply chain: Considering flexible lead times, nonlinear purchase and shortage cost functions. *European Journal of Operational Research, 230*(1), 26–41.

Modak, N. M., Kazemi, N., & Cárdenas-Barrón, L. E. (2019). Investigating structure of a two-echelon closed-loop supply chain using social work donation as a corporate social responsibility practice. *International Journal of Production Economics, 207*, 19–33.

Mohajeri, A., & Fallah, M. (2016). A carbon footprint-based closed-loop supply chain model under uncertainty with risk analysis: A case study. *Transportation Research Part D: Transport and Environment, 48*, 425–450.

Morseletto, P. (2020). Targets for a circular economy. *Resources, Conservation and Recycling, 153*, 104553.

Mota, B., Gomes, M. I., Carvalho, A., & Barbosa-Povoa, A. P. (2018). Sustainable supply chains: An integrated modeling approach under uncertainty. *Omega, 77*, 32–57.

Najjar, M. S., Dahabiyeh, L., & Nawayseh, M. (2019). Share if you care: The impact of information sharing and information quality on humanitarian supply chain performance-a social capital perspective. *Information Development, 35*(3), 467–481.

Nakamba, C. C., Chan, P. W., & Sharmina, M. (2017). How does social sustainability feature in studies of supply chain management? A review and research agenda. *Supply Chain Management: An International Journal, 22*(6), 522–541.

Namagembe, S., Ryan, S., & Sridharan, R. (2019). Green supply chain practice adoption and firm performance: Manufacturing SMEs in Uganda. *Management of Environmental Quality: An International Journal, 30*(1), 5–35.

Nandi, S., Sarkis, J., Hervani, A., & Helms, M. (2021). Do blockchain and circular economy practices improve post COVID-19 supply chains? A resource-based and resource dependence perspective. *Industrial Management & Data Systems, 121*(2), 333–363.

Nazam, M., Hashim, M., Ahmad Baig, S., Abrar, M., Ur Rehman, H., Nazim, M., & Raza, A. (2020). Categorizing the barriers in adopting sustainable supply chain initiatives: A way-forward towards business excellence. *Cogent Business & Management, 7*(1), 1825042.

Neto, B., Dias, A. C., & Machado, M. (2013). Life cycle assessment of the supply chain of a Portuguese wine: From viticulture to distribution. *The International Journal of Life Cycle Assessment, 18*, 590–602.

Nowicka, K. (2021). Circular economy values perspectives on digital supply chain business models. In *The economics of sustainable transformation* (pp. 139–166). Routledge.

Ntabe, E. N., LeBel, L., Munson, A. D., & Santa-Eulalia, L. A. (2015). A systematic literature review of the supply chain operations reference (SCOR) model application with special attention to environmental issues. *International Journal of Production Economics, 169*, 310–332.

Nurpribadi, G., & Rulianti, E. (2022). Getting countries alternative to resolve supply chain management regarding wheat commodity for Indonesia during war between Ukraine and Russia. *Journal of Economics and Business Letters, 2*(3), 25–28.

Ofori, E. K., Onifade, S. T., Ali, E. B., Alola, A. A., & Zhang, J. (2023). Achieving carbon neutrality in post COP26 in BRICS, MINT, and G7 economies: The role of financial development and governance indicators. *Journal of Cleaner Production, 387*, 135853.

Olatunji, O. O., Akinlabi, S. A., Ayo, O. O., Madushele, N., Adedeji, P. A., & Fatoba, S. O. (2019). Drivers and barriers to competitive carbon footprint reduction in manufacturing supply chain: A brief review. *Procedia Manufacturing, 35*, 992–1000.

Oliveira, C., Coelho, D., & Antunes, C. H. (2016). Coupling input–output analysis with multiobjective linear programming models for the study of economy–energy–environment–social (E3S) trade-offs: A review. *Annals of Operations Research, 247*, 471–502.

Orji, I. J., Kusi-Sarpong, S., & Gupta, H. (2020). The critical success factors of using social media for supply chain social sustainability in the freight logistics industry. *International Journal of Production Research, 58*(5), 1522–1539.

Orji, I., & Wei, S. (2016). A detailed calculation model for costing of green manufacturing. *Industrial Management & Data Systems, 116*(1), 65–86.

Ossio, F., Salinas, C., & Hernández, H. (2023). Circular economy in the built environment: A systematic literature review and definition of the circular construction concept. *Journal of Cleaner Production*, 137738.

Özceylan, E., & Paksoy, T. (2014). Interactive fuzzy programming approaches to the strategic and tactical planning of a closed-loop supply chain under uncertainty. *International Journal of Production Research, 52*(8), 2363–2387.

Özkır, V., & Başlıgıl, H. (2012). Modelling product-recovery processes in closed-loop supply-chain network design. *International Journal of Production Research, 50*(8), 2218–2233.

Padhi, S. S., Pati, R. K., & Rajeev, A. (2018). Framework for selecting sustainable supply chain processes and industries using an integrated approach. *Journal of Cleaner Production, 184*, 969–984.

Paksoy, T., Bektaş, T., & Özceylan, E. (2011). Operational and environmental performance measures in a multi-product closed-loop supply chain. *Transportation Research Part E: Logistics and Transportation Review, 47*(4), 532–546.

Papamichael, I., Chatziparaskeva, G., Voukkali, I., Navarro Pedreno, J., Jeguirim, M., & Zorpas, A. A. (2023). The perception of circular economy in the framework of fashion industry. *Waste Management & Research, 41*(2), 251–263.

Patterson, J., Schulz, K., Vervoort, J., Van Der Hel, S., Widerberg, O., Adler, C., Hurlbert, M., Anderton, K., Sethi, M., & Barau, A. (2017). Exploring the governance and politics of transformations towards sustainability. *Environmental Innovation and Societal Transitions, 24*, 1–16.

Paulraj, A., Chen, I. J., & Blome, C. (2017). Motives and performance outcomes of sustainable supply chain management practices: A multi-theoretical perspective. *Journal of Business Ethics, 145*, 239–258.

Peters, N. J., Hofstetter, J. S., & Hoffmann, V. H. (2011). Institutional entrepreneurship capabilities for interorganizational sustainable supply chain strategies. *The International Journal of Logistics Management, 22*(1), 52–86.

Pfajfar, G., Shoham, A., Małecka, A., & Zalaznik, M. (2022). Value of corporate social responsibility for multiple stakeholders and social impact–Relationship marketing perspective. *Journal of Business Research, 143*, 46–61.

Piyathanavong, V., Garza-Reyes, J. A., Kumar, V., Maldonado-Guzmán, G., & Mangla, S. K. (2019). The adoption of operational environmental sustainability approaches in the Thai manufacturing sector. *Journal of Cleaner Production, 220*, 507–528.

Potting, J., Hekkert, M. P., Worrell, E., & Hanemaaijer, A. (2017). Circular economy: Measuring innovation in the product chain. *Planbureau voor de Leefomgeving, 2544*.

Prokesch, S. (2010). The sustainable supply chain. *Harvard Business Review, 88*(10), 70–72.

Qin, Z., & Chen, P. K. (2022). Enhancing the resilience of sustainable supplier management through the combination of win-win lean practices and auditing mechanisms–An analysis from the resource-based view. *Frontiers in Environmental Science, 10*, 1541.

Qorri, A., Mujkić, Z., & Kraslawski, A. (2018). A conceptual framework for measuring sustainability performance of supply chains. *Journal of Cleaner Production, 189*, 570–584.

Ramanathan, R., He, Q., Black, A., Ghobadian, A., & Gallear, D. (2017). Environmental regulations, innovation and firm performance: A revisit of the Porter hypothesis. *Journal of Cleaner Production, 155*, 79–92.

Ramanathan, U., He, Q., Subramanian, N., Gunasekaran, A., & Sarpong, D. (2023). Collaborative closed-loop supply chain framework for sustainable manufacturing: Evidence from the Indian packaging industry. *Technological Forecasting and Social Change, 191*, 122489.

Ramezani, M., Bashiri, M., & Tavakkoli-Moghaddam, R. (2013). A robust design for a closed-loop supply chain network under an uncertain environment. *The International Journal of Advanced Manufacturing Technology, 66*, 825–843.

Rao, P., & Holt, D. (2005). Do green supply chains lead to competitiveness and economic performance? *International Journal of Operations & Production Management, 25*(9), 898–916.

Reefke, H., & Sundaram, D. (2018). Sustainable supply chain management: Decision models for transformation and maturity. *Decision Support Systems, 113*, 56–72.

Rehman, S. U., Kraus, S., Shah, S. A., Khanin, D., & Mahto, R. V. (2021). Analyzing the relationship between green innovation and environmental performance in large manufacturing firms. *Technological Forecasting and Social Change, 163*, 120481.

Reike, D., Vermeulen, W. J., & Witjes, S. (2018). The circular economy: New or refurbished as CE 3.0?—Exploring controversies in the conceptualization of the circular economy through a focus on history and resource value retention options. *Resources, Conservation and Recycling, 135*, 246–264.

Saeed, M. A., & Kersten, W. (2017). Supply chain sustainability performance indicators: A content analysis based on published standards and guidelines. *Logistics Research, 10*(12), 1–19.

Saeed, M. A., & Kersten, W. (2019). Drivers of sustainable supply chain management: Identification and classification. *Sustainability, 11*(4), 1137.

Sajjad, A. (2021). The COVID-19 pandemic, social sustainability and global supply chain resilience: A review. *Corporate Governance: The International Journal of Business in Society, 21*(6), 1142–1154.

Sajjad, A., Eweje, G., & Tappin, D. (2015). Sustainable supply chain management: Motivators and barriers. *Business Strategy and the Environment, 24*(7), 643–655.

Salema, M. I. G., Barbosa-Povoa, A. P., & Novais, A. Q. (2007). An optimization model for the design of a capacitated multi-product reverse logistics network with uncertainty. *European Journal of Operational Research, 179*(3), 1063–1077.

Schoenherr, T., Modi, S. B., Talluri, S., & Hult, G. T. M. (2014). Antecedents and performance outcomes of strategic environmental sourcing: An investigation of resource-based process and contingency effects. *Journal of Business Logistics, 35*(3), 172–190.

Schulze, H., & Bals, L. (2020). Implementing sustainable purchasing and supply management (SPSM): A Delphi study on competences needed by purchasing and supply management (PSM) professionals. *Journal of Purchasing and Supply Management, 26*(4), 100625.

Seuring, S., & Müller, M. (2008). From a literature review to a conceptual framework for sustainable supply chain management. *Journal of Cleaner Production, 16*(15), 1699–1710.

Sgarbossa, F., & Russo, I. (2017). A proactive model in sustainable food supply chain: Insight from a case study. *International Journal of Production Economics, 183*, 596–606.

Sharma, M., Luthra, S., Joshi, S., & Kumar, A. (2022). Developing a framework for enhancing survivability of sustainable supply chains during and post-COVID-19 pandemic. *International Journal of Logistics Research and Applications, 25*(4–5), 433–453.

Sheehy, B., & Farneti, F. (2021). Corporate social responsibility, sustainability, sustainable development and corporate sustainability: What is the difference, and does it matter? *Sustainability, 13*(11), 5965.
Shibin, K. T., Gunasekaran, A., Papadopoulos, T., Dubey, R., Singh, M., & Wamba, S. F. (2016). Enablers and barriers of flexible green supply chain management: A total interpretive structural modeling approach. *Global Journal of Flexible Systems Management, 17*, 171–188.
Silva, M. E., & Ruel, S. (2022). Inclusive purchasing and supply chain resilience capabilities: Lessons for social sustainability. *Journal of Purchasing and Supply Management, 28*(5), 100767.
Silvestre, B. (2016). Sustainable supply chain management: Current debate and future directions. *Gestão & Produção, 23*, 235–249.
Simonetto, M., Sgarbossa, F., Battini, D., & Govindan, K. (2022). Closed loop supply chains 4.0: From risks to benefits through advanced technologies. A literature review and research agenda. *International Journal of Production Economics*, 108582.
Singh, S., Ghosh, S., Jayaram, J., & Tiwari, M. K. (2019). Enhancing supply chain resilience using ontology-based decision support system. *International Journal of Computer Integrated Manufacturing, 32*(7), 642–657.
Sodhi, M. S., & Tang, C. S. (2021). Extending AAA capabilities to meet PPP goals in supply chains. *Production and Operations Management, 30*(3), 625–632.
Spence, L., & Bourlakis, M. (2009). The evolution from corporate social responsibility to supply chain responsibility: The case of Waitrose. *Supply Chain Management: An International Journal, 14*(4), 291–302.
Srivastava, A. K., Dixit, S., & Srivastava, A. A. (2022). Criticism of triple bottom line: TBL (with special reference to sustainability). *Corporate Reputation Review*, 1–12.
Stindt, D. (2017). A generic planning approach for sustainable supply chain management-How to integrate concepts and methods to address the issues of sustainability? *Journal of Cleaner Production, 153*, 146–163.
Subulan, K., Baykasoğlu, A., Özsoydan, F. B., Taşan, A. S., & Selim, H. (2015). A case-oriented approach to a lead/acid battery closed-loop supply chain network design under risk and uncertainty. *Journal of Manufacturing Systems, 37*, 340–361.
Sudarto, S., Takahashi, K., & Morikawa, K. (2017). Efficient flexible long-term capacity planning for optimal sustainability dimensions performance of

reverse logistics social responsibility: A system dynamics approach. *International Journal of Production Economics, 184*, 179–192.

Sudarto, S., Takahashi, K., Morikawa, K., & Nagasawa, K. (2016). The impact of capacity planning on product lifecycle for performance on sustainability dimensions in Reverse Logistics Social Responsibility. *Journal of Cleaner Production, 133*, 28–42.

Tachizawa, M. E., & Yew Wong, C. (2014). Towards a theory of multi-tier sustainable supply chains: A systematic literature review. *Supply Chain Management: An International Journal, 19*(5/6), 643–663.

Taghipour, A., & Beneteau-Piet, C. (2020). Sustainable supply chain management performance. *International Journal of Innovation, Management and Technology, 11*(6), 897.

Talaei, M., Moghaddam, B. F., Pishvaee, M. S., Bozorgi-Amiri, A., & Gholamnejad, S. (2016). A robust fuzzy optimization model for carbon-efficient closed-loop supply chain network design problem: A numerical illustration in electronics industry. *Journal of Cleaner Production, 113*, 662–673.

Tang, C. S. (2018). Socially responsible supply chains in emerging markets: Some research opportunities. *Journal of Operations Management, 57*, 1–10.

Tate, W. L., Ellram, L. M., & Kirchoff, J. F. (2010). Corporate social responsibility reports: A thematic analysis related to supply chain management. *Journal of Supply Chain Management, 46*(1), 19–44.

Touboulic, A., & Walker, H. (2015). Theories in sustainable supply chain management: A structured literature review. *International journal of physical distribution & logistics management, 45*(1/2), 16–42.

Tsai, W. H., Chen, H. C., Liu, J. Y., Chen, S. P., & Shen, Y. S. (2011). Using activity-based costing to evaluate capital investments for green manufacturing systems. *International Journal of Production Research, 49*(24), 7275–7292.

Tsang, Y. P., Fan, Y., & Feng, Z. P. (2023). Bridging the gap: Building environmental, social and governance capabilities in small and medium logistics companies. *Journal of Environmental Management, 338*, 117758.

Tseng, M. L., Wu, K. J., Hu, J., & Wang, C. H. (2018). Decision-making model for sustainable supply chain finance under uncertainties. *International Journal of Production Economics, 205*, 30–36.

Tseng, M. L., Bui, T. D., Lim, M. K., Fujii, M., & Mishra, U. (2022). Assessing data-driven sustainable supply chain management indicators for the textile industry under industrial disruption and ambidexterity. *International Journal of Production Economics, 245*, 108401.

Tundys, B. (2016, June). Sustainable supplier selection criteria in the context of developing of green supply chain. In *Proceedings of the 5th IEEE International Conference on Advanced Logistics & Transport (ICALT), Krakow, Poland* (pp. 1–3).

Tundys, B. (2018). *Zielony łańcuch dostaw: zarządzanie, pomiar, ocena.* CeDeWu Sp. z oo.

Tundys, B., & Fernando, Y. (2019). Sustainable supply chain management-Key performance indicators (KPI) as an element for measuring of processes. *Transport Economics and Logistics, 83*, 31–50.

Tunn, V. S., Van den Hende, E. A., Bocken, N. M., & Schoormans, J. P. (2021). Consumer adoption of access-based product-service systems: The influence of duration of use and type of product. *Business Strategy and the Environment, 30*(6), 2796–2813.

Unger, S., & Landis, A. (2016). Assessing the environmental, human health, and economic impacts of reprocessed medical devices in a Phoenix hospital's supply chain. *Journal of Cleaner Production, 112*, 1995–2003.

Uyar, A., Karaman, A. S., & Kilic, M. (2020). Is corporate social responsibility reporting a tool of signaling or greenwashing? Evidence from the worldwide logistics sector. *Journal of Cleaner Production, 253*, 119997.

Vachon, S. (2007). Green supply chain practices and the selection of environmental technologies. *International Journal of Production Research, 45*(18–19), 4357–4379.

Vachon, S., & Klassen, R. D. (2008). Environmental management and manufacturing performance: The role of collaboration in the supply chain. *International Journal of Production Economics, 111*(2), 299–315.

Vishwakarma, A., Dangayach, G. S., Meena, M. L., & Gupta, S. (2022). Analysing barriers of sustainable supply chain in apparel & textile sector: A hybrid ISM-MICMAC and DEMATEL approach. *Cleaner Logistics and Supply Chain, 5*, 100073.

Walker, H., & Brammer, S. (2012). The relationship between sustainable procurement and e-procurement in the public sector. *International Journal of Production Economics, 140*(1), 256–268.

Wang, Z., & Sarkis, J. (2017). Corporate social responsibility governance, outcomes, and financial performance. *Journal of Cleaner Production, 162*, 1607–1616.

Wang, J., Zhu, L., Feng, L., & Feng, J. (2023). A meta-analysis of sustainable supply chain management and firm performance: Some new findings on sus-

tainable supply chain management. *Sustainable Production and Consumption, 38*, 312–330.
Weber, M. (2008). The business case for corporate social responsibility: A company-level measurement approach for CSR. *European Management Journal, 26*(4), 247–261.
Wilson, M., & Goffnett, S. (2022). Reverse logistics: Understanding end-of-life product management. *Business Horizons, 65*(5), 643–655.
Winter, S., & Lasch, R. (2016). Environmental and social criteria in supplier evaluation–Lessons from the fashion and apparel industry. *Journal of Cleaner Production, 139*, 175–190.
Wu, J., Zhang, X., & Lu, J. (2018). Empirical research on influencing factors of sustainable supply chain management—Evidence from Beijing, China. *Sustainability, 10*(5), 1595.
Wuyts, W., Marin, J., Brusselaers, J., & Vrancken, K. (2020). Circular economy as a COVID-19 cure? *Resources, Conservation, and Recycling, 162*, 105016.
Xu, X., & Gursoy, D. (2015). A conceptual framework of sustainable hospitality supply chain management. *Journal of Hospitality Marketing & Management, 24*(3), 229–259.
Yadav, G., Luthra, S., Jakhar, S. K., Mangla, S. K., & Rai, D. P. (2020). A framework to overcome sustainable supply chain challenges through solution measures of industry 4.0 and circular economy: An automotive case. *Journal of Cleaner Production, 254*, 120112.
Yoo, S., Keeley, A. R., & Managi, S. (2021). Does sustainability activities performance matter during financial crises? Investigating the case of COVID-19. *Energy Policy, 155*, 112330.
Yoon, J., Talluri, S., Yildiz, H., & Ho, W. (2018). Models for supplier selection and risk mitigation: A holistic approach. *International Journal of Production Research, 56*(10), 3636–3661.
Yu, Y., Xu, J., Huo, B., Zhang, J. Z., & Cao, Y. (2023). The impact of supply chain social responsibility on sustainable performance. *Journal of Cleaner Production, 385*, 135666.
Yuen, K. F., & Lim, J. M. (2016). Barriers to the implementation of strategic corporate social responsibility in shipping. *The Asian Journal of Shipping and Logistics, 32*(1), 49–57.
Yuen, K. F., Thai, V. V., & Wong, Y. D. (2017). Corporate social responsibility and classical competitive strategies of maritime transport firms: A contingency-fit perspective. *Transportation Research Part A: Policy and Practice, 98*, 1–13.

Żak, A. (2015). Triple bottom line concept in theory and practice. *Social Responsibility of Organizations Directions of Changes, 387*(1), 251–264.

Zhang, H., & Kim, H. (2022). Institutional quality and FDI location: A threshold model. *Economic Modelling, 114*, 105942.

Zhang, K., Liu, Z., & Wang, P. (2020). Exploring the supply chain management of fair trade business: Case study of a fair trade craft company in China. *Cogent Business & Management, 7*(1), 1734345.

Zhao, J. (2021). Reimagining corporate social responsibility in the era of COVID-19: Embedding resilience and promoting corporate social competence. *Sustainability, 13*(12), 6548.

Zhu, Q., Cordeiro, J., & Sarkis, J. (2013). Institutional pressures, dynamic capabilities and environmental management systems: Investigating the ISO 9000–Environmental management system implementation linkage. *Journal of Environmental Management, 114*, 232–242.

3

Challenges for Resilient and Sustainable Supply Chains

3.1 Environmental, Social, and Economic Factors as Sources of Risk to Supply Chains

A discussion of resilient, sustainable supply chains first requires clarification of the relevant risk terminology. Since the issue of risk and risk management has been a subject of research for many years, most established and generally accepted definitions have appeared in facultative management standards, both national and international. Therefore, when explaining the fundamental issues, it is worth referring to documents commonly implemented by organizations, emphasizing that the interpretations of risk, risk management process, or risk treatment methods, presented in standards, are consistent with each other.

Risk is understood as a combination of two parameters, that is, the probability of occurrence of an event (P) and its consequences (C) that may affect the achievement of the objective of a given system. In turn, risk management requires the realization of several successive stages, including risk analysis (risk identification and risk measurement with the use of two parameters, probability and consequences), risk evaluation

B. Tundys et al., *Sustainable Supply Chains 2.0*,
https://doi.org/10.1007/978-3-031-50337-5_3

(decision of risk acceptance), risk treatment (influencing the risk parameters with adequate methods, e.g., avoidance, reduction, transfer, mitigation), and risk monitoring (implementation controls, measures and procedures, gathering information, and knowledge) (ISO/IEC Guide 73:2002, 2002; FERMA, 2003; COSO, 2004, p. 25; ISO 9001:2005, 2005; ISO 31000:2018, 2018). This standardized approach, which constitutes best practice, is to ensure effective prevention and response to risk, while understanding business activity, protecting assets, and making strategic decisions more accurately. Consequently, comprehensive risk management, especially with the use of supply chain innovations and information technology, drives long-term competitive advantage (Elahi, 2013; Kwak et al., 2018; Saeidi et al., 2019).

Risk management from the perspective of a single organization (Enterprise Risk Management, ERM) is insufficient today due to a number of dependencies between suppliers and buyers as well as a highly volatile business environment. Therefore, over the years, the concept of supply chain risk management (SCRM) has been developed. SCRM includes long-term cooperation of various supply chain links in order to design and implement sufficient risk management strategies (Zsidisin et al., 2000). Mature communication at different levels in terms of risk prevention and response is primarily aimed at ensuring a continuous flow of physical goods and information, from the initial supplier to the consumer (Waters, 2007, p. 86). The latest definition based on the results of the systematic literature review says that SCRM means "the identification, assessment, treatment, and monitoring of supply chain risks, with the aid of the internal implementation of tools, techniques and strategies and of external coordination and collaboration with supply chain members so as to reduce vulnerability and ensure continuity coupled with profitability, leading to competitive advantage" (Fan & Stevenson, 2018).

Risk is closely related to uncertainty. These are basically inseparable concepts and often interchangeably used terms. Risk management is understood as the way companies deal with uncertainty. Especially in the context of disruptions occurring in supply chains, it is suggested that risk and uncertainty should be considered in a similar way, or even treated analogously (Marcos et al., 2021; Vilko et al., 2014). Risk is measurable and is regarded as an outcome of uncertainty, while uncertainty is unmeasurable (the inability to measure the exact probability or severity of potential situations due to lack or difficulty of relying on the history of events and forecasts), involves having less information (when making strategic decisions), and may result in various scenarios and consequences (Zimmermann, 2000; Van Der Vorst & Beulens, 2002; Ghadge et al., 2012; Sinha & Sinha, 2020). Uncertainty is also understood as a source of risk or chances (COSO, 2004, p. 15). In this meaning, risk is related to the negative, while chances have a positive impact on the organization.

Events and sequences of events of various natures may occur and negatively impact supply chain performance. Therefore, both supply chain risk and supply chain uncertainty can hinder the achievement of supply chain goals and lead to serious problems with the continuity of flow processes. Supply chain risk is understood as "an exposure to an event which causes disruption" (Ghadge et al., 2012) and any event that may negatively affect the flow of information or goods in the supply chain (Jüttner et al., 2003), whereas supply chain uncertainty "is a state of lack of information that restrains the ability of decision-makers to accurately predict the right outcome of scenarios and the impact of control actions in the supply chain"(Marcos et al., 2021).

Risk can be considered in relation to various aspects which are related to specific classifications (Fig. 3.1). Depending on the managers' awareness and knowledge of the event, four forms of supply chain risk can be distinguished (Aggarwal & Bohinc, 2012; Browning & Ramasesh, 2015; Feduzi et al., 2022; Lu & Shen, 2020; Paltrinieri et al., 2019; Paltrinierin et al., 2012; Ramani & Okwudire, 2020):

- 'known known'—Risk analysis of the event or scenario is based on the statistical methods and models. Information is available about similar events that have occurred in the past, their frequency, and their impact. There are effective methods for risk treatment.
- 'unknown known'—The event occurred in the past, but there is no actual awareness of it. The risk can be managed with certain confidence as some records exist.
- 'known unknown'—There is some awareness of an event that may occur, but its probability and potential consequences are not specified

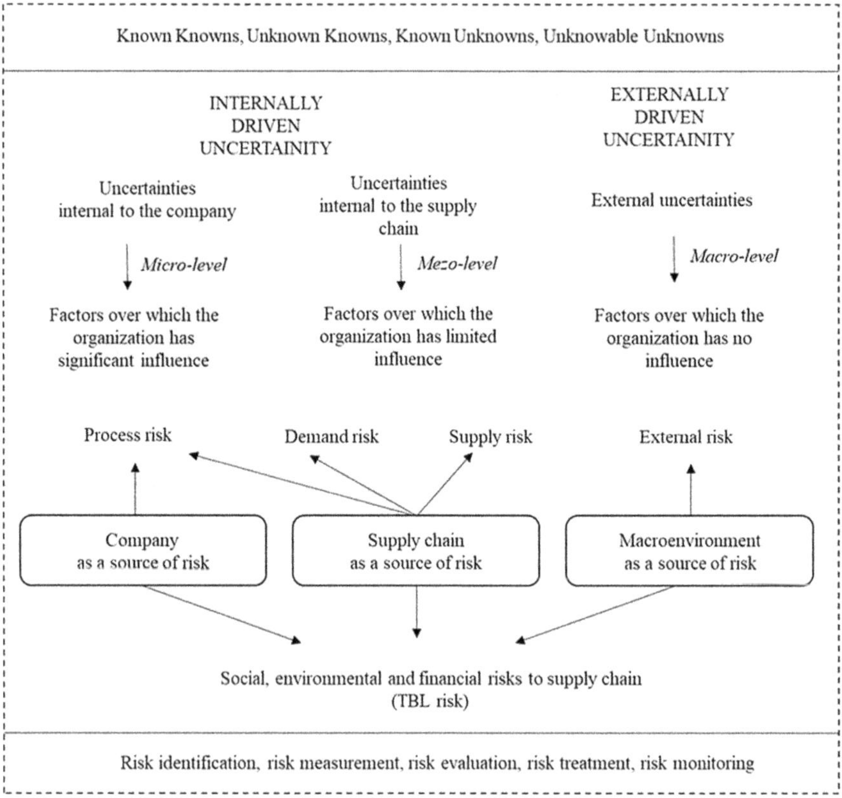

Fig. 3.1 Various aspects of sustainable risk to supply chains. Source: own study

and known. This can be conditioned by the overly high cost of measurement in relation to the size of the effects of uncertainty as well as the variability of the probability due to the changing factors (e.g., activities of supply chain links). The risk is managed with prevention and learning capabilities.

- 'unknowable unknown'—These are unexpected events, of which there is no awareness or knowledge. Risk cannot be managed. This refers to black swans or ignorance.

Managing the risk of "known known' events seems to be highly accessible and less uncertain. In this case, it is based on common and well-described methods of assessing and responding to risk. Knowledge about such events is available and well described. Further, events are not sudden and surprising; on the contrary, sometimes it is almost certain that they will occur. The conditions are getting more and more difficult for the next forms of supply chain risk, firstly because of the burden of increasingly poor information on the risk parameters of a potential event and decreasing awareness of the possibility of its occurrence. The most difficult situation to manage concerns "unknowable unknowns." It is characterized by both the lack of awareness and knowledge about the potential event and scenarios. Therefore, it is actually not possible to manage (e.g., identify, measure, and control) such risks. Black swans are almost impossible to predict. They are completely unexplored, and the development of a crisis situation can be the most surprising and indescribable due to the lack of similar experiences in the past. Even more so, when an event occurs, ignorance can lead to serious losses. Thus, increasing awareness and knowledge of potential adverse events is crucial to minimizing the probability of occurrence or effects of various disruptions and enhancing supply chain resilience.

Supply chain risk management should start with the implementation of the risk identification stage. This stage is related to recognizing main risk types, understanding where and under what conditions adverse events may occur and possibly develop into disruption or even a crisis situation. Effective supply chain risk recognition is possible only if organizations understand the context of their functioning, that is, key processes, business partners, main locations, as well as critical external environment factors.

In the literature on the subject there are several main categories of supply chain risk (uncertainty) that need to be understood and analyzed (Johnson, 2001; Russell & Saldanha, 2003; Manuj & Mentzer, 2008; Directive 2009/138/EC; Pfohl et al., 2011; Angkiriwang et al., 2014; Marcos et al., 2021):

- supply risk
- demand risk

- process risk
- external risk

The first category is related to the supplies, poor performance of suppliers, and problems with meeting customer requirements (e.g., untimely and poor-quality deliveries), as well as each potential threat coming from the supplier's side that can negatively impact the company's objectives. The volatility and uncertainty of demand is the second category that is also associated with the bullwhip effect, product specification changes, and product life cycle. Process risk includes all adverse events that occur during information, money, and material/service flows, and can hinder continuity of operation of the production or distribution system. It is closely related to operational risk, which includes such risk sources as internal processes (inadequate or failed), people (human errors, intentional deviations from procedures, lack of sufficient competence), systems (machines and devices, IT systems), and business environment (strikes). It is also related to the problems linked to the physical security of infrastructure, people, information, trading partners, and supplies (US Customs and Border Protection, 2006; Wieteska, 2011). Finally, external risk comes outside the supply chain in the form of changing political, economic, social, technological, legislative, and environmental (PESTLE) factors.

From the point of view of the supply chain structure, the supply chain risk can be (Wieteska, 2013):

- internally driven, when the uncertainty is related to functioning of each supply chain link (strategic, tactical, operational levels), supplier–buyer dependences (resulting from close cooperation, asymmetry of power), supply chain attributes (e.g., demand, product), supply chain configuration
- externally driven, when the uncertainty is related to competitive supply chains and macroenvironmental changes

According to this approach, the following sources of risk can also be distinguished (Jüttner et al., 2003):

- organizational risk sources, related to the operational level of the company
- network risk sources, related to the dependences between supplier and buyers and possible mismatch between supply and demand
- environmental risk sources, related to the disruptions outside the supply chain

Risk factors that may negatively affect the functioning of the supply chain should not only be identified, but above all minimized in the context of both probability and various consequences (e.g., financial, environmental). However, as experience has shown, risk factors can be controlled to varying degrees. In this understanding, there are three groups of risk factors (Gil, 2001, pp. 105–107):

- factors over which the organization has significant influence
- factors over which the organization has limited influence
- factors over which the organization has no influence

When analyzing the structure of the supply chain, the enterprise (e.g., focal company) may have a different impact on risk, depending on where it arises. If internal processes are the source of adverse events, the company has a significant influence on them, especially through preventive actions toward the probability parameter. Events that occur inside the company are the most known by managers, and may occur relatively often (e.g., absences, technical infrastructural problems). Such events are well known, records are available, and controls are implemented. The risk that arises in cooperation with suppliers and customers is under the limited influence of the company. Thus, it can be partially managed by, for example, initial and periodic supplier assessment or certain terms in the business contracts signed by both parties. Finally, the uncertainty coming from the external environment of the supply chain is beyond the control of companies. Mainly, supply chain links have no influence on the volatility of external risk factors. Especially low-probability high- impact events may disrupt supply chains significantly.

Examples for each group of factors and supply chain structure perspective are as follows (Simangunsong et al., 2012):

- uncertainties internal to the company: product characteristics, manufacturing process, control uncertainty, decision complexity, organizational and behavioral, information technology and information systems complexity
- uncertainties internal to the supply chain: end-customer demand, demand amplification, supplier, parallel interaction, order forecast horizon, supply chain configuration, infrastructure and facilities
- external uncertainties: environment, disasters

Uncertainty understood as lack of information or ambiguity can also be considered in relation to the micro, meso, and macro levels of a supply chain (Flynn et al., 2016). Micro-level supply chain uncertainty refers to the variations in information and material flow processes, especially in terms of demand volatility. Uncertainty at the meso level concerns the difference between the information possessed by the company (including the information received from business partners, who may be opportunistic in cooperation) and full information needed to make the right strategic, tactical, and operational decisions. Finally, macro-level uncertainty is related to a turbulent business environment with unknowns and unexpectedly changing conditions.

It is understandable that when managing risk, companies first focus on events with a high probability of occurrence, which bring measurable and known losses. These are usually internally driven events from quadrants I and IV of the risk matrix (Fig. 3.2). In contrast, low-probability events are often overlooked, intentionally unconsidered, or ignored. As history has shown, it can be especially detrimental to underestimate externally driven low-probability but high-consequence events (quadrat II), which are not under the influence of supply chain links. In fact, such events can cause very serious effects extending as disruptions on a global scale (e.g., COVID-19 pandemic, war in Ukraine).

Depending on the scale of the probability and effects, different methods for risk treatment are recommended (Norrman & Jansson, 2004):

- for high-probability high-effects events—risk avoidance
- for high-probability low-effects events—risk reduction or risk mitigation

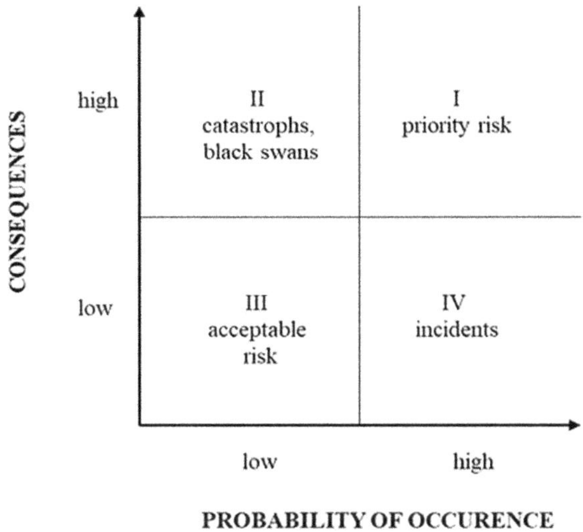

Fig. 3.2 Risk matrix. Source: own study

- for low-probability low-effects events—risk acceptance
- for low-probability high-effects events—risk sharing or risk transfer

Risk avoidance means not exposing the company and the supply chain to the risk unnecessarily and not making too uncertain decisions, for example not to cooperate with X supplier, or not to locate the factory at Y location. Risk reduction and risk mitigation mean reducing probability and effects through preventive actions, for example employee training or security monitoring in the warehouse. The risk acceptance method is used for events whose risk level is acceptable, and both probability and impact are very low. Another situation is when an event with a low probability can cause huge losses. Then we can use the risk sharing (e.g., appropriate terms of the contract, supplier involvement in product development) or risk transfer (e.g., Incoterms, insurance, outsourcing).

Especially for events with a low probability and high potential impact on the company or supply chain, internally or externally driven, the business continuity management (BCM) approach is used. While the methodical basis of risk management is risk analysis (using the probability and impact parameters), in BCM, the key method is Business Impact

Analysis (BIA), which takes into account the impact and time of disruption (Business Continuity Institute, 2007, p. 7; Wieteska, 2018). Namely, it expresses how the effects of the critical event will grow over time. The supply chain vulnerability to disruptions is therefore of particular importance to BCM. Vulnerability is understood as "susceptibility of the supply chain to the consequences of disruptive events" (Chowdhury & Quaddus, 2015). In response to the most realistic results of the BIA, appropriate procedures are prepared to be launched at the right moment as the situation develops. Firstly, business continuity plans are prepared in order to maintain key processes at least at the minimum required performance level when the crisis arises. Consequently, business continuity plans ensure customer service in accordance with the critical goals. Secondly, recovery plans are being developed that aim to rebuild and return to the pre-disruption level of operations or to a new, higher performance of the system. The key elements of the supply chain business continuity management are (Zsidisin et al., 2005):

- creating awareness (both in company and in supply chain)
- prevention (risk identification, assessment, treatment and monitoring)
- remediation (plan how to minimize impact and duration of disruption; execution)
- knowledge management (track results, positive and negative experiences, future action list)

Risk and business continuity aspects should be analyzed in terms of the most important goals of companies. Therefore, risk management is an approach considered to be a crucial part of sustainable supply chain management today. Risk assessment is crucial to support decision-making in a sustainable supply chain and should take into account a number of risk indicators (environmental, sociopolitical, economic) which can disturb the material and information flow processes (Hadiguna, 2012). The sources of sustainable risk are the three dimensions of a sustainable supply chain: environmental, social, and economic (Xu et al., 2019). Triple bottom line (3BL) risk to a sustainable supply chain can be perceived through the prism of different forms, categories, and sources, the level of knowledge, and influence possibilities (Fig. 3.1). Regardless of the place of occurrence in the supply chain (e.g., purchase market, production, distribution processes), three main types of sustainable risk are indicated (Teuscher et al., 2006):

- internal/external ecological risks
- internal/external social risks
- internal/external economic risks

Internal sustainability risk is related to the company's activities and supplier–buyer relationship and supply chain network, whereas exogenous sustainability risk comes from the environment in which supply chains are functioning.

In order to effectively manage sustainable risk, it is necessary to identify all its potential sources and types. Therefore, it is important to understand exactly what events, situations, threats, and factors are directly related to 3BL risk. Taking into account the source of risk, the following sustainability risk examples can be listed (Christopher & Gaudenzi, 2015; Giannakis & Papadopoulos, 2016; Wang et al., 2022; Wieteska-Rosiak, 2017):

- endogenous environmental risk: environmental incidents (e.g., fires, explosions, accidents), pollution (air, water, soil), non-compliance with sustainability laws, emission of greenhouse gases, industrial emissions, ozone depletion, energy consumption (unproductive use of energy), excessive or unnecessary packaging, product waste; inefficient use of resources
- exogenous environmental risk: natural disasters (e.g., hurricanes, floods, earthquakes), water scarcity, heatwaves, droughts, rising sea level
- endogenous social risk: excessive working time and work–life imbalance, unfair payment, child labor/forced labor, discrimination (race, sex, religion, disability, age, political views), human rights (infringe on the rights of others), employee health and safety, healthy and safe working environment, exploitative hiring policies (lack of contract, insurance), unethical treatment of animals, labor strikes
- exogenous social risk: pandemic, social instability/uncertainty (mass demonstrations, migrations), demographic challenges/aging

population, crime/terrorist attacks, political instability, corruption, cultural risk, law risk
- endogenous financial/economic risk: bribery, false claims/dishonesty, price fixing accusations, antitrust claims, patent infringements, tax evasion, R&D investment risk, reputational risk
- exogenous financial/economic risk: boycotts, litigations, energy prices volatility, volatile oil/fuel prices, interest rate risk, tax-related risk, exchange rate risk (currency fluctuations), credit uncertainty, financial crises, economic recession

In addition to the three basic sustainability risk dimensions for supply chains, two more are also distinguished (Fig. 3.3). The first, institutional risk, includes: carelessness of top management in policymaking, absence of strategic planning, lack of laws and legislations, lack of health and safety management facility, lack of eco-literacy and eco-designed system, and lack of internal auditing programs. The second, technical risk, is related to lack of technical expertise, machine breakdowns, damage to products in logistics processes, poor process output at supply source (low

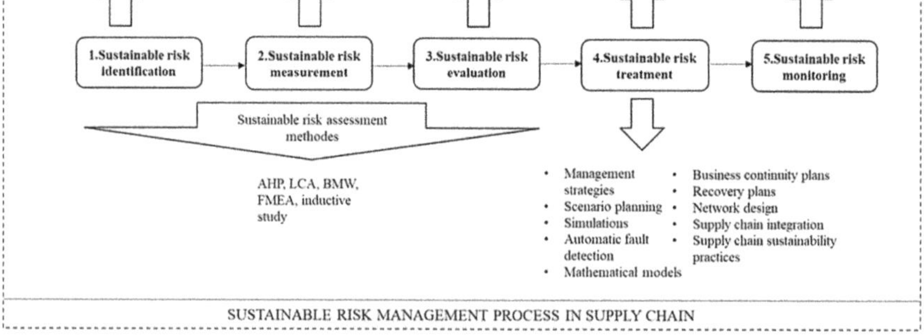

Fig. 3.3 Sustainable risk management process in the supply chain. Source: own study

supplier performance), supplier failures, changes in consumer preference/changes in demand, raw material scarcity, and wrong (insufficient) supplier selection (Moktadir et al., 2021).

In addition to the sustainability risk classifications, another perspective is considered by researchers, namely the risk categories to sustainable supply chains. This perspective is much broader. Therefore, except the environmental, social, and economic risks, others are indicated. For example, among risks faced by sustainable supply chains, operations risk is additionally mentioned (Christopher & Gaudenzi, 2015). Operations risk is similar to technical risk; however, it also covers traditional risk occurring at the operational level:

- constraint on supplier capacity
- lack of availability of raw material
- supplier bankruptcy
- losing the competitive advantage of supplier
- demand volatility/seasonality
- inaccuracy in forecast
- inventory stock-out
- excess inventory risk
- quality-related risk
- non-confirming products
- product design changes
- fluctuation in lead time
- labor strikes in supplier's company

In recent years, sustainable supply chain risk management includes more and more aspects. The next example is the following classification, which consists of seven sustainable supply chain risk categories and identifies specific sub-criteria for each to be evaluated and controlled (Rostamzadeh et al., 2018):

- environmental risks (sub-criteria: wars, terrorism, political unsteadiness, concerns related to economic, natural events, common work conflicts)

- organizational risks (sub-criteria: management policy failures, government policy risks, human error, poor interrelationships between supply chain partners, lack of commitment in the supply chain to go green)
- sustainable supply risks (sub-criteria: capacity constraints, key supplier failures, supplier quality, supplier uncertainty, material order risks, inventory risks, limited number of green suppliers to choose from, supplier's financial instability)
- sustainable production risks (sub-criteria: risk related to design of product, risk related to production capacity, risk in demand, quality-related risk, poor planning and scheduling, forecasting errors, labor strike, machines and equipment risks, long product lead times for green products/materials, change in technologies due to going green)
- sustainable distribution risks (sub-criteria: proximity to airports, quality of roads, demand fluctuations, demand forecasting risks, market-related risks, inability to use green fuel, product perishability risk)
- sustainable recycling risks (sub-criteria: lack of proper sewage infiltration, inability in use of other companies wastes, discharging of wastes risks, groundwater pollution risks)
- IT-related risk (sub-criteria: IT security, bullwhip effect, fail to access information, IT system failure)

A similar approach was pointed out recently. In addition to 3BL risk (environmental, social, and economic risk), sustainable operational risk, economic risk factors, as well as sustainable distribution and recycling risk are indicated (Wang & Rani, 2022). Due to the development of new approaches in the modern economy, other types of risk are also recognized on an ongoing basis. An example is the risks for sustainable supply chains related to the circular economy (CE) implementation with the use of new technologies, that is, risk of management, decision process, and supply chain integration, risk related to labor and human resources, risk related to material costs and suppliers, quality- and design-related risk, and performance-related risk (Kazancoglu et al., 2021).

Conducting traditional risk management activities may result in underestimating or failing to note sustainable risk. Therefore, detailed knowledge of the sustainable risk types becomes very important. The essential issue is emphasized, which is the role of stakeholders in recognizing sustainable supply chain risk sources (Hofmann et al., 2014). For managing sustainability-related risk, a slightly different perspective is also recommended for individual stages of the process, in order to achieve competitive advantage. Mainly, during risk identification, a deterioration of ecosystems, effect on societal values, and responsible management should be taken into account (Giannakis & Papadopoulos, 2016). When it comes to risk causes and implications, both for a traditional supply chain and a sustainable supply chain management, they are the same (Rebs et al., 2018). For example, the consequences of sustainable risk may be of various natures, for example financial, operational, social, environmental, relational, or strategic (Giannakis & Papadopoulos, 2016). It is also indicated that various disruptive risks can negatively affect the sustainability parameters of the supply chain. Especially such problems as low accuracy in demand forecasting, poor supplier assessment, or lack of supply chain coordination and information sharing can lead to the most serious sustainable supply chain disruptions (Shareef et al., 2020).

It is statistically confirmed that the implementation of appropriate supply chain sustainability practices and governance mechanisms allows for the reduction of sustainability risks and improves market performance (Chowdhury & Quaddus, 2021). Interestingly, some sustainable supply chain management risk practices can be influential or dependent, which results from the relationship between them. Practices that are influential and dependent at the same time are, in particular, practices implemented in the design process (delayed differentiation, sharing with upstream and/or downstream partners knowledge or ideas around the design of new products and simplification of the dismantling of products/anticipation of the end of the product life), practices implemented in cooperation with suppliers during buy, supply, and distribution processes (evaluation of suppliers/subcontractors, pooling of supplies for several suppliers or service providers, establishment of contracts with carriers), and a practice implemented in the return process (management of return logistics) (Elmsalmi et al., 2021).

Once a risk has been identified, it must be measured and then, based on appropriate criteria, a decision should be made as to whether the risk is acceptable, tolerable, or unacceptable (Fig. 3.3). Various models are primarily used for sustainable supply chain risk assessment (Wang et al., 2022). These models may include the following:

- analytic hierarchy process (AHP) (Lyu et al., 2020; Mangla et al., 2015)
- life cycle assessment (LCA) (Muazu et al., 2021)
- BMW model (Dobrin, 2021; Zhang et al., 2020)
- Failure mode and effects analysis (FMEA) and inductive study (Giannakis & Papadopoulos, 2016)

Immediate actions are required to reduce unacceptable risk. Prevention, mitigation, avoidance, sharing, or transfer methods are appropriate as a response to risk, depending on the type of sustainability risk. Sustainable risk treatment should be aimed at management strategies, scenario planning, simulations, as well as automatic fault detection and recovery (Giannakis & Papadopoulos, 2016). A large role for risk mitigation and response is also attributed to models (linear programming, stochastic programming, Game Theory), traditional risk management strategies, supply chain configuration, as well as sustainable supply chain integration through innovation, coordination, and demand management (Wang et al., 2022).

Irrespective of the type of risk, the same risk management process can be applied. However, for each step of the process, specific methods and techniques for its implementation are selected, depending on the needs. In the case of sustainable development, environmental, social, and economic factors are the main sources of risk to supply chains. Over the years, however, these categories have been expanded to include new ones more akin to traditional supply chain risk management. Within each analyzed sustainable risk category, there are numerous undesirable events that can negatively affect the supply chain.

The main classification of sustainable risk to the supply chain is based on the place of origin. On the one hand, sustainable risk to the supply chain can be external, arising outside the supply chain and negatively affecting the companies cooperating with each other. In this case, the aim of risk management is specifically to reduce vulnerability to the effects of events occurring in the macro-environment, over which companies have no influence, and which affect the supply chain links and flow processes with different strengths. On the other hand, the sustainable risk to the supply chain can also be internal. In this case, the sources of adverse events are the companies and flow processes in the supply chain. In this case, risk management should be focused especially on prevention through minimizing the probability of adverse events (which is possible because these are factors over which the organizations have influence) as well as mitigating negative consequences. Summing up, managing sustainable risk to the supply chain should be carried out in two ways. Firstly, it should deal with risk factors with a vector of impact directed toward the supply chain, and secondly, it should deal with factors with a vector directed in the opposite direction, that is, outside the supply chain.

3.2 COVID-19 and War in Ukraine as a Part of Supply Chain Risk

Nowadays, in the external environment of the supply chains, there are more and more low-probability high-effects events that hinder the continuity of key operations of companies and cause long-term crises. These are particularly threatening situations, as it is problematic to influence the likelihood of their occurrence (Fig. 3.2). As history shows, externally driven situations may severely disrupt the functioning of international and global supply chains. Such situations can be referred to the critical changes in the each type of PESTLE factors (Fig. 3.4).

Recent years have been extremely turbulent for many companies. Political factors that hinder business processes are related mainly to the decisions of governments (Banham, 2014). Recently, the war in Ukraine has become particularly disruptive to supply chains (Ngoc et al., 2022; Paché, 2022). The military conflict has also impacted the global economy, determining, among others, increase in energy prices and inflation (Cui et al., 2023). The previous most difficult economic period was the global financial crisis that started at the end of 2008 with the collapse of Lehman Brothers. Russia's aggression against Ukraine has hit the already weakened economy after the most significant social risk in recent years. The COVID-19 pandemic has had multidimensional effects on global supply chains, societies, and the natural environment (Pujawan & Bah,

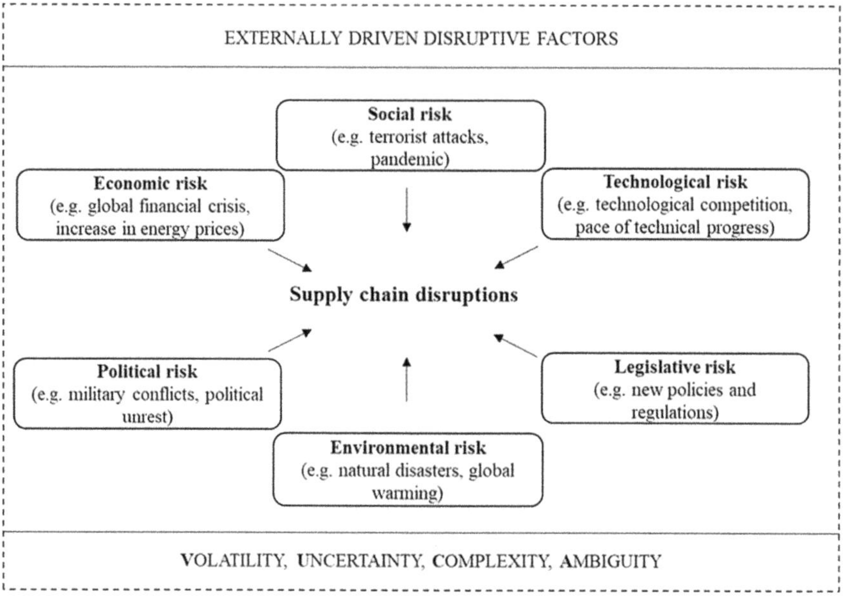

Fig. 3.4 Externally driven supply chain disruptive factors in a volatility, uncertainty, complexity, ambiguity (VUCA) world. Source: own study

2022; Verma & Prakash, 2020). In addition to the impact on the economy, the pandemic increased the importance of new technologies, especially in the area of communication. However, technological changes can be perceived not only as a source of benefits, but also as a factor disrupting various industries (Friedlmaier et al., 2018). The next type of external risk that may bring crises in supply chains is environmental risk. The forces of nature, in the form of natural disasters, paralyze large areas of regions and, at the same time, the product flow processes carried out on them. This was demonstrated, among others, by events such as the volcanic eruption in Iceland causing a global paralysis of air connections with Europe, or the flood in Thailand disrupting global supply chains of hard drives (Alexander, 2013; Haraguchi & Lall, 2015). On the one hand, natural forces pose a threat to society and the economy; on the other hand, it is society and the economy that pose a threat to the natural environment. Therefore, new policies and regulations (especially under sustainable development and circular economy concepts) are being introduced in order to force the expected changes in consumer behavior and supply chain operations. However, the introduced legislative changes may be perceived as disruptive factors as they may become significant financial issues for both companies and households.

Supply chain managers need to deal with many challenges posed by the world of VUCA (volatility, uncertainty, complexity, ambiguity). External uncertainty and risks are often extremely difficult to anticipate and mitigate. The dynamics of changes in the business environment can be characterized by two variables (Bennett & Lemoine, 2014):

- the ability to predict the results of a company's actions (higher for complexity and volatility, lower for ambiguity and uncertainty)
- the scale of the knowledge about the situation (higher for volatility and uncertainty, lower for complexity and ambiguity)

In most cases, the only option to treat the risk of externally driven situations is to minimize the impact and multidimensional losses by implementing appropriate reactions. The response can be carried out using both proactive and reactive/recovery strategies aimed at building supply chain resilience (SCRES) in the era of VUCA (Gao et al., 2021).

The situation that has greatly affected supply chains is the COVID-19 pandemic caused by a new type of coronavirus, SARS-CoV-2. It has spread very fast and affected almost all countries in the world. The first known case of acute respiratory disease was identified in Wuhan (China) in December 2019. The virus quickly spread to other countries and the situation was declared a pandemic by the World Health Organization in March 2020. The virus not only caused widespread illness and the deaths of millions of people, but also had a significant impact on industries and economies around the world. Over the two-year period, there were several waves of the pandemic. The first and second occurred in 2020 and the third and fourth in 2021. The severity of the waves varied by region, with some countries experiencing more severe outbreaks of disease than others.

The situation, considered as a black swan, developed very dynamically. Due to the lack of comprehensive knowledge about the rapidly spreading threat, the number of positively diagnosed cases and secondary outbreak increased day by day. Especially the ambiguity related to the new business situation made it difficult to make the right decisions and deal with event scenarios (Gunessee & Subramanian, 2020). COVID-19 pandemic uncertainty affected companies in various dimensions, inducing strong pressures and difficulties in maintaining a balance between capacity and demand in individual supply chains as well as pressures related to increasing sustainable supply chain risk (Fig. 3.5).

The externally driven situation disturbed supply management, demand management, and operational management simultaneously. The COVID-19 pandemic impacted supply chains of many products, causing demand and supply shocks and continuity problems of product flow processes. The supply, demand, and operational risk pressure has resulted in huge losses for companies worldwide, revealing many weaknesses in

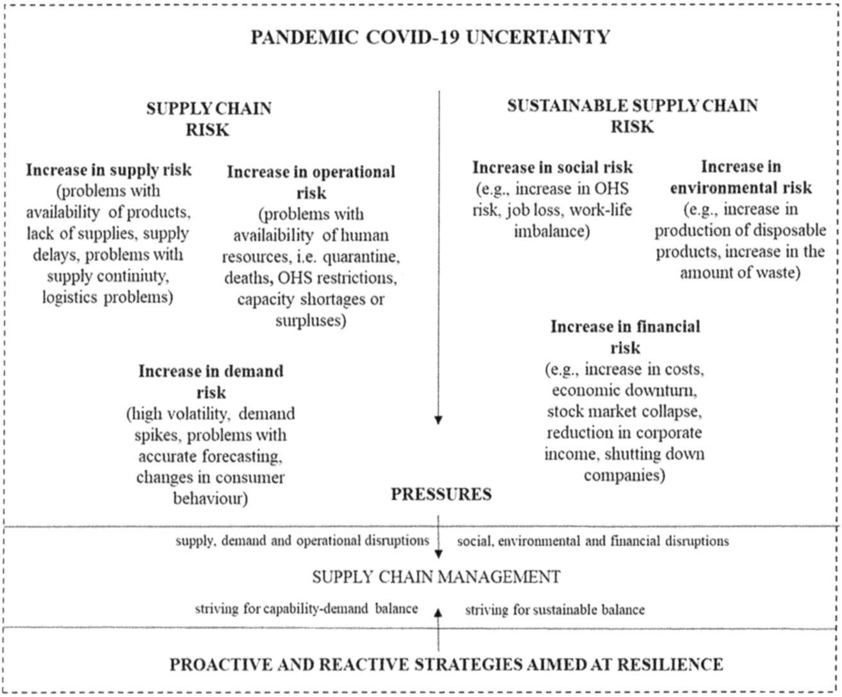

Fig. 3.5 COVID-19 pandemic uncertainty, increased risk and pressure on supply chains. Source: own study

the management of modern supply chains. Unpredictable changes in demand and supplies as well as operational disruptions spilled over to global value chains.

First, for some products (e.g., food, medicines, hospital services) the demand was growing rapidly, whereas for other products (e.g., luxury goods, public transport, clothes, cosmetics) the demand was stable or declining in an unpredictable way (Handfield et al., 2020; Nikolopoulos et al., 2021). In some industries, demand volatility was extremely high. An example is food products, for which demand suddenly increased as a result of public panic, and then gradually decreased due to excess stocks in households and a stabilizing situation (Hobbs, 2020). Except for the extremely high uncertainty of demand, there were also serious problems with the availability of raw materials, components, and final products (Gupta et al., 2021; Lozano-Diez et al., 2020; Paul & Chowdhury, 2021; Rowan & Laffey, 2020; Singh et al., 2020). That was also related to the disrupted global logistics, mainly due to the shortages in the labor force, closing borders, shutting down of airports, and suspended movement of people (Hirata & Matsuda, 2022; Ikotun et al., 2021; Xu et al., 2020). One of the main problems was the disruption of international trade as borders were closed and travel restrictions were imposed. Delays, lack of deliveries of products, as well as insufficient inventory hindered the continuity of flows in production and distribution systems. Finally, operational process capacities were also hampered by problems with human resources accessibility due to quarantine, deaths, and occupational and safety restrictions introduced by authorities (Bochtis et al., 2020; Dubey et al., 2020; Poudel et al., 2020). As a consequence, there were backlogs and delays in the execution of orders. Enterprises that wanted to take advantage of the opportunity associated with increased demand had problems with increasing production capacity and the limited capacity of the supplier base. On the other hand, companies that noted suddenly reduced demand struggled to maintain existing production and distribution resources and at the same time financial liquidity. Due to multi-level problems, some enterprises were also shutting down (Alabi & Ngwenyama, 2023). The pandemic had a significant impact on global supply chains, leading to an economic slowdown and widespread job losses.

The COVID-19 pandemic was also a major challenge for managing increasing risk for sustainable supply chains (Fig. 3.5). The "unknowable unknown" impacted the three dimensions of sustainable development in enterprises and supply chain processes, that is, sourcing, manufacturing, and distribution (Begum et al., 2022; Kumar et al., 2022; Sarkis, 2020; Sharma et al., 2022; Verma & Prakash, 2020). The list of key sustainability issues related to the pandemic is as follows (Chowdhury et al., 2021):

- social issues: health and safety, labor law, social security, job loss, modern slavery risk, domestic violence, economic inequality
- environmental issues: increase in negative impact (e.g., increase in production of pharmaceutical products, uncollected medical waste, problems with effective recycling and circular economy, increase in household, medical, plastic food, and single-use waste, damaging the trend of green energy), and decrease in negative impact (e.g., reduction in air pollution, oil consumption, greenhouse gas emissions, energy consumption)
- economic issues: increase in supply chain costs (e.g., storage costs), global economy shock (e.g., slowdown in economic activity, stock market collapse, decrease in price of gas fuel), looking for solutions that minimize total cost in supply chain

The COVID-19 pandemic was significantly related to social and cultural repercussions, with people around the world experiencing changes in their daily habits and way of life. Many people had to adapt to remote work or distance learning, often feeling the negative impact of this situation not only on their physical but especially their mental health (Pragholapati, 2020; Ravi et al., 2021).

The pandemic confirmed the vulnerability of supply chains and the global economy to black swan events. The multidimensional problems spread in the form of the ripple effect in supply chains (Buera et al., 2021; Dolgui & Ivanov, 2021). To successfully deal with observed challenges (changing consumer behaviors, labor mismatch, demand and supply mismatch, changing health and safety behaviors) companies were trying to implement different types of responses (Mollenkopf et al.,

2021). SCRES turned out to be essential to survive the long-term crisis. Various strategies and capabilities were recognized as crucial to implement in supply chains during and/or in a post-pandemic reality:

- contingency planning and risk management, moving from just-in-time to just-in-case (Fonseca & Azevedo, 2020)
- supply chain flexibility (Chenarides et al., 2021)
- agility, collaboration, flexibility, redundancy (Scala & Lindsay, 2021)
- automation integration to increase manufacturing flexibility, omni-channel distribution, artificial intelligence (Ahmed et al., 2022)
- collaboration efficiency, that is,. collaborative planning, forecasting, and replenishment, resource sharing, network resources, co-creation (Friday et al., 2021; Sharma et al., 2021)
- collaboration, risk management culture, visibility, and flexibility strategies (Spieske et al., 2022)
- strategic sourcing (Frederico, Kumar, & Garza-Reyes, 2021)
- supporting supply chain partners (especially SMEs), production of protective products, flexibility, responsiveness and visibility, re-shoring (Xu et al., 2020)
- conversions in supply chain processes and resources: production location, production line, storage, usage, distribution and workforce (Haraguchi et al., 2023)
- localized sourcing, reserve inventory, and capacity deployment (Bastas & Garza-Reyes, 2022)
- diversification (Sajjad, 2021)
- knowledge management (de Sousa Jabbour et al., 2020)
- supply chain innovation (Ozdemir et al., 2022)
- logistics improvements (Goel et al., 2021)
- 4.0 technologies, digital technologies (Balakrishnan & Ramanathan, 2021 Frederico, Kumar, Garza-Reyes, Kumar, & Agrawal, 2021; Kumar et al., 2022)
- big data analytics tools (Bag et al., 2021; Bastas & Garza-Reyes, 2022)
- blockchain technology (Xiong et al., 2021)
- artificial intelligence (Modgil et al., 2022)
- sustainability focus (Lau et al., 2022)

The development of the situation during the pandemic was extremely difficult to predict. Decisions on risk and continuity management were often intuitive due to the lack of similar experiences based on historical data and accurate forecasts in supply chains. Managers reacted on an ongoing basis by considering the most likely scenarios of events. The unusual turbulence of the environment has affected not only companies, but also governments and, above all, societies and economics of almost all countries worldwide.

The global economic slowdown caused by the pandemic rapidly overlapped with the negative effects of the escalating Russian-Ukrainian war on February 24, 2022, when Russia invaded Ukraine (International Monetary Fund, 2022). According to European research, 68% of logistics and supply chain managers from the EMEA region anticipate that in 2023, the war will negatively impact supply chains, which is the most important concern (Reuters Events Supply Chains and JLL, 2023, p. 6). The effects of the war are projected to be multidimensional (Bin-Nashwan et al., 2022). The disruptions spread through the supply chains with the global ripple effect. First, the war increased the externally driven uncertainty, which resulted in increase of external risk (e.g., political risk, economic risk, social risk, legislative risk), supply chain risk (e.g., demand risk, supply risk, and operational risk), as well as sustainability risk worldwide (Fig. 3.6).

Before 2022, Russia was the largest energy products exporter to the EU. For example, in 2020, the EU imported more than 25% of petroleum oil from Russia (Eurostat, 2023). Russia's full-scale invasion of Ukraine has started the implementation of a plan that aims to make the EU independent of fossil fuels purchased from Russia until 2030 (European Commission, 2022). The aim of such activities is primarily to increase energy security. In turn, the USA immediately banned trade in oil, natural gas, and coal (all energy-related products), under an Executive Order signed by President Joe Biden on March 8, 2022 (The White House, 2022). The situation resulted in an important reduction in the supply of crude oil and, consequently, in a significant increase in the prices of energy raw materials on the global market. In the following months, despite the relative stabilization of the price, it remained at a high level, for example 85.95 USD per oil barrel on April 17, 2023

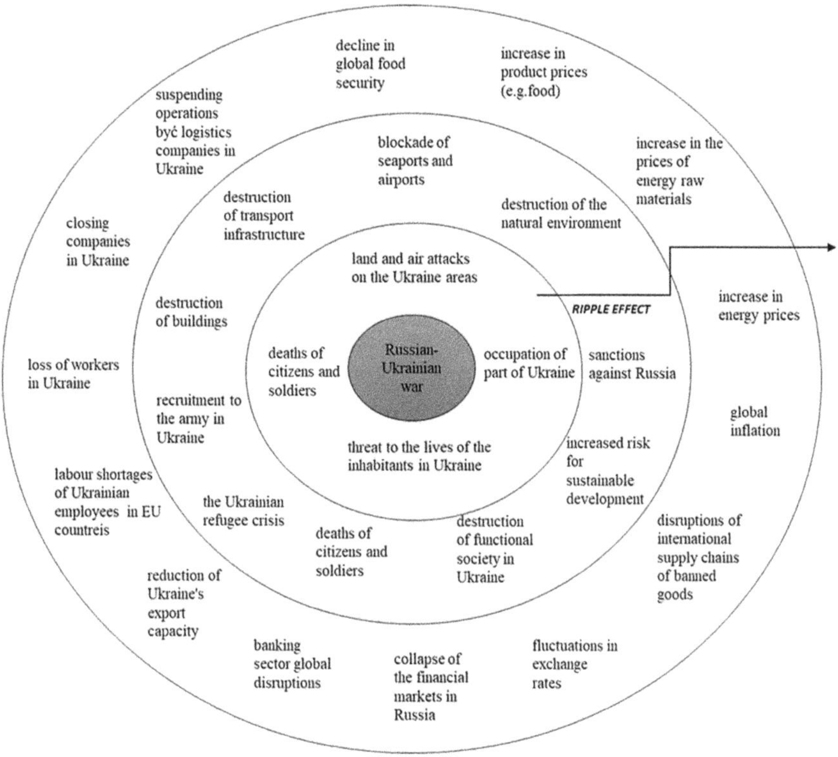

Fig. 3.6 The ripple effect of war on the Ukraine on the global economy and supply chains. Source: own study

(Bankier.pl, 2023). High prices of natural gas, petroleum, and electricity translate into an increase in the operating costs of enterprises from all sectors and an increase in the prices of consumer products. Despite the well-assessed resilience, Russia's aggression against Ukraine has confirmed that, apart from sea piracy and terrorism, the greatest security threat to energy supply chains is war (Urciuoli et al., 2014).

The increase in the prices of energy raw materials resulted in an understandable increase in energy prices. Consequently, the increase in energy prices has a negative impact on the supply chain costs and financial performance of companies (Ferriani & Gazzani, 2023). Among the most exposed industrial sectors in terms of energy intensity are paper and forest products, airlines, and construction materials (Ferriani & Gazzani, 2023). The increase in the prices of essential commodities which resulted from the war initially affected European countries and then countries worldwide. However, it was recognized that the severity of inflation is greater for countries that are in close proximity to Russia and Ukraine and countries with a more intensive trade with countries in military conflict (Maurya et al., 2023). Global inflation significantly hinders consumer buying power and consequently decline in demand. The effects of price increase extend to all participants in supply chains. However, most companies indicate that costs will be transferred to consumers in the end (Reuters Events Supply Chains and JLL, 2023, pp. 6, 10).

Within a year of launching a full-blown invasion of Ukraine, 10 sanctions packages against Russia were introduced. The sanctions are aimed at weakening the Russian economy by depriving the aggressor of markets, access to technology, and, consequently, the possibility of conducting military operations. Thus, the ban on imports from Russia also extended to other goods, including gold, steel, cement, cosmetics, cigarettes, seafood, and liquor. Similarly, many goods cannot be exported to Russia, especially new technology, luxury goods, and products related to transportation, aviation, and space industries (European Council, 2023). In this way, many flows of goods in international supply chains have been disrupted as a result of the introduced legal regulations. The sanctions of the EU and the USA led to the collapse of the financial markets in Russia. Ukraine's stock market also suffered, but with lower losses (Najaf et al., 2023). Global trade was affected by strong fluctuations in exchange rates, including for the euro and US dollar (Aliu et al., 2023). The war also hit the banking sector and bank stocks, especially in Europe, Asia, and North America (Boubaker et al., 2023). The immediate cause of this situation was the economic interdependence between the neighboring EU, Ukraine, and Russia.

The military conflict in Ukraine has a negative impact on the functioning of international supply chains, disrupting road, air, and sea transport. Many logistics companies have had to suspend operations in the threatened area (Ngoc et al., 2022). Some enterprises (e.g., Azovstal, Antonow) located in the war-torn area lost their locations as a result of total or partial destruction of buildings and labor shortages (Świetlińska, 2022).

In neighboring countries (e.g., Poland), from which large groups of Ukrainians returned to their country to defend it, there were labor shortages in production, construction, and transport (Szkwarek, 2023). The main impact of the war in Ukraine on logistics is especially (Krykavskyy et al., 2023):

- occupation of part of Ukraine by Russia and non-kinetic warfare
- supply chain disruptions
- destruction of logistics infrastructure
- destruction of functional society

The direct threat to the lives of the inhabitants of the area covered by the military conflict resulted in a mass emigration of the population from Ukraine, especially to the neighboring countries. Within a year of the start of the war, nearly 8.1 million refugees from Ukraine have been recorded across Europe (the International Organization for Migration, 2023). For example, according to the data of the Polish Border Guard, from February 24, 2022 to April 23, 2023, the Polish-Ukrainian border was crossed by 11.151 million refugees from Ukraine, mainly women and children (Turaieva, 2023).

Not only society but also the natural environment is suffering from the military conflict in Ukraine. Disturbances of the balance in ecosystems are related to (Pereira et al., 2022; Rawtani et al., 2022):

- reduction of biodiversity
- deforestation and destruction of habitat of wild animals
- soil degradation and damage of landscape morphology
- pollution of sweet water
- deterioration of air quality
- the risk of nuclear accidents

Russia's military invasion of Ukraine has a wide impact on sustainable development, threatening in particular the following goals worldwide: peace and justice, no poverty, zero hunger, and responsible consumption and production (Ben Hassen & El Bilali, 2022; Bin-Nashwan et al., 2022).

The war has caused particularly severe problems in the food sector due to the fact that Russia and Ukraine are two of the largest exporters of grains and oilseeds, and in addition, Russia, apart from the world's gas supplies, is an important supplier of fertilizers. For example, in 2021, Ukraine exported the most wheat to Asia and Africa (Matuszak, 2022). The key aspects related to the functioning of food supply chains in the conditions of the current war are (Ben Hassen & El Bilali, 2022; Jagtap et al., 2022; Shams Esfandabadi et al., 2022):

- negative impact on supply chains by disrupting sourcing, production, and logistics processes
- reduction of Ukraine's export capacity
- disruption of grain transport by blocking key sea and river ports and paralysis of major shipping routes
- delays as the result of insufficient efficiency of customs
- labor shortages due to conscription and displacement of the population
- increase in global prices of wheat, corn, sunflower seeds, and oil
- increase in global prices of fertilizers, which can cause their reduced use and lower yields
- a shift from the demand for Ukrainian products to substitutes of other imports
- inflation causing consumers to search for inexpensive alternatives

In the light of all kinds of repercussions, it is necessary to build both resilient and sustainable food supply chains (Shams Esfandabadi et al., 2022). Certain directions can be indicated in this regard. Mostly, they include cooperation with suppliers. It is important to have alternative suppliers of raw materials located in close proximity and preferably in the same country. Companies should concentrate on developing innovations with supply chain partners in order to ensure product safety and quality. Increasing global transport flexibility is another resilience factor. Next, the digital transformation would allow for the minimization of labor risks and support maintaining food flow processes (Jagtap et al., 2022). Finally, there is an urgent need for renewable energy transition (Bin-Nashwan et al., 2022). Among strategies also strengthening the resilience of other supply chains in times of war, managers point to: diversification, cooperation and coopetition, and business–government–society partnership (Krykavskyy et al., 2023).

Modern supply chains have been hit hard by black swans and ripple effects in recent years. Global disruptions have caused problems in the manufacturing and distribution systems at different levels and stages of adding value. Uncertainty and risk associated with the pandemic and war have induced great difficulties, above all with planning. These crises have affected the areas of supply and demand, as well as resources and operational activities in enterprises. Companies without a culture of risk management and business continuity have often made reactive and intuitive decisions, which in many cases have had catastrophic results. Therefore, with the challenges of managing in such turbulent times, more and more organizations are focusing their attention on strengthening supply chain resilience. The COVID-19 pandemic and the war in Ukraine have made food supply chains the focus of research on risk and resilience (e.g., Ali et al., 2022; Dyson et al., 2023; Kumar & Kumar Singh, 2022; Saleheen & Habib, 2023). At the same time, however, there is an urgent need for constant attention to activities aimed at sustainable development. Mainly, it has turned out that during global crises, it is extremely difficult to effectively achieve a balance in the implementation of environmental, social, and financial goals.

3.3 Supply Chain Resilience

Over the past three decades a broad concept of supply chain resilience (SCRES) has been developed. Despite its multidimensionality, it is described in the literature in a transparent and comprehensive way. The foundation of understanding this concept is the three phases: before, during, and after the disruption. For each of them, the specific strategies are assigned and then the detailed directions for their implementation. The guidelines in this area are a variety of principles, recommendations, elements, enablers, capabilities, and practices (Fig. 3.7).

SCRES was first mentioned in 2003, when highlighting the need for configuring not only secure but also resilient supply chains capable of responding to various threats, especially terrorism. It was explained that

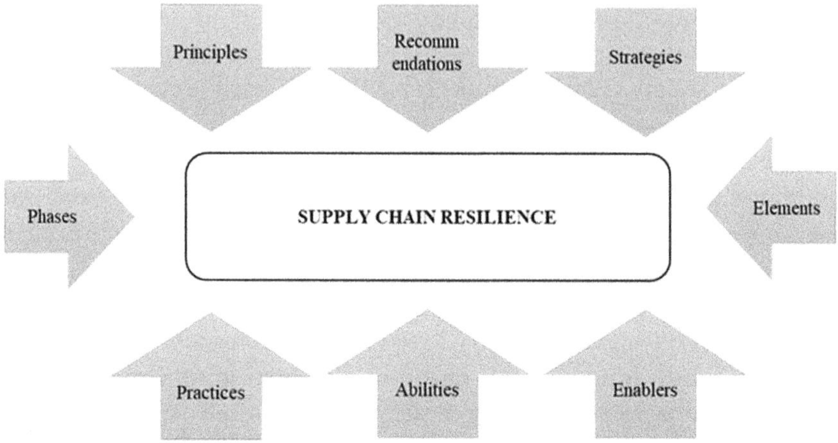

Fig. 3.7 Comprehensive understanding of SCRES in the literature. Source: own study

building SCRES is possible mainly by enhancing flexibility and redundancy (Rice & Caniato, 2003a, 2003b).

Supply chain flexibility is "the ability of an organization to manage the internal (e.g. manufacturing) and interfacing (e.g. procurement and distribution) processes, as well as its key suppliers/customers to respond to expected changes in supply, product and demand in an efficient manner enabled by both technological and social platforms" (Fayezi et al., 2014). Flexibility may characterize various areas of the supply chain. There are several dimensions of supply chain flexibility, including (Fantazy et al., 2009):

- logistics/delivery/distribution/access flexibility
- sourcing/supply/volume/procurement flexibility
- product development flexibility
- new product/launch flexibility
- information systems/spanning flexibility
- production flexibility, manufacturing flexibility, operations system flexibility

Upstream risk can lead to particularly intense disruptions, causing a domino effect in the entire supply chain. Therefore, building flexibility in a supplier relationship is considered particularly important. This type of flexibility consists of sourcing flexibility (procurement flexibility) and supplier flexibility (vendor/supply flexibility). Sourcing flexibility is primarily the ability to reconfigure the supply base and/or shift the orders among the suppliers quickly, whereas supplier flexibility refers to the supplier's ability to respond to volume, delivery time, mix, and product changes (Duclos et al., 2003; Pujawan, 2004; Sanchez & Perez, 2005; Lummas et al., 2005; Fantazy et al., 2009; Chu et al., 2012).

Redundancy allows for preparation for uncertainties and global disruptions by keeping various types of reserve resources in the supply chain (Sheffi, 2001). These can be safety stocks (Christopher & Peck, 2004), including high buffers of critical components (Stecke & Kumar, 2009), as well as spare capacity (Rice & Caniato, 2003b). The redundancy in the supplier relationship is usually understood as having back-up suppliers and performing multi-sourcing strategies (Tang, 2006; Zsidisin & Wagner, 2010). Depending on the research context, the latter may increase both flexibility and redundancy (Mackay et al., 2020).

There are four main SCRES principles (Christopher & Peck, 2004; Kamalahmadi & Parast, 2016).The first is "supply chain reengineering." Mainly, resilient strategies should be based on several open options and a new trade-off between efficiency and redundancy must be reconsidered. This is possible thanks to flexibility and redundancy. The second principle refers to the "collaboration" which is developed on trust, information sharing, and visibility. Visibility is understood as having knowledge about the structure and resources of the entire supply chain. Such an approach makes it possible to recognize upstream and downstream uncertainties, quickly identify the places where disruptions arise, and adequately react to the crisis (Christopher & Peck, 2004; Pettit et al., 2013). All activities aimed at building supplier–buyer cooperation based on joint-decision-making, information and knowledge sharing, supplier certification, and supplier development co-create collaboration (Hohenstein et al., 2015). The third principle is "agility," which consists of visibility and velocity, that is, the pace of flexible adjustments. The last principle, "supply chain risk management culture," is based on innovation implementation, risk management leadership, and team (Christopher & Peck, 2004; Kamalahmadi & Parast, 2016).

The above principles can be enriched by the following recommendations that should guide the strengthening of supply chain resilience (World Economic Forum, 2013, p. 27):

- partnership
- policy
- strategy
- IT

As part of the "partnership" recommendation, attention is paid to the cooperation between business, government, and policymakers in minimizing the impact of low-probability and high-consequence events on supply chains. There is a need to involve various supply chain stakeholders in the risk management process. In particular, risk assessment can be supported by increasing the use of data sharing platforms, which is included in the "IT" recommendation. The "policy" recommendation also emphasizes the importance of establishing new international resilience standards by organizations for standardization. Finally, the "strategy" recommendation indicates that companies should implement strategies focused especially on strengthening agility and adaptability (World Economic Forum, 2013, p. 27). This is consistent with the so-called triple A supply chain, namely, a supply chain that is to gain a sustainable advantage over competition is characterized by (Lee, 2004):

- agility—dealing with short-term changes in demand and supply quickly as well as with external disruptions
- adaptability—reconfiguring supply chain design to market changes, new strategy product, or technology
- alignment—stimulating partnership cooperation based on the exchange of information, dedicated roles and risk, and costs and benefits sharing

The first integrated definition of SCRES was developed on the basis of the analysis of the issue of resilience in various disciplines (e.g., psychology, ecology): "the adaptive capability of the supply chain to prepare for unexpected events, respond to disruptions, and recover from them by maintaining continuity of operations at the desired level of connectedness and control over structure and function" (Ponomarov & Holcomb, 2009). It identifies key characteristics that are the foundation of resilient supply chains. The first aspect is preparation for all kinds of adverse events. This requires understanding the context of functioning of supply chain participants, anticipation of threats, and risk assessment skills. The second attribute is related to the ability to respond to various types of disruptive events through launching appropriate contingency and business continuity plans. The last component involves the issue of returning to the balance and level of functioning before the disruption and learning from the experience. Over the years, many other definitions of SCRES have appeared. Their analysis allowed for recognition of three or four of the most frequently indicated phases and elements of supply chain resilience. The three-phase division is as follows (Kamalahmadi & Parast, 2016):

- anticipation phase—elements: proactive thinking, time before the disturbance occurs, planning, preparing, looking for the best solutions
- resistance phase—elements: time during a disruption, actions to maintain the structure and functions
- recovery and response phase—elements: reactive thinking, reactive actions

In turn, the four-phase division includes (Hohenstein et al., 2015):

- readiness (the most frequent elements: flexibility, redundancy, agility, collaboration, information sharing, and visibility)
- response (the most frequent elements: flexibility, visibility, capacity, collaboration, redundancy, and agility)
- recovery (the most frequent elements: flexibility, capacity, redundancy, visibility, and collaboration)
- growth (the most frequent elements: flexibility, collaboration, visibility, agility, capacity, and redundancy)

In addition to flexibility, redundancy, agility, visibility, and collaboration, which were explained earlier, the capacity is mentioned in the four-phase approach. Capacity is understood as an ability of the supply chain to "survive, adapt and grow" in the face of a high-turbulence environment (Fiksel, 2006; Pettit et al., 2010; Sawik, 2013).

Readiness, response, and recovery can be measured with the use of several sub-constructs and items (Chowdhury & Quaddus, 2016):

- readiness construct—sub-constructs: flexibility (items: production flexibility, customization, multi-skilled workforce, contract flexibility, distribution flexibility), redundancy (items: reserve capacity, stock, back-up utility), visibility (items: information sharing, tracking information on operations, business intelligence), collaboration (items: collaborative demand forecasting, collaborative decision, investing in suppliers plants), disaster planning (items: readiness training, readiness resource, contingency planning)
- response-recovery—sub-constructs: response (items: quick response, response team), recovery (items: quick recovery, loss absorption, reduction of impact)

SCRES principles and elements can also be named as enablers. In the literature, the most frequently mentioned SCRES enablers are the following five: collaboration, visibility, flexibility, agility, and redundancy (de Lima et al., 2018).

Another systematic review of the literature on the subject provided a comprehensive compilation of strategies aimed at strengthening the resilience of the supply chain. They are identified taking into account the moment of strategy performance, that is, before and after the disruption (Tukamuhabwa et al., 2015):

- proactive SCRES strategies: appropriate supplier selection, building logistics capabilities, building security, building social capital and relational competences, coopetition, creating appropriate contractual agreements, creating public–private partnerships, creating risk management culture, increasing innovativeness, increasing visibility, increasing visibility, knowledge management, portfolio diversification,

supplier development, supply chain collaboration, supply chain network structure/ design, sustainability compliance, use of information technology
- reactive SCRES strategies: building logistics capabilities, building social capital and relational competences, contingency planning, creating redundancy, demand management, ensuring supply chain agility, increasing flexibility, increasing velocity, increasing visibility, supply chain collaboration, use of information technology

In the classification, some of the proactive and reactive strategies are the same. What is interesting is that among the proactive strategies the aspects of sustainability compliance and risk management appear and among the reactive strategies the issue of contingency planning is listed. Sustainability protects value, awareness, and reputation, as well as determining supplier–buyer partnership. Therefore, it can be regarded as one of the supply chain resilience factors (Faisal, 2010; Zhao et al., 2017). It is also widely noted that risk management (assessment, mitigation, control) and business continuity management (identification of high-impact and low-probability events as well as business continuity plans) are particularly important for supply chain resilience in terms of both preventing and responding to internal and external disruptions (Colicchia et al., 2010; Jüttner & Maklan, 2011; Wedawatta & Ingirige, 2012).

The most comprehensive SCRES understanding, which is based on systematic literature review (SLR), lists three main strategies and assigns specific abilities, elements, and practices to them (Ali et al., 2022). The proactive strategy is performed during the readiness phase, before a disruption occurs. The key ability that should be developed at this time is the ability to anticipate. The concurrent strategy is implemented in the responsiveness phase. During-disruption actions require two abilities: the ability to adapt and the ability to respond. Finally, the reactive strategy is related to recovery and growth phases and is based on the ability to recover and the ability to learn. Achieving each of these abilities is possible using certain elements (Ali et al., 2022):

- ability to anticipate—elements: situation awareness, robustness, increasing visibility, building security and knowledge management

- ability to adapt—elements: increasing flexibility and building redundancy;
- ability to respond—elements: collaboration and agility
- ability to recover—elements: contingency planning and market position
- ability to learn—elements: knowledge management and building social capital

For each element there can be several practices. However, there are still not many in-depth studies on if and how exactly they influence SCRES. For example, one of the still underappreciated practices that determine processes and supply chain resources and structure is supplier involvement in product development (SIPD). Recently, it was confirmed in a quantitative way that partnership during SIPD reduces supply risk, and that communication during SIPD reduces operational risk in a buyer company (Wieteska, 2020; Kędzia, 2023). However, at the same time the ambiguous impact of supplier involvement in product development on supplier relationship resilience was revealed (Kędzia, 2023).

SCRES is also analyzed with the use of CIMO (context, interventions, mechanisms, outcomes) logic. Behind the context are the external and internal uncertainties and risks that supply chains are exposed to. Interventions cover both the supply chain vulnerabilities and supply chain capabilities relevant to managing disturbances effectively. Various theories (e.g., dynamic capabilities, resource-based view, systems and control theories) create mechanisms. Finally, expected SCRES outcomes are related to improved performance and sustained competitiveness as well as risk reduction and better recovery time (Datta, 2017; Kochan & Nowicki, 2018).

The issue of SCRES is a highly relevant concept today. Global crises are prompting in-depth work on the factors that strengthen the ability of enterprises and supply chains to cope with business uncertainty and unexpected disruptions. Undoubtedly, further research is needed in this area, both qualitative and quantitative. Nowadays, it is particularly interesting to search for detailed relationships between the concept of sustainable development and the concept of supply chains resilience.

References

Aggarwal, R., & Bohinc, J. (2012). Black swans and supply chain strategic necessity. *Journal of Transportation Security, 5*, 39–49.

Ahmed, T., Karmaker, C. L., Nasir, S. B., & Moktadir, M. A. (2022). Identifying and analysis of key flexible sustainable supply chain management strategies toward overcoming the post-COVID-19 impacts. *International Journal of Emerging Markets, 18*(6), 1472–1492.

Alabi, M. O., & Ngwenyama, O. (2023). Food security and disruptions of the global food supply chains during COVID-19: Building smarter food supply chains for post COVID-19 era. *British Food Journal, 125*(1), 167–185.

Alexander, D. (2013). Volcanic ash in the atmosphere and risks for civil aviation: A study in European crisis management. *International Journal of Disaster Risk Science, 4*, 9–19.

Ali, I., Sadiddin, A., & Cattaneo, A. (2022). Risk and resilience in agri-food supply chain SMEs in the pandemic era: A cross-country study. *International Journal of Logistics Research and Applications, 26*, 1–19.

Aliu, F., Hašková, S., & Bajra, U. Q. (2023). Consequences of Russian invasion on Ukraine: Evidence from foreign exchange rates. *The Journal of Risk Finance, 24*(1), 40–58.

Angkiriwang, R., Pujawan, I. N., & Santosa, B. (2014). Managing uncertainty through supply chain flexibility: Reactive vs. proactive approaches. *Production & Manufacturing Research, 2*(1), 50–70.

Bag, S., Dhamija, P., Luthra, S., & Huisingh, D. (2021). How big data analytics can help manufacturing companies strengthen supply chain resilience in the context of the COVID-19 pandemic. *The International Journal of Logistics Management, 34*(4), 1141–1164.

Balakrishnan, A. S., & Ramanathan, U. (2021). The role of digital technologies in supply chain resilience for emerging markets' automotive sector. *Supply Chain Management: An International Journal, 26*(6), 654–671.

Banham, R. (2014). Political risk and the supply chain. *Risk Management, 61*(5), 22–27.

Bankier.pl. (2023). Notowania surowców, https://www.bankier.pl/surowce/notowania. Accessed 17 Apr 2023.

Bastas, A., & Garza-Reyes, J. A. (2022). Impact of the COVID-19 pandemic on manufacturing operations and supply chain resilience: Effects and response strategies. *Journal of Manufacturing Technology Management, 33*(5), 962–985.

Begum, H., Abbas, K., Alam, A. F., Song, H., Chowdhury, M. T., & Abdul Ghani, A. B. (2022). Impact of the COVID-19 pandemic on the environment and socioeconomic viability: A sustainable production chain alternative. *Foresight, 24*(3/4), 456–475.

Ben Hassen, T., & El Bilali, H. (2022). Impacts of the Russia-Ukraine war on global food security: Towards more sustainable and resilient food systems? *Foods, 11*(15), 2301.

Bennett, N., & Lemoine, J. (2014). What VUCA really means for you. *Harvard Business Review, 92*(1/2), 27–27.

Bin-Nashwan, S. A., Hassan, M. K., & Muneeza, A. (2022). Russia–Ukraine conflict: 2030 agenda for SDGs hangs in the balance. *International Journal of Ethics and Systems*. (ahead-of-print).

Bochtis, D., Benos, L., Lampridi, M., Marinoudi, V., Pearson, S., & Sørensen, C. G. (2020). Agricultural workforce crisis in light of the COVID-19 pandemic. *Sustainability, 12*(19), 8212.

Boubaker, S., Nguyen, N., Trinh, V. Q., & Vu, T. (2023). Market reaction to the Russian Ukrainian war: A global analysis of the banking industry. *Review of Accounting and Finance, 22*(1), 123–153.

Browning, T. R., & Ramasesh, R. V. (2015). Reducing unwelcome surprises in project management. *MIT Sloan Management Review, 56*(3), 53–62.

Buera, F. J., Fattal-Jaef, R. N., Hopenhayn, H., Neumeyer, P. A., & Shin, Y. (2021). *The economic ripple effects of COVID-19 (No. w28704)*. National Bureau of Economic Research.

Business Continuity Institute. (2007). Business continuity management good practice guidelines, part I.

Chenarides, L., Manfredo, M., & Richards, T. J. (2021). COVID-19 and food supply chains. *Applied Economic Perspectives and Policy, 43*(1), 270–279.

Chowdhury, P., Paul, S. K., Kaisar, S., & Moktadir, M. A. (2021). COVID-19 pandemic related supply chain studies: A systematic review. *Transportation Research Part E: Logistics and Transportation Review, 148*, 102271.

Chowdhury, M. M. H., & Quaddus, M. A. (2015). A multiple objective optimization based QFD approach for efficient resilient strategies to mitigate supply chain vulnerabilities: The case of garment industry of Bangladesh. *Omega, 57*, 5–21.

Chowdhury, M. M. H., & Quaddus, M. (2016). Supply chain readiness, response and recovery for resilience. *Supply Chain Management: An International Journal, 21*(6), 709–731.

Chowdhury, M. M. H., & Quaddus, M. A. (2021). Supply chain sustainability practices and governance for mitigating sustainability risk and improving market performance: A dynamic capability perspective. *Journal of Cleaner Production, 278*, 123521.

Christopher, M., & Gaudenzi, B. (2015). Managing risks in sustainable supply chains. *Sinergie Italian Journal of Management, 33*(Jan-Apr), 57–74.

Christopher, M., & Peck, H. (2004). Building the resilient supply chain. *International Journal of Logistics Management, 15*(2), 1–14.

Chu, P.-Y., Chang, K.-H., & Huang, H.-F. (2012). How to increase supplier flexibility through social mechanisms and influence strategies? *Journal of Business & Industrial Marketing, 27*(2), 115–131.

Colicchia, C., Dallari, F., & Melacini, M. (2010). Increasing supply chain resilience in a global sourcing context. *Production Planning & Control, 21*(7), 680–694.

COSO. (2004). Enterprise risk management framework.

Cui, L., Yue, S., Nghiem, X. H., & Duan, M. (2023). Exploring the risk and economic vulnerability of global energy supply chain interruption in the context of Russo-Ukrainian war. *Resources Policy, 81*, 103373.

Datta, P. (2017). Supply network resilience: A systematic literature review and future research. *The International Journal of Logistics Management, 28*(4), 1387–1424.

de Lima, F. R. P., Da Silva, A. L., Godinho Filho, M., & Dias, E. M. (2018). Systematic review: Resilience enablers to combat counterfeit medicines. *Supply Chain Management: An International Journal, 12*(3), 117–135.

de Sousa Jabbour, A. B. L., Jabbour, C. J. C., Hingley, M., Vilalta-Perdomo, E. L., Ramsden, G., & Twigg, D. (2020). Sustainability of supply chains in the wake of the coronavirus (COVID-19/SARS-CoV-2) pandemic: Lessons and trends. *Modern Supply Chain Research and Applications, 2*(3), 117–122.

Dobrin, G. I. (2021). Analysis of risks and opportunities in the BMW group. *Journal of Public Administration, Finance and Law, 10*(22), 164–168.

Dolgui, A., & Ivanov, D. (2021). Ripple effect and supply chain disruption management: New trends and research directions. *International Journal of Production Research, 59*(1), 102–109.

Dubey, P., Singh, G., Nagaraju, G., Gharat, K., Bharambe, S. D., & Vajarekar, A. (2020). Reduction of workforce due to impact of covid-19 and occupational health and safety management at workplace. *International Journal of Occupational Safety and Health, 10*(2), 92–99.

Duclos, L. K., Vokurka, R. J., & Lummus, R. R. (2003). A conceptual model of supply chain flexibility. *Industrial Management & Data Systems, 103*(6), 446–456.

Dyson, E., Helbig, R., Avermaete, T., Halliwell, K., Calder, P. C., Brown, L. R., Ingram, J., Popping, B., Verhagen, H., Bobies, A. R., Guelinckx, I., Dye, L., & Boyle, N. (2023). Impacts of the Ukraine–Russia conflict on the global food supply chain and building future resilience. *EuroChoices, 22*(1), 14–19.

Elahi, E. (2013). Risk management: The next source of competitive advantage. *Foresight, 15*(2), 117–131.

Elmsalmi, M., Hachicha, W., & Aljuaid, A. M. (2021). Prioritization of the best sustainable supply chain risk management practices using a structural analysis based-approach. *Sustainability, 13*(9), 4608.

European Commission. (2022). REPowerEU: Joint European action for more affordable, secure and sustainable energy, https://ec.europa.eu/commission/presscorner/detail/en/ip_22_1511. Accessed 17 Apr 2023.

European Council. (2023). EU sanctions against Russia explained. https://www.consilium.europa.eu/en/policies/sanctions/restrictive-measures-against-russia-over-ukraine/sanctions-against-russia-explained/#sanctions. Accessed 24 Apr 2023.

Eurostat. (2023). EU Imports of energy products - recent developments. https://ec.europa.eu/eurostat/statistics-explained/index.php?title=EU_imports_of_energy_products_-_recent_developments&oldid=558719#Overview. Accessed 17 Apr 2023.

Faisal, M. N. (2010). Sustainable supply chains: A study of interaction among the enablers. *Business Process Management Journal, 16*(3), 508–529.

Fan, Y., & Stevenson, M. (2018). A review of supply chain risk management: Definition, theory, and research agenda. *International Journal of Physical Distribution & Logistics Management, 48*(3), 205–230.

Fantazy K. A., Kumar V., & Kumar U. (2009). An empirical study of the relationships among strategy, flexibility, and performance in the supply chain context. *Supply Chain Management: An International Journal, 14*(3), 177–188.

Fayezi, S., Zutshi, A., & O'Loughlin, A. (2014). Developing an analytical framework to assess the uncertainty and flexibility mismatches across the supply chain. *Business Process Management Journal, 20*(3), 362–391.

Feduzi, A., Faulkner, P., Runde, J., Cabantous, L., & Loch, C. H. (2022). Heuristic methods for updating small world representations in strategic situations of Knightian uncertainty. *Academy of Management Review, 47*(3), 402–424.

FERMA. (2003). AIRMIC/ALARM/IRM:2002.

Ferriani, F., & Gazzani, A. G. (2023). The impact of the war in Ukraine on energy prices: Consequences for firms' financial performance. *SUERF Policy Brief, 554*, 1–6. https://www.suerf.org/docx/f_0846e37d7c994c87aa8b4cfcf327c3b8_64153_suerf.pdf. Accessed 17 Apr 2023

Fiksel, J. (2006). Sustainability and resilience: Toward a systems approach. *Sustainability: Science, Practice and Policy, 2*(2), 14–21.

Flynn, B. B., Koufteros, X., & Lu, G. (2016). On theory in supply chain uncertainty and its implications for supply chain integration. *Journal of Supply Chain Management, 52*(3), 3–27.

Fonseca, L. M., & Azevedo, A. L. (2020). COVID-19: Outcomes for global supply chains. *Management & Marketing. Challenges for the Knowledge Society, 15*(s1), 424–438.

Frederico, G. F., Kumar, V., & Garza-Reyes, J. A. (2021). Impact of the strategic sourcing process on the supply chain response to the COVID-19 effects. *Business Process Management Journal, 27*(6), 1775–1803.

Frederico, G. F., Kumar, V., Garza-Reyes, J. A., Kumar, A., & Agrawal, R. (2021). Impact of I4. 0 technologies and their interoperability on performance: Future pathways for supply chain resilience post-COVID-19. *The International Journal of Logistics Management, 34*(4), 1020–1049.

Friday, D., Savage, D. A., Melnyk, S. A., Harrison, N., Ryan, S., & Wechtler, H. (2021). A collaborative approach to maintaining optimal inventory and mitigating stockout risks during a pandemic: Capabilities for enabling health-care supply chain resilience. *Journal of Humanitarian Logistics and Supply Chain Management, 11*(2), 248–271.

Friedlmaier, M., Tumasjan, A., & Welpe, I. M. (2018, January). Disrupting industries with blockchain: The industry, venture capital funding, and regional distribution of blockchain ventures. In *Venture capital funding, and regional distribution of blockchain ventures (September 22, 2017). Proceedings of the 51st annual Hawaii international conference on system sciences (HICSS).*

Gao, Y., Feng, Z., & Zhang, S. (2021). Managing supply chain resilience in the era of VUCA. *Frontiers of Engineering Management, 8*(3), 465.

Ghadge, A., Dani, S., & Kalawsky, R. (2012). Supply chain risk management: Present and future scope. *The International Journal of Logistics Management, 23*(3), 313–339.

Giannakis, M., & Papadopoulos, T. (2016). Supply chain sustainability: A risk management approach. *International Journal of Production Economics, 171*, 455–470.

Gil, Z. (2001). *Zarządzanie ryzykiem i antyryzykiem w działalności gospodarczej i społecznej*. AGH University of Science and Technology in Kraków, Uczelniane Wydawnictwo Naukowo-Dydaktyczne.

Goel, R. K., Saunoris, J. W., & Goel, S. S. (2021). Supply chain performance and economic growth: The impact of COVID-19 disruptions. *Journal of Policy Modeling, 43*(2), 298–316.

Gunessee, S., & Subramanian, N. (2020). Ambiguity and its coping mechanisms in supply chains lessons from the Covid-19 pandemic and natural disasters. *International Journal of Operations & Production Management, 40*(7/8), 1201–1223.

Gupta, V., Ivanov, D., & Choi, T. M. (2021). Competitive pricing of substitute products under supply disruption. *Omega, 101*, 102279.

Hadiguna, R. A. (2012). Decision support framework for risk assessment of sustainable supply chain. *International Journal of Logistics Economics and Globalisation, 4*(1–2), 35–54.

Handfield, R. B., Graham, G., & Burns, L. (2020). Corona virus, tariffs, trade wars and supply chain evolutionary design. *International Journal of Operations & Production Management, 40*(10), 1649–1660.

Haraguchi, M., & Lall, U. (2015). Flood risks and impacts: A case study of Thailand's floods in 2011 and research questions for supply chain decision making. *International Journal of Disaster Risk Reduction, 14*, 256–272.

Haraguchi, M., Neise, T., She, W., & Taniguchi, M. (2023). Conversion strategy builds supply chain resilience during the covid-19 pandemic: A typology and research directions. *Progress in Disaster Science, 100276*, 1–7.

Hirata, E., & Matsuda, T. (2022). Uncovering the impact of COVID-19 on shipping and logistics. *Maritime Business Review, 7*(4), 305–317.

Hobbs, J. E. (2020). Food supply chains during the COVID-19 pandemic. *Canadian Journal of Agricultural Economics/Revue canadienne d'agroeconomie, 68*(2), 171–176.

Hofmann, H., Busse, C., Bode, C., & Henke, M. (2014). Sustainability-related supply chain risks: Conceptualization and management. *Business Strategy and the Environment, 23*(3), 160–172.

Hohenstein, N. O., Feisel, E., Hartmann, E., & Giunipero, L. (2015). Research on the phenomenon of supply chain resilience: A systematic review and paths for further investigation. *International Journal of Physical Distribution & Logistics Management, 45*(1/2), 90–117.

Ikotun, O., Akhigbe, A., & Okunade, S. (2021). Sustainability of borders in a post-COVID-19 world. *Politikon, 48*(2), 297–311.

International Monetary Fund. (2022). Inflation and uncertainty, https://www.imf.org/en/Publications/WEO/Issues/2022/10/11/world-economic-outlook-october-2022. Accessed 17 Apr 2023.
ISO 31000:2018. (2018). Risk management – Principles and guidelines. International Organization for Standardization.
ISO 9001:2005. (2005). Quality management systems – Requirements.
ISO/IEC Guide 73:2002. (2002). Risk management – Vocabulary.
Jagtap, S., Trollman, H., Trollman, F., Garcia-Garcia, G., Parra-López, C., Duong, L., Martindale, W., Munekata, P. E. S., Lorenzo, J. M., Hdaifeh, A., Hassoun, A., Salonitis, K., & Afy-Shararah, M. (2022). The Russia-Ukraine conflict: Its implications for the global food supply chains. *Food, 11*(14), 2098.
Johnson, M. E. (2001). Learning from toys: Lessons in managing supply chain risk from toy industry. *California Management Review, 43*(3), 106–124.
Jüttner, U., & Maklan, S. (2011). Supply chain resilience in the global financial crisis: An empirical study. *Supply Chain Management: An International Journal, 16*(4), 246–259.
Jüttner, U., Peck, H., & Christopher, M. (2003). Supply chain risk management: Outlining an agenda for future research. *International Journal of Logistics: Research and Applications, 6*(4), 197–210.
Kamalahmadi, M., & Parast, M. M. (2016). A review of the literature on the principles of enterprise and supply chain resilience: Major findings and directions for future research. *International Journal of Production Economics, 171*, 116–133.
Kazancoglu, Y., Ozkan-Ozen, Y. D., Sagnak, M., Kazancoglu, I., & Dora, M. (2021). *Framework for a sustainable supply chain to overcome risks in transition to a circular economy through industry 4.0* (Vol. 34, pp. 1–16). Production Planning & Control.
Kędzia, G. (2023). The ambiguous impact of supplier involvement in product development on supplier relationship resilience and company performance. *Central European Management Journal.* (in press).
Kochan, C. G., & Nowicki, D. R. (2018). Supply chain resilience: A systematic literature review and typological framework. *International Journal of Physical Distribution & Logistics Management, 48*(8), 842–865.
Krykavskyy, Y., Chornopyska, N., Dovhun, O., Hayvanovych, N., & Leonova, S. (2023). Defining supply chain resilience during wartime. *Eastern-European Journal of Enterprise Technologies, 1*(13), 121.
Kumar, P., & Kumar Singh, R. (2022). Strategic framework for developing resilience in Agri-Food Supply Chains during COVID 19 pandemic. *International Journal of Logistics Research and Applications, 25*(11), 1401–1424.

Kumar, V., Yetkin Ekren, B., Wang, J., Shah, B., & Frederico, G. F. (2022). Investigating the impact of COVID-19 on sustainable food supply chains. *Journal of Modelling in Management, 18*(4), 1250–1273.

Kwak, D. W., Seo, Y. J., & Mason, R. (2018). Investigating the relationship between supply chain innovation, risk management capabilities and competitive advantage in global supply chains. *International Journal of Operations & Production Management, 38*(1), 2–21.

Lau, Y. Y., Ranjith, P. V., Hin, C. E. M., Kanrak, M., & Varma, A. J. (2022). A new shape of the supply chain during the COVID-19 pandemic. *Foresight*. (ahead-of-print).

Lee, H. L. (2004). The triple-A supply chain. *Harvard Business Review, 82*(10), 102–113.

Lozano-Diez, J. A., Marmolejo-Saucedo, J. A., & Rodriguez-Aguilar, R. (2020). Designing a resilient supply chain: An approach to reduce drug shortages in epidemic outbreaks. *EAI Endorsed Transactions on Pervasive Health and Technology, 6*, 1–12.

Lu, M., & Shen, Z. J. M. (2020). A review of robust operations management under model uncertainty. *Production and Operations Management, 30*, 1927–1943.

Lummas, R. R., Vokurka, R. J., & Duclos, K. L. (2005). Delphi study on supply chain flexibility. *International Journal of Production Research, 43*(13), 2687–2708.

Lyu, H. M., Sun, W. J., Shen, S. L., & Zhou, A. N. (2020). Risk assessment using a new consulting process in fuzzy AHP. *Journal of Construction Engineering and Management, 146*(3), 04019112.

Mackay, J., Munoz, A., & Pepper, M. (2020). Conceptualising redundancy and flexibility towards supply chain robustness and resilience. *Journal of Risk Research, 23*(12), 1541–1561.

Mangla, S. K., Kumar, P., & Barua, M. K. (2015). Risk analysis in green supply chain using fuzzy AHP approach: A case study. *Resources, Conservation and Recycling, 104*, 375–390.

Manuj, I., & Mentzer, J. T. (2008). Global supply chain risk management strategies. *International Journal of Physical Distribution & Logistics Management, 38*(3), 192–223.

Marcos, J. T., Scheller, C., Godina, R., Spengler, T. S., & Carvalho, H. (2021). Sources of uncertainty in the closed-loop supply chain of lithium-ion batteries for electric vehicles. *Cleaner Logistics and Supply Chain, 1*, 100006.

Matuszak, S. (2022). *Produkcja i eksport żywności z Ukrainy w warunkach wojny z Rosją*. OSW. https://www.osw.waw.pl/pl/publikacje/komentarze-

osw/2022-05-06/produkcja-i-eksport-zywnosci-z-ukrainy-w-warunkach-wojny-z. Accessed 21 Apr 2023
Maurya, P. K., Bansal, R., & Mishra, A. K. (2023). Russia–Ukraine conflict and its impact on global inflation: An event study-based approach. *Journal of Economic Studies.* (ahead-of-print).
Modgil, S., Singh, R. K., & Hannibal, C. (2022). Artificial intelligence for supply chain resilience: Learning from Covid-19. *The International Journal of Logistics Management, 33*(4), 1246–1268.
Moktadir, M. A., Dwivedi, A., Khan, N. S., Paul, S. K., Khan, S. A., Ahmed, S., & Sultana, R. (2021). Analysis of risk factors in sustainable supply chain management in an emerging economy of leather industry. *Journal of Cleaner Production, 283*, 124641.
Mollenkopf, D. A., Ozanne, L. K., & Stolze, H. J. (2021). A transformative supply chain response to COVID-19. *Journal of Service Management, 32*(2), 190–202.
Muazu, R. I., Rothman, R., & Maltby, L. (2021). Integrating life cycle assessment and environmental risk assessment: A critical review. *Journal of Cleaner Production, 293*, 126120.
Najaf, K., Joshipura, M., & Alshater, M. M. (2023). War build-up and stock returns: Evidence from Russian and Ukrainian stock markets. *Journal of Risk Finance, 24*(3), 354–370. https://doi.org/10.1108/JRF-05-2022-0107
Ngoc, N. M., Viet, D. T., Tien, N. H., Hiep, P. M., Anh, N. T., Anh, L. D. H., & Dung, V. T. P. (2022). Russia-Ukraine war and risks to global supply chains. *International Journal of Mechanical Engineering, 7*(6), 633–640.
Nikolopoulos, K., Punia, S., Schäfers, A., Tsinopoulos, C., & Vasilakis, C. (2021). Forecasting and planning during a pandemic: COVID-19 growth rates, supply chain disruptions, and governmental decisions. *European Journal of Operational Research, 290*(1), 99–115.
Norrman, A., & Jansson, U. (2004). Ericsson's proactive supply chain risk management approach after a serious sub-supplier accident. *International Journal of Physical Distribution & Logistics Management, 34*(5), 434–456.
Ozdemir, D., Sharma, M., Dhir, A., & Daim, T. (2022). Supply chain resilience during the COVID-19 pandemic. *Technology in Society, 68*, 101847.
Paché, G. (2022). The invasion of Ukraine by Russian troops: A violent shock for supply chains. *Strategic Management Quarterly, 10*(1), 1–8.
Paltrinieri, N., Comfort, L., & Reniers, G. (2019). Learning about risk: Machine learning for risk assessment. *Safety Science, 118*, 475–486.
Paltrinierin, N., Dechy, N., Salzano, E., Wardman, M., & Cozzani, V. (2012). Lessons learned from Toulouse and Buncefield Disasters: From risk analysis

failures to the identification of atypical scenarios through a better knowledge management. *Risk Analysis, 32*(8), 1404–1419.

Paul, S. K., & Chowdhury, P. (2021). A production recovery plan in manufacturing supply chains for a high-demand item during COVID-19. *International Journal of Physical Distribution & Logistics Management, 51*(2), 104–125.

Pereira, P., Bašić, F., Bogunovic, I., & Barcelo, D. (2022). Russian-Ukrainian war impacts the total environment. *Science of the Total Environment, 837*, 155865.

Pettit, T. J., Fiksel, J., & Croxton, K. L. (2010). Ensuring supply chain resilience: Development of a conceptual framework. *Journal of Business Logistics, 31*(1), 1–21.

Pettit T. J., Croxton K. L., & Fiksel J. (2013). Ensuring supply chain resilience: Development and implementation of an assessment tool. *Journal of Business Logistics, 34*(1) 46–76.

Pfohl, H. C., Gallus, P., & Thomas, D. (2011). Interpretive structural modelling of supply chain risks. *International Journal of Physical Distribution & Logistics Management, 41*(9), 839–859.

Ponomarov, S. Y., & Holcomb, M. C. (2009). Understanding the concept of supply chain resilience. *The International Journal of Logistics Management, 20*(1), 124–143.

Poudel, P. B., Poudel, M. R., Gautam, A., Phuyal, S., Tiwari, C. K., Bashyal, N., & Bashyal, S. (2020). COVID-19 and its global impact on food and agriculture. *Journal of Biology and Today's World, 9*(5), 221–225.

Pragholapati, A. (2020). Mental health in pandemic covid-19. Available at SSRN, 3596311.

Pujawan, I. N. (2004). Assessing supply chain flexibility: A conceptual framework and case study. *International Journal of Integrated Supply Management, 1*(1), 79–97.

Pujawan, I. N., & Bah, A. U. (2022, January). Supply chains under COVID-19 disruptions: Literature review and research agenda. In *Supply chain forum: An international journal* (Vol. 23(1), pp. 81–95). Taylor & Francis.

Ramani, K. S., & Okwudire, C. E. (2020, October). Two-stage robust tracking controller for linear systems with known uncertainty using filtered basis functions. In *Dynamic systems and control conference* (Vol. 84287, p. V002T35A001). American Society of Mechanical Engineers.

Ravi, P., Ismail, A., & Kumar, N. (2021). The pandemic shift to remote learning under resource constraints. *Proceedings of the ACM on Human-Computer Interaction, 5*(CSCW2), 1–28.

Rawtani, D., Gupta, G., Khatri, N., Rao, P. K., & Hussain, C. M. (2022). Environmental damages due to war in Ukraine: A perspective. *Science of the Total Environment, 850*, 157932.

Rebs, T., Brandenburg, M., Seuring, S., & Stohler, M. (2018). Stakeholder influences and risks in sustainable supply chain management: A comparison of qualitative and quantitative studies. *Business Research, 11*, 197–237. Research 2 (1), 50–70.

Reuters Events Supply Chains, & JLL. (2023). The state of European Supply Chains, report, 01.03.2023.

Rice, J. B., & Caniato, F. (2003a). Building a secure and resilient supply network. *Supply Chain Management Review, 7*(5), 22–30.

Rice, J. B., & Caniato, F. (2003b). *Supply chain response to terrorism: Creating resilient and secure supply chains* (pp. 1–59). Report by MIT Center for Transportation and Logistics.

Rostamzadeh, R., Ghorabaee, M. K., Govindan, K., Esmaeili, A., & Nobar, H. B. K. (2018). Evaluation of sustainable supply chain risk management using an integrated fuzzy TOPSIS-CRITIC approach. *Journal of Cleaner Production, 175*, 651–669.

Rowan, N. J., & Laffey, J. G. (2020). Challenges and solutions for addressing critical shortage of supply chain for personal and protective equipment (PPE) arising from coronavirus disease (COVID19) pandemic – Case study from the Republic of Ireland. *Science of the Total Environment, 725*, 138532.

Russell, D. M., & Saldanha, J. P. (2003). Five tenets of security-aware logistics and supply chain operation. *Transportation Journal*, 44–54.

Saeidi, P., Saeidi, S. P., Sofian, S., Saeidi, S. P., Nilashi, M., & Mardani, A. (2019). The impact of enterprise risk management on competitive advantage by moderating role of information technology. *Computer Standards & Interfaces, 63*, 67–82.

Sajjad, A. (2021). The COVID-19 pandemic, social sustainability and global supply chain resilience: A review. *Corporate Governance: The International Journal of Business in Society, 21*(6), 1142–1154.

Saleheen, F., & Habib, M. M. (2023). Supply chain resilience during disruption: A study on supply chain performance measurement. *International Supply Chain Technology Journal, 9*(2), 1–14.

Sanchez, A., & Perez, M. (2005). Supply chain flexibility and firm performance: A conceptual model and empirical study in the automotive industry. *International Journal of Operations & Production Management, 25*(7), 681–700.

Sarkis, J. (2020). Supply chain sustainability: Learning from the COVID-19 pandemic. *International Journal of Operations & Production Management, 41*(1), 63–73.
Sawik, T. (2013). Selection of resilient supply portfolio under disruption risks. *Omega, 41*(2), 259–269.
Scala, B., & Lindsay, C. F. (2021). Supply chain resilience during pandemic disruption: Evidence from healthcare. *Supply Chain Management: An International Journal, 26*(6), 672–688.
Shams Esfandabadi, Z., Ranjbari, M., & Scagnelli, S. D. (2022). The imbalance of food and biofuel markets amid Ukraine-Russia crisis: A systems thinking perspective. *Biofuel Research Journal, 9*, 1640–1647.
Shareef, M. A., Dwivedi, Y. K., Kumar, V., Hughes, D. L., & Raman, R. (2020). Sustainable supply chain for disaster management: Structural dynamics and disruptive risks. *Annals of Operations Research*, 1–25.
Sharma, M., Luthra, S., Joshi, S., & Kumar, A. (2021). Accelerating retail supply chain performance against pandemic disruption: Adopting resilient strategies to mitigate the long-term effects. *Journal of Enterprise Information Management, 34*(6), 1844–1873.
Sharma, V., Singh, A., & Rai, S. S. (2022). Disruptions in sourcing and distribution practices of supply chains due to COVID-19 pandemic: A sustainability paradigm. *Journal of Global Operations and Strategic Sourcing, 15*(2), 235–261.
Sheffi, Y. (2001). Supply chain management under the threat of international terrorism. *International Journal of Logistics Management, 12*(2), 1–11.
Simangunsong, E., Hendry, L. C., & Stevenson, M. (2012). Supply-chain uncertainty: A review and theoretical foundation for future research. *International Journal of Production Research, 50*(16), 4493–4523.
Sinha, D., & Sinha, S. (2020). Managing in a VUCA world: Possibilities and pitfalls. *Journal of Technology Management for Growing Economies, 11*(1), 17–21.
Singh, S., Kumar, R., Panchal, R., & Tiwari, M. K. (2020). Impact of COVID-19 on logistics systems and disruptions in food supply chain. *International Journal of Production Research, 59*(7), 1993–2008.
Spieske, A., Gebhardt, M., Kopyto, M., Birkel, H., & Hartmann, E. (2022). How did supply chain networks handle the COVID-19 pandemic? Empirical evidence from an automotive case study. *International Journal of Physical Distribution & Logistics Management, 52*(7), 567–601.

Stecke, K. E., & Kumar, S. (2009). Sources of supply chain disruptions, factors that breed vulnerability, and mitigating strategies. *Journal of Marketing Channels, 16*(3), 193–226.
Świetlińska, M. (2022). Te firmy ukraińskie zostały zrównane z ziemią. Straty na 80 MLD dolarów. https://www.dziennikprawny.pl/pl/a/te-firmy-ukrainskie-zostaly-zrownane-z-ziemia-straty-na-80-mld-dolarow. Accessed 21 Apr 2023.
Szkwarek, W. (2023). Rok po wybuchu wojny. "Nowi-starzy" Ukraińcy na polskim rynku pracy. https://www.money.pl/gospodarka/rok-po-wybuchu-wojny-nowi-starzy-ukraincy-na-polskim-rynku-pracy-6866199745804928a.html. Accessed 21 Apr 2023.
Tang, C. S. (2006). Robust strategies for mitigating supply chain disruptions. *International Journal of Logistics: Research and Applications, 9*(1), 33–45.
Teuscher, P., Grüninger, B., & Ferdinand, N. (2006). Risk management in sustainable supply chain management (SSCM): Lessons learnt from the case of GMO-free soybeans. *Corporate Social Responsibility and Environmental Management, 13*(1), 1–10.
The International Organization for Migration. (2023). Key figures: Mobility within and from Ukraine, 2020–2023. https://www.migrationdataportal.org/sites/g/files/tmzbdl251/files/2023-02/ukraine-key-figures-2023.pdf. Accessed 24 Apr 2023.
The White House. (2022). FACT SHEET: United States Bans Imports of Russian Oil, Liquefied Natural Gas, and Coal. https://www.whitehouse.gov/briefing-room/statements-releases/2022/03/08/fact-sheet-united-states-bans-imports-of-russian-oil-liquefied-natural-gas-and-coal/. Accessed 15 Apr 2023.
Tukamuhabwa, B. R., Stevenson, M., Busby, J., & Zorzini, M. (2015). Supply chain resilience: Definition, review and theoretical foundations for further study. *International Journal of Production Research, 53*(18), 5592–5623.
Turaieva, I. (2023). Aktualna sytuacja granicy ukraińsko-polskiej, Ukrainian in Poland, 18.04.2023 https://www.ukrainianinpoland.pl/how-many-ukrainians-have-crossed-the-ukrainian-polish-border-since-the-beginning-of-the-war-current-data-pl/#:~:text=Wed%C5%82ug%20danych%20Stra%C5%BCy%20Granicznej%20od%2024%20lutego%202022,Ukrai%C5%84c%C3%B3w%2C%20kt%C3%B3rzy%20wyjechali%20do%20Polski%2C%20si%C4%99gn%C4%99%C5%82a%20751%20tysi%C4%99cy. Accessed 24 Apr 2023.
Urciuoli, L., Mohanty, S., Hintsa, J., & Gerine Boekesteijn, E. (2014). The resilience of energy supply chains: A multiple case study approach on oil and

gas supply chains to Europe. *Supply Chain Management: An International Journal, 19*(1), 46–63.
US Customs and Border Protection. (2006). *Supply chain security best practices catalog*. Customs-Trade Partnership against Terrorism (C-TPAT).
Van Der Vorst, J. G., & Beulens, A. J. (2002). Identifying sources of uncertainty to generate supply chain redesign strategies. *International Journal of Physical Distribution & Logistics Management, 32*(6), 409–430.
Verma, A. K., & Prakash, S. (2020). Impact of covid-19 on environment and society. *Journal of Global Biosciences, 9*(5), 7352–7363.
Vilko, J., Ritala, P., & Edelmann, J. (2014). On uncertainty in supply chain risk management. *The International Journal of Logistics Management, 25*(1), 3–19.
Wang, L., Cheng, Y., & Wang, Z. (2022). Risk management in sustainable supply chain: A knowledge map towards intellectual structure, logic diagram, and conceptual model. *Environmental Science and Pollution Research, 29*(44), 66041–66067.
Wang, L., & Rani, P. (2022). Sustainable supply chains under risk in the manufacturing firms: An extended double normalization-based multiple aggregation approach under an intuitionistic fuzzy environment. *Journal of Enterprise Information Management, 35*(4/5), 1067–1099.
Waters, D. (2007). *Supply chain risk management: Vulnerability and resilience in logistics*. Kogan Page Limited.
Wedawatta, G., & Ingirige, B. (2012). Resilience and adaptation of small and medium-sized enterprises to flood risk. *Disaster Prevention and Management: An International Journal, 21*(4), 474–488.
Wieteska, G. (2011). Security of supply networks. *Acta Universitatis Lodziensis, Folia Oeconomica, 258*, 149–162.
Wieteska, G. (2013). Supply chain risk management. In *Managing towards supply chain maturity: Business process outsourcing and offshoring* (pp. 133–159).
Wieteska, G. (2018). Business impact analysis of supply chain disruptions. In *8th international conference on management, economics and humanities, Barcelona, Spain* (pp. 110–119).
Wieteska, G. (2020). The impact of supplier involvement in product development on supply chain risks and supply chain resilience. *Operations and Supply Chain Management: An International Journal, 13*(4), 359–374.
Wieteska-Rosiak, B. (2017). Directions in climate change adaptation: Case of delta cities network. *Economics and Environment, 61*(2), 20–30.
World Economic Forum. (2013). Building resilience in supply chains. https://www.weforum.org/reports/building-resilience-supply-chains

Xiong, Y., Lam, H. K., Kumar, A., Ngai, E. W., Xiu, C., & Wang, X. (2021). The mitigating role of blockchain-enabled supply chains during the COVID-19 pandemic. *International Journal of Operations & Production Management, 41*(9), 1495–1521.

Xu, M., Cui, Y., Hu, M., Xu, X., Zhang, Z., Liang, S., & Qu, S. (2019). Supply chain sustainability risk and assessment. *Journal of Cleaner Production, 225*, 857–867.

Xu, Z., Elomri, A., Kerbache, L., & El Omri, A. (2020). Impacts of COVID-19 on global supply chains: Facts and perspectives. *IEEE Engineering Management Review, 48*(3), 153–166.

Zhang, X., Sun, B., Chen, X., Chu, X., & Yang, J. (2020). An approach to evaluating sustainable supply chain risk management based on BWM and linguistic value soft set theory. *Journal of Intelligent & Fuzzy Systems, 39*(3), 4369–4382.

Zhao, G., Liu, S., & Lopez, C. (2017). A literature review on risk sources and resilience factors in Agri-food supply chains. In *Collaboration in a data-rich world: 18th IFIP WG 5.5 working conference on virtual enterprises, PRO-VE 2017, Vicenza, Italy, September 18–20, 2017, proceedings 18* (pp. 739–752). Springer International Publishing.

Zimmermann, H. J. (2000). An application-oriented view of modelling uncertainty. *European Journal of Operational Research, 122*(2), 190–198.

Zsidisin, G. A., Melnyk, S. A., & Ragatz, G. L. (2005). An institutional theory perspective of business continuity planning for purchasing and supply management. *International Journal of Production Research, 43*(16), 3401–3420.

Zsidisin, G. A., Panelli, A., & Upton, R. (2000). Purchasing organization involvement in risk assessments, contingency plans, and risk management: An exploratory study. *Supply Chain Management: An International Journal, 5*(4), 187–198.

Zsidisin, G. A., & Wagner, S. M. (2010). Do perceptions become reality? The moderating role of supply chain resiliency on disruption occurrence. *Journal of Business Logistics, 31*(2), 1–20.

4

Modeling of Sustainable Supply Chain 2.0. (Framework)

4.1 Environmental, Social and Economic Resilience in Sustainable Supply Chain

Resilience is one of the most important issues in the modern economic world. Organizations and their supply chains that are resilient to unfavorable economic, environmental or negative social pressures may effectively protect themselves against uncertainty, risk, and loss of competitive position, with the implication that they may have to abandon business, while at the same time being flexible and adaptive to negative phenomena and threats arising from different directions and to different extents (Manurung et al., 2023). Recent events that have affected all global economies are contributing to a greater importance and attention to preparing supply chains to respond to sudden disruptions (Chowdhury, Sarkar, et al., 2020; Paul et al., 2021). They have different sources and nature (Fig. 3.1). They also bring companies problems with maintaining business continuity and all types of consequences (financial, environmental, social, reputational) at once, what needs proper resilient strategies and practices implementation (Wieteska, 2018a). This means there is need for changing the approach and remodeling, reconfiguring, and rethinking how the long-term goals of supply chains can be achieved both with resilience and sustainability in mind (Frederico, 2023).

B. Tundys et al., *Sustainable Supply Chains 2.0*,
https://doi.org/10.1007/978-3-031-50337-5_4

Resilience in terms of social, environmental, and economic dimensions can protect against new risk factors that have emerged in recent years, negative factors such as the ripple effect, which is becoming increasingly important in global governance and business, black swans or the effects of emerging armed conflicts, or the threat of changing settlements in financial markets and the development of financial markets toward demonetization (Dolgui & Ivanov, 2021; Jaggi et al., 2018; Manning et al., 2020; Vishwakarma et al., 2022). At the same time, both observation of global markets and business units and research indicate that the unusual, unforeseen events that have occurred in recent years and have definitely had a negative impact on supply chains have contributed to many difficulties in managing and dealing with them, not only in the phase of occurrence, but also with the consequences and uncertainty of further and actions. They can spread in unexpected ways, multidirectional, with different strengths and impacts and consequently disrupt supply chain processes with different degrees and an interference phenomenon, and according to past research—production process, the most seriously (Wieteska, 2018b). The reason for this may be the increasingly globalized and dynamic environment, as a disruption or breakdown in the execution of processes, even in the remotest corners of the world, may affect customers, producers and all subsequent processes in a completely different part of the globe (Chowdhury et al., 2020).

In the context of a sustainable supply chain, it is important to recognize uncertainty sources and dimensions but also resilience factors that allow organizations and their chains to connect, understand, and become resilient, and to use the weaknesses and identified risk factors as an element to support competitiveness and highlight the positive elements of the concept indicated.

Figure 4.1 presents the theoretical framework of a new sustainable supply chain concept—namely sustainable supply chain 2.0, which incorporates risk and resilience factors in its structure, activities, elements, and processes, as a basis for an innovative concept. This concept can be considered in the context of the traditional view of a sustainable supply chain and risk factors that are present and determining the functioning of a

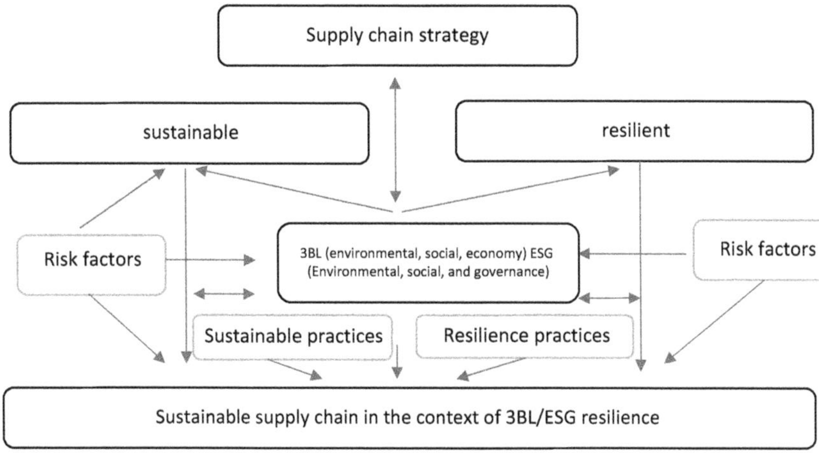

Fig. 4.1 Sustainable supply chain in the context of 3BL/ESG resilience. Source: own elaborations

given strategy. By adding the criteria of resilience, variously understood, one can expand sustainable supply chain strategies and try to create an even more innovative competitive strategy.

Environmental, social, and economic resilience in sustainable supply chain should be considered in this context. TBL issues can become a criterion I component of sustainable supply chain resilience.

Each element can be considered separately, but also as a component of the TBL concept (holistic view). It seems reasonable to identify the interrelationships and relationships between sustainability and resilience in the supply chain and then to consider the individual elements as drivers of the whole and as a strategic element of the new concept of supply chain management. Supply chains can thus enhance their resilience by using their abilities to 'anticipate', 'adapt' and 'respond' to external disruptions in order to cope with disruptions, ultimately moving to state before the disruption or a better state (Ali et al., 2017; Carissimi et al., 2023; Munir et al., 2022; Ocicka et al., 2022; Singh et al., 2019). In addition to managing disruption through the use of resilient elements (especially flexibility redundancy), the stage of learning and improvement is important; that comes last and thus becomes an input to the risk and uncertainties anticipation for the pre-disruption phase (Wieteska, 2020).

Therefore, it can be said that by combining the issues of sustainability and resilience, a new paradigm is emerging that can be described as SSC2.0—incorporating both the principles of sustainability as the basis for building a sustainable supply chain and resilience and the ability to respond to unexpected crisis, as well as identified and unidentified or underestimated (low probability-high impact) adverse events. (Fahimnia et al., 2019; Perera et al., 2019). There is no consensus or strongly supported basis in literature indicating a convergence and specific elements, actions or conceptual scope between sustainability, especially in the context of TBL, and resilience and combining these elements into a single whole. The need to skillfully link and combine these elements, can positively influence the effectiveness of managerial decision-making and the ways in which they are interpreted, and communicated to external and internal stakeholders (Marchese et al., 2018; Negri et al., 2021).

To date, however, the paradigms indicated are most often referred to as independent concepts (Dolgui et al., 2018; Jabbarzadeh et al., 2018). There is a rich literature and research in this area. There is a growing body of research in the context of a resilient sustainable supply chain, but it does not attempt to link the concept in such a way that resilience can be understood as one element of a sustainable (Daryanian et al., 2023; Foroozesh et al., 2023; Izadikhah et al., 2021; Mohammed et al., 2023; Sazvar et al., 2021; Vergara et al., 2023). The range of studies indicated is predominantly quantitative and mathematical-statistical in nature, not providing simple and concrete answers and operational solutions for managers. The literature review indicates that resilience is often added to aspects of sustainability, but there is no clear definition, understanding, and presentation of a theoretical framework as to whether sustainability includes attributes of resilience and vice versa (Carissimi et al., 2023; Ivanov, 2022; Zhu & Krikke, 2020). Lack of guidance and clarity on what elements of TBL can create supply chain resilience (Tundys & Wiśniewski, 2023), and which may give rise to distortions and risks (Golan et al., 2020), often, a certain degree of over-interpretation can also contribute to potential problems in their implementation (Marchese et al., 2018). Resilience can be achieved through sustainable development and sustainability can also be determined by resilience. It seems unjustified to use both terms as synonyms. Mainly, sustainable development may strengthen organizations and supply chains in the context of achieving TBL goals, through efficient sustainable practices implementation as well as financial, environmental, and social risk management for endogenous and exogenous sources. Consequently, it shapes processes and resources toward robustness and resilience. On the other hand, the resilience of organizations and supply chains achieved in the context of three phases of disruption enables effective TBL risks management what may translate into sustainable development and the maintaining systemic homeostasis in the future.

There are many sources of literature, including systematic literature reviews (Xu et al., 2020) containing aspects of sustainability and resilience; however, these are usually based on bibliometric studies (Larrea-Gallegos et al., 2022; López-Castro & Solano-Charris, 2021; Negri et al., 2021; Tsai et al., 2021; Zavala-Alcívar et al., 2020a). They do not result in theoretical frameworks or management models that can be verified or reflected in business practice and focus on risk management rather than building a system whose resilience will be both integral to sustainability and such a supply chain strategy.

The result of the research undertaken in the literature is most often assumptions about how to interpret and study the phenomena indicated, without further exploration of their relationship on a more conceptual basis. In this view, an analysis of the literature linking resilience and sustainability in supply chain network design, with a breakdown and distinction between the characteristic aspects of sustainability and resilience, has been presented, for example, in the publications of López-Castro & Solano-Charris, 2021, Larrea-Gallegos et al., 2022, Holgado & Niess, 2023, Al-Humaiqani & Al-Ghamdi, 2023. In another context, existing knowledge is reviewed through four dimensions of analysis (Negri et al., 2021): concepts and theory building, implementation (practices, pressures or drivers, decision-making and barriers, performance and measurement, and barriers), outcomes and measurement, and the future research agenda. It is difficult to explicitly address both elements indicated and to develop one common definition and concept. The areas can be considered in different dimensions. From one perspective, it can be pointed out that resilience builds sustainability (Davidson et al., 2019; Roostaie et al., 2019). In support of this thesis, it can be said that organizations and supply chains, if they are resilient, are sustainable; if they are not sustainable, they lose resilience at the same time (Carissimi et al., 2023). Only sustainable systems can operate effectively and counter sudden, unforeseen emergencies. The application of TBL principles alone is not sufficient for systems to be resilient to various types of disruption. TBL needs to be integrated with other risk management functions (He et al., 2021; Wu et al., 2019). Therefore, when building sustainable and resilient supply chains, one should think about integrating these concepts by developing management of external and internal TBL risks and disruptions of a financial, environmental nature, in relation to the comprehensive understanding of SCRES framework (Fig. 3.7), that is, taking into account especially SCRES strategies, phases, abilities and elements.

The context of resilience and sustainability can be understood as achieving environmental, social, and economic objectives while being able to mitigate and adapt to a variety of (often simultaneous internal and external) risks and uncertainties, through the appropriate identification and application of resilience attributes (Settembre-Blundo et al., 2021). It is important to ensure the durability of the chain despite the many adverse conditions (Vroegindewey & Hodbod, 2018) Implementation of defense mechanisms contributes to balancing systems and entire supply chains (Zavala-Alcívar et al., 2020b). In such cases, a skillful risk management, collaborative, proactive approach is required, both to the sustainability aspect and to building a supply chain resilience system. A proactive approach will allow the creation of defenses and the skillful management of potential risks, not only operationally, but also in the long term. To effectively manage a sustainable supply chain, supply chain must be resilient at the same time. This is a prerequisite if TBL is to achieve its objectives (Yılmaz et al., 2021). LCA also helps to realize these goals. Life Cycle Assessment (LCA) is an effective tool, not only for assessing sustainability, but also for resilience (Berr et al., 2022). In this perspective, it is necessary to be able to assess, interpret, and critically analyze issues related to social, environmental and economic risks, but also geopolitical risks, including the management of natural resources (Cimprich et al., 2017; Elluru et al., 2019; Negri et al., 2021; Shashi et al., 2020; Sonnemann et al., 2015). Supplier involvement in product development, (understood as cooperation with a partner during designing product), processes, and supply chain, also impacts supply chain resilience positively, but under the condition of a mediating role of communication (Kędzia & Staniec, 2022). Another perspective suggests that sustainability builds resilience. Implementing sustainability leads to having a socially, economically, and environmentally coherent supply chain that meets common goals and is most likely to withstand damaging situations (Marchese et al., 2018). Being sustainable reduces risk while increasing the level of resilience (Khot & Thiagarajan, 2019), where resilience can be considered from two points of view: small scale (demand fluctuations, production risks, employee fluctuations) and large scale (natural disasters, climate change, political and financial crises) (Elluru et al., 2019; Kaur & Singh, 2019). The aim of the measures taken is to build a system that is resilient to competition and to gain a competitive advantage, to reduce environmental risks (lowering of emissions). Reducing risks and increasing resilience will contribute to a forward-looking view and perspective on the future and give a greater chance of survival. The limitations of the traditional approach focusing on the short term must be overcome and a broader framework and assumptions on resilience and sustainability adopted (Paul et al., 2023).

More resilient chains can be created through a sustainability approach in an adaptive long-term planning situation and taking this perspective (Ivanov et al., 2023; Ongkowijoyo & Christian, 2020; Queiroz et al., 2022); this means that supply chains need to be rethought and reconfigured, taking into account other management perspectives, and also other elements and practices that affect the achievement of long-term sustainability goals while building a resilient system that supports and promotes sustainable and resilient behavior, while dynamically adapting to an ever-changing economic environment, creating long-term social, environmental and economic value (Paul et al., 2023; Queiroz et al., 2022).

4.2 The Role of Financial, Social and Governance Aspects in Strengthening a Sustainable Resilient Supply Chain

Analyzing ESG or TBL issues, one can see that the purpose of the efforts made in their implementation is to improve the performance and assessment of supply chains, while at the same time improving the efficiency and degree of implementation of the indicated concepts. The Covid-19 pandemic as well as geopolitical crises and other global events have made it clear what vulnerabilities global supply chains have, what disruptions they lead to and how networked a world we live and function in. Disruptions in the remotest corners of the world, can affect entire economies, societies, but also the environment. The effects of disturbances often spread in an unpredictable and multidirectional way, both in a domino effect and especially in situations like a black swan—in the ripple effect driven by external uncertainty, which is very difficult to control and mitigate. The high awareness of the risks and their potential impact, resulting from the global experience of recent years, clearly indicates that there is a need to implement and operate in more sustainable yet resilient systems and supply chains that will contribute to good performance and increase ESG efficiency and scope.

Sustainability and resilience in supply chains also play a key role in environmental, social, and governance (ESG) performance, which is why global economies are putting in place various types of systems and requirements that allow for disclosure, transparency, and unambiguity in understanding assumptions, as well as indications of how to implement due diligence in supply chains in relation to ESG factors. Disclosure on the environment, human rights, protection of designated areas, fair and ethical practices toward its stakeholders and reinforcing their importance in doing business unequivocally contributes to supply chain resilience, sustainability, and improved ESG performance.

The supply chain context that reflects the ESG criteria relates to due diligence reflected, as an indicator of the social and governance aspects of ESG performance. Namely, it is, among other things, about carrying out supply chains' due diligence on human rights, including the prohibition of forced labor and slavery. This is reflected in the establishment of a risk management system for human rights, social and environmental issues. Such legal solutions (relevant laws) have been implemented, among others, in Germany, France, the Netherlands, and Japan, and are reflected in EU directives (EU Corporate Sustainability Due Diligence Directive, which came into force on June 1, 2023) (https://ec.europa.eu/commission/presscorner/detail/en/IP_22_1145, 39.06.2023). In 2022, a similar legislative solution was introduced in the US—the Uyghur Forced Labor Prevention Act (UFLPA). In this case, the application of the requirements relates to the protection of a designated national minority, but also applies generally. Similar solutions taking into account the protection and enforcement of human and workers' rights are concluded in the framework of agreements (e.g., US-Mexico-Canada, as well as in the UK or Australia).

Actions to improve ESG performance (Mio et al., 2023) should include not only those initiatives that are enforced by legislation, but also bottom-up, widespread, and voluntary practices that revolve around actions that reduce negative environmental impacts, improve labor rights, and ensure fair business practices at every link and relating to every company operating in the supply chain. There are many examples and initiatives that can contribute to the implementation and improvement of ESG performance so as to support and build a sustainable yet resilient supply chain without unnecessary risk and uncertainty.

Effective SCRES building begins with the first stage, which means anticipation of threats, risks, disruptions and their potential development scenarios. In subsequent phases, the disruption response and recovery plans are launched. The first phase of SCRES is therefore largely about the preparation and thus the success of crisis management in the system. Enterprises and supply chains wanting to comprehensively strengthen their resilience should first assess and treat the risk from each quadrant of the matrix (Fig. 3.2.). This means at the same time the need to manage not only the traditional risk for the supply chain, but also the risk for sustainable development, including ESG criteria and risks associated with them. ESG reporting is closely related to risk management. For example, the suggested indicators include climate change risks and opportunities (indicator E-P3) (Krzysztofik et al., 2021, p. 27). A history shows, global disruptions may bring financial, environmental, and social effects at once (Fig. 3.5). In strengthening the resilience of the economy, the public sector is of key importance, for example by shaping the legal or infrastructural environment in an appropriate way in order to increase the degree of adaptation of cities to climate change (Wieteska-Rosiak, 2017). Another aspect critical for sustainable and resilient supply chains is also the need of cooperation with authorities (public-private partnership, PPP), especially when building response and recovery plans prepared for the situation of various threats to business continuity, for example, disaster management (The Business Continuity Institute, 2007, pp. 10, 14; Busch & Givens, 2013; Ma et al., 2022; Ampratwum et al., 2022).

Reducing the environmental impact of chains is key to achieving long-term sustainability. In this regard, organizations and their supply chains need to adopt various strategies to minimize ESG risks. The measures taken to minimize ESG risks can therefore include resource efficiency, the use of sustainable materials, renewable energy, or life cycle assessment in the scope of operations. An important aspect of the environmental component will be the construction and implementation of environmental management systems, with activities supported by appropriate certification, which provides a structured approach to managing environmental performance, including the reduction of emissions throughout the supply chain. The social context and risks associated with these activities relate primarily to the introduction of an effective system to ensure the full protection of workers' rights. Actions taken in this area can not only minimize the disruption caused by labor disputes, but also improve their reputation and meet the expectations of ethical consumers and investors. Risk minimization in this area includes the creation of conditionalities in the form of a code of ethical conduct and good practice (e.g., in the cooperation undertaken with suppliers), as well as the creation of a system of audits and monitoring. In the area indicated, it is also possible to speak of building a system of training and development programs to implement best practices and to assess risks in an appropriate manner, with the implementation of a due diligence system, by setting priorities and strategies for an effective mechanism to address the risks of the environmental and social elements indicated. Such activities contribute to the visibility and transparency not only of processes but also of business practices in terms of the overall strategy. An important element will be the use of technology and its support systems to manage environmental and social issues, including to improve communication. There is another important issue to be implemented that relates to the implementation of fair business practices, both in terms of procurement and customer service processes.

4.3 Analysis of the Research Data

Management in the twenty-first century should increasingly be based on predicting the future on the basis of a well-diagnosed past and present. Theories developing in the management sciences require empirical confirmation. For this purpose, elements of statistics are most often used. Since the 1990s, there has been a shift in the way statistics is used in the management sciences, moving away from simple description and statistical exploration (Staniec, 2018), and moving toward causal explanation and modeling that allows for causal inference. This approach stimulates the use of structural equation models (SEM) to test hypothesized cause-effect relationships between variables. The goal of SEM is to define a theoretical causal model consisting of a set of predicted covariances between variables, and then test whether it is reliable compared to observed data (Bielby & Hauser, 1977). Hence, in modern research methodology, the importance of structural models is so important. Path analysis models were first developed by Sewall Wright (1921), a biostatistician, in the early 1920s. Structural models as applied in the social sciences only began appearing in the 1970s (Bollen, 1989; Jöreskog, 1973) with their increasing application paralleling the availability of software (Bentler, 1995) all of which executed covariance-based SEM. The popularity of the method can be attributed to the sophistication of the underlying statistical theory, its potential to address important substantive issues, and the availability and simplicity of software dedicated to structural equation modeling (Kaplan, 2001). SEM is a collection of statistical techniques that allow the determination of relationships between one or more independent variables, continuous or discrete, and one or more dependent variables, continuous or discrete. Structural equation modeling is also referred to as causal modeling, causal analysis, simultaneous equation modeling, analysis of covariance structures, path analysis, or confirmatory factor analysis. The latter two are actually special types of SEM (Ullman & Bentler, 2012).

The complexity of the reality under study, including the difficulty of representing certain theoretical constructs (e.g., supply chain resilience) with a single endogenous variable, has prompted the increasing use of advanced statistical methods in management science. Structural equation models are fundamentally similar to multiple regression models, but are more flexible when describing interactions between variables, especially qualitative ones, for which classical regression assumptions are not met. In contrast to multiple regression models, where regression coefficients are obtained from minimizing the sum of squares of the differences between the observed and predicted dependent variables, SEM minimizes the difference between the observed covariance structure and that implied by a structural or path model. This is done by iteratively modifying the path coefficients and variances of the residuals until there is no further improvement in the fit. The identified best-fit path coefficient reflects the influence of one area (variable) on another area (variable). SEM can be put as a method that uses patterns of functional relationships (covariances) to derive information about effective relationships (path coefficients) (McIntosh & Misic, 2013).

SEM has the advantage of being able to identify the directionality of the effect of the activity of one area on the activity of another area. In addition, SEM allows the researcher to test the validity of the theoretical model regarding network interactions between areas. SEM methodology has been successfully used to show the impact of various aspects of the supply chain on its efficiency, for example, in Dey et al. (2021) or Zhang et al. (2022).

The fundamental tool used in structural modeling is the path diagram, which graphically depicts the causal relationships between variables. In the graphical presentation of the diagram, explicit variables are usually placed in boxes, latent variables in an ellipse/circle, and residual variables are not marked with any figure. Relationships between the variables included in the model are presented by arrows, the arrowhead of which indicates the effect variable. In the case of residual variables, the arrow points to the observable variable with an error (Fig. 4.2).

Table 4.1 shows the symbols used in structural equation modeling. In the measurement model of the latent exogenous variable, the explicit

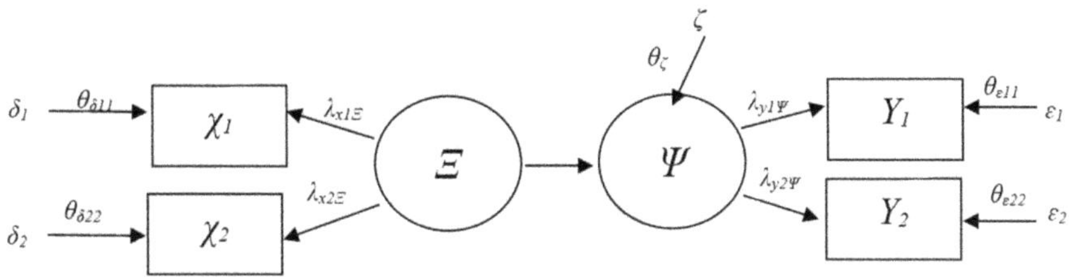

Fig. 4.2 Diagram of an example structural equation model

Table 4.1 Variables and parameters of the structural equation model

The symbol	Meaning
Model variables	
Ψ	Hidden endogenous variable
ζ	Residual (error) variables for latent endogenous variables
Y	Explicit endogenous variables, measurement variables for hidden endogenous variables
ε	Residual (error) variables for explicit endogenous variables
Ξ	Hidden exogenous variables
χ	Explicit exogenous variables, measurement variables for hidden exogenous variables
Model parameters	
γ	Coefficients representing the influence of latent exogenous variables on latent endogenous variables
λ	Factor loadings representing the strength of the relationship between latent and explicit variables
θ	Correlations/covariances between error variables and explicit or latent variables

Based on Sagan (2003a)

exogenous variables (χ_1, χ_2), which are observable representatives of the latent exogenous variable (Ξ), are treated as variables that provide information about them. For this reason, they have been assigned the title of indicator variables. The residual variables occurring in the model (δ_1, δ_2) for the explicit exogenous variables (χ_1, χ_2), represent the impact of measurement errors made, and other non-observable factors. The measurement model of the latent endogenous variable has an analogous design, where the variable (Ψ) is represented by explicit endogenous variables (*Y1, Y2*), which are its representatives. As in the previous measurement model, the residual variables (ε_1, ε_2) inform about measurement errors. Mapping the relationship between the exogenous (Ξ) and endogenous (Ψ) latent variables thus represented, which is an essential element of structural modeling, is done using a structural model (Korol, 2005). From the point of view of the purpose of modeling, the structural model provides the most important information.

In the process of analysis, explicit exogenous and endogenous variables are often subjected to a standardization procedure. For standardized values of indicator variables, the system of equations of the structural model presented in Fig. 4.1 takes the following form:

Structural model:

$$\Psi_k = \gamma_{\Psi\Xi}\, \xi_k + \theta_\zeta\, \zeta_k$$

Model of the latent exogenous variable:

$$u_{k\chi 1} = \lambda_{x1\Xi}\, \xi k + \theta_{\delta 11}\, \delta_{k1}$$

$$u_{k\chi 2} = \lambda_{x2\Xi}\, \xi k + \theta_{\delta 22}\, \delta_{k2}$$

Model of the latent endogenous variable.

$$u_{kY1} = \lambda_{y1\Psi}\, \Psi + \theta_{\varepsilon 11}\, \varepsilon_{k1}$$

$$u_{kY2} = \lambda_{y2\Psi}\, \Psi + \theta_{\varepsilon 22}\, \varepsilon_{k2}$$

The parameter *k* determines the number of observations, and latent variables are treated as variables that have a "hidden" feature value. The estimation of parameters determining the strengths and directions of individual relationships is carried out in the structural equation model on the basis of empirical information. Most often, this information is recorded in the form of a correlation matrix. The essence of parameter estimation is to find such parameter values for which the determined theoretical correlations take on the closest possible values of empirical correlations (Sroka, 2010). In practice, estimation is carried out by solving a system of equations with one of the iterative methods.

An integral step in the application of SEM methodic is its verification. Over the years, researchers have developed a number of indicators to answer the question of whether the model built has a good fit. The most common indicator of the fit of the model to the real data is the value of the chi-square statistic $\chi2$. This test applies to the null hypothesis, stating that the standardized residuals of the empirical and theoretical matrices are 0, i.e. that the constraints imposed by the researcher resulting from the adopted model are accurate (Sagan, 2003b). However, various scholars argue that this statistic is susceptible to numerous sampling fluctuations (e.g., sample size; model complexity, non-normality), leading to limited insights concerning the model's quality (e.g., Hu & Bentler, 1999). Hence, it is reasonable to evaluate the model fit by a number of alternative indices, which may be classified as (1) stand-alone or absolute, (2) comparative or incremental, and (3) parsimony-based fit indices (Weitzl et al., 2017). Hu and Bentler (1999) suggest reporting at least one fit index of each category:

- Stand-alone fit measures were obtained: the goodness-of-fit index (GFI) (Jöreskog & Sörbom, 1993) and the adjusted goodness-of-fit index (AGFI) (Jöreskog & Sörbom, 1993), which both can range from 0 to 1, whereas higher values suggest a better fit.
  In assessing the goodness of the model, the root-mean-square error-of-approximation RMSEA can also be used—values less than 0.05 indicate a good fit (Steiger & Lind, 1980). In contrast, values over 0.10 have been advocated to be indicative of a bad fit (Browne & Cudeck, 1993; Worthington & Whittaker, 2006).

- Most commonly used incremental fit indices, which compare the estimated model to a baseline or "null" (or independence) model, which assumes no relationships among the data and measures the improvement in a model's fit, are: the comparative fit index (CFI) proposed by Bentler (1990), for which a value of 0.90 or larger is regarded to indicate acceptable model fit (Hu & Bentler, 1999), and the normed fit index (NFI) (Bentler & Bonett, 1980).
- Parsimony-based indices typically adjust fit in order to compare models with differing numbers of estimated parameters (i.e., fit per coefficient) (Netemeyer et al., 2003). Degrees of freedom (df) are defined as the number of unique correlations or covariances in the data output matrix minus the number of estimated coefficients (Aaker & Bagozzi, 1979). Specifically, the normed chi-square (chi-square/degrees of freedom (df) ratio) for which acceptance levels range from less than 2 to less than 5 (Schumacker & Lomax, 2004; Ullman, 2001)

Other indicators of goodness of fit can be found in the literature; however, it is good practice to usually use one of each type.

4.3.1 Data Collection

The data collection process is one of the most important elements of the research methodology. The research area identified as a research gap was reflected in the conducted study. Its main research objective was to recognize the impact of sustainable concept and practices on building supply chain resilience (SCRES). A quantitative approach to data collection using deductive reasoning was adopted. In order to collect data from research respondents, a survey questionnaire was designed. The assumptions that the surveyed companies were expected to meet were:

- companies in the processing industry sector
- the company implements the concept of sustainable development
- the size of the company is medium and large (more than 50 employees)

The constructed questionnaire was divided into two main sections. The first section included general information about the companies—representatives of the companies, such as the size of the company, origin of the capital, possession of foreign branches. The survey sample included 550 companies operating in Poland. Those who were responsible for responding most often held managerial positions, such as production manager, manager or leader of the logistics department. A summary of company profiles is provided in Table 4.2. The survey was properly carried out using the CATI (Computer-Assisted Telephone Interviewing) method, between September 5, 2022 and September 16, 2022. They were preceded by a pilot study to ensure that all questions are understandable to the respondents.

The second section of the questionnaire survey included variables to form theoretical constructs in confirmatory factor analysis (CFA) and also for structural equation models—shown in Table 4.3. The constructs for sustainable supply chain was mainly develop on the past research presented by many authors. The most important primary sources of literature include Seuring & Müller (2008) and Silvestre (2016). Various aspects were taken into account when constructing the model: product development (Das & Posinasetti, 2015), reverse logistics (Haddadsisakht & Ryan, 2018; Sgarbossa & Russo, 2017), collaborative planning (Allaoui et al., 2019), sustainable supply chain practices (Paulraj et al., 2017),

Table 4.2 Company profiles

Number of people employed by the company	
51–250	62%
251–500	23%
Over 500	15%
Company with foreign branches	
No	68%
Yes	32%
Origin of the capital	
Domestic	69%
Domestic and foreign	21%
Foreign	10%

Table 4.3 The set of variables included in the study

Sustainable supply chain—a process view	(PV1)	The company implements the principles of sustainable development in the process: Supplier relationship management
	(PV2)	The company implements the principles of sustainable development in the process: Customer relationship management
	(PV3)	The company implements the principles of sustainable development in the process: Customer service management
	(PV4)	The company implements the principles of sustainable development in the process: Demand management
	(PV5)	The company implements the principles of sustainable development in the process: Order fulfillment
	(PV6)	The company implements the principles of sustainable development in the process: Production flow management
	(PV7)	The company implements the principles of sustainable development in the process: Returns management
Sustainable development practices—external	(SDE1)	The company selects and periodically evaluates suppliers for environmental and social responsibility
	(SDE2)	The company has supplier development programs (e.g., training, financial support) aimed at improving their sustainability performance
	(SDE3)	The company jointly implements projects (product development, process improvement) with suppliers aimed at achieving sustainability goals
	(SDE4)	The company has and monitors financial indicators dedicated to sustainable development
	(SDE5)	The company reports ESG indicators (regarding corporate, environmental and social governance)
	(SDE6)	The company reduces the negative impact of its value rendering processes on the environment (e.g., reducing the amount of raw materials and materials used, reducing energy consumption, reducing the amount of waste generated, reducing harmful emissions)
	(SDE7)	The company takes care to reduce the impact of its activities on the local community (responsible behavior)
	(SDE8)	The company improves its social image by introducing CSR practices
	(SDE9)	The company meets the expectations and needs of customers
	(SDE10)	The company responds quickly to changes in demand and supply through integrated information systems
	(SDE11)	The company selects and periodically evaluates suppliers for environmental and social responsibility

(*continued*)

Table 4.3 (continued)

Sustainable development practices—internal	(SDI1)	The company introduces new products with reduced negative impact on the natural environment
	(SDI2)	The company designs products and processes taking into account the principles of a closed-loop economy
	(SDI3)	The company increases the use of eco-friendly packaging for its products
	(SDI4)	The company systematically monitors and implements environmental protection requirements and regulations
	(SDI5)	The company complies with the requirements of ISO 14001
	(SDI6)	The company monitors the state of technical infrastructure to reduce environmental risks
	(SDI7)	The company's management is committed to implementing environmental protection activities
	(SDI8)	The company cares about human rights
	(SDI9)	The company systematically increases the level of occupational health and safety
	(SDI10)	The company supports building career paths and development of its employees
	(SDI11)	The company implements CSR (corporate social responsibility) activities
	(SDI12)	The company takes the greatest care in launching products that are safe for the health and life of users
	(SDI13)	The company cares about the safety of processes carried out in the supply chain
The ability of the company's supply chain to anticipate risks	(AR1)	The company is aware of the types and locations of risks in the supply chain and takes measures to mitigate those risks
	(AR2)	The company configures the supply chain (its structure—density, complexity and resources, including critical resources) to ensure that it is as capable as possible of sustaining operations during a disruption
	(AR3)	The company has the ability to track the flow of materials, components and products in the supply chain, through activities such as sharing information with partners, implementing IT solutions, monitoring KPIs
	(AR4)	The company ensures the security (protection) of information and product flow processes in cooperation with various stakeholders (e.g., suppliers, government)
	(AR5)	The company trains and educates employees on risk and business continuity management

(*continued*)

Table 4.3 (continued)

The ability of the company's supply chain to respond to disruptions	(RD1)	The company has flexibility in various supply chain processes, for example, procurement, production, transportation
	(RD2)	The company maintains various types of buffers in the supply chain, for example, safety stock, capacity reserves
	(RD3)	The company jointly implements planning and information sharing with supply chain partners
	(RD4)	The company shapes the agility of the supply chain ensuring its ability to respond quickly to changes in demand and supply
The ability of a company's supply chain to recover from a disruption	(RFD1)	The company has plans to restore operations and recover from the disruption
	(RFD2)	The company has the market position, market share and customer relationships that will increase the chance of maintaining financial stability after a disruption occurs
	(RFD3)	The company learns from its experience, managing knowledge and making appropriate changes in risk management and business continuity after a disruption occurs
	(RFD4)	The company has inter-organizational partnerships and extensive cooperation with stakeholders in for example, strategy implementation, product development.
The resilience of the company's supply chain to disruption	(RSCD1)	The company's supply chain is capable of responding to unexpected disruptions by quickly restoring the continuity of goods flow processes
	(RSCD2)	The company's supply chain can quickly return to its original state before the disruption
	(RSCD3)	The company's supply chain can transition to a new, more desirable state after a disruption
	(RSCD4)	The company's supply chain is well equipped to deal with the financial impact of disruption
	(RSCD5)	The company's supply chain has the ability to maintain the desired level of control over structure and functions during a disruption
	(RSCD6)	The company's supply chain has the ability to learn from the lessons and experience of disruption

supplier selection (Dai & Blackhurst, 2012), pro-environmental, social, and economics aspects (Hou et al., 2019; Taghipour & Beneteau-Piet, 2020), a combination of corporate social responsibility, environmental management and supply chain management (Hendiani et al., 2022; Saeed and Kersten, 2017; Tundys et al., 2019; Calzolari et al., 2022;

Tseng et al., 2022). The model was also based on the green supply chain management model: (Bag et al., 2017; de Oliveira et al., 2018; Petljak, 2019; Tundys, 2020). The constructs for SCRES abilities based on abilities presented by Ali et al. (2017), whereas the construct for the resilience of the company's supply chain to disruption were developed following mainly the work of Ponomarov (2012, p. 72).

4.3.2 Confirmatory Factor Analysis

The first step in SEM analysis is model specification; either exploratory or confirmatory factor analysis is used here. Both exploratory and confirmatory factor analysis aim to reproduce the observed relationships among a group of indicators using a smaller set of latent variables (constructs). If we assign specific measurable variables (e.g., survey questions) to specific constructs then, as in this paper, Confirmatory Factor Analysis (CFA) is used. CFA is a statistical strategy specifically designed to identify and test hypothesized constructs. The attractiveness of CFA compared to other approaches to testing hypothesized constructs lies in its ability to test detailed hypotheses in a deductive mode. CFA also enable to test for aspects of convergent validity, discriminant validity among the factors, as well as internal consistency of the preliminary form of the scale (Fornell & Larcker, 1981). In addition, CFA models can be incorporated directly into general structural equation modeling (SEM), which includes directional relationships between the constructs under study. A central issue of CFA is the modeling of factors, sometimes referred to as latent variables. Factors are influences that are not directly measured, but account for commonality among a set of measurements (Brown & Moore, 2012).

The research used a measurement model to identify the number of factors in the latent variables, as well as a structural model showing the effect–cause relationships between the variables. The existence of correlations between the theoretical exogenous constructs was also investigated. First, CFA was conducted, based upon which a set of variables (specific questions in the survey) was extracted that was most able to explain the latent variables. CFA was deemed a primary step toward the application of the SEM model, and it was used to decide how the proposed model fits the data (Jenatabadi & Ismail, 2014). The application of CFA and other procedures enabled the confirmation of the construct's order, dimensionality, and the measure's reliability. Additionally with CFA, any item that does not fit the measurement model due to low factor loading should be removed. CFA needs to be performed for every latent construct that is involved in a model.

Based on the literature analysis presented in earlier chapters and the authors' experience, it was assumed that a model would be investigated to include theoretical constructs that create latent variables relating to sustainable supply chain elements and also to supply chain resilience (Table 4.3). Variables were created from questions that respondents answered using a Likert scale from 1 to 5. The five-point Likert scale is a highly acceptable and reliable scale for questionnaire research (Dillman et al., 2014).

Table 4.4 presents the CFA of a measurement model with three latent constructs representing elements of a sustainability supply chain and four latent constructs representing the resilience of the supply chain. Model was conducted using Statistica Software (Statsoft v. 13).

The basis for factor inclusion was that the eigenvalue should be greater than one, the total variance explained should be greater than 50%, and that the factor loading of each item should be greater than 0.50. Of the list of 50 variables forming constructs (Table 4.3) after applying factor analysis 31 variables remained in the study. It can be seen that the largest number of variables were discarded from constructs related to sustainable supply chains (due to factor loadings of < 0.50), and most of the variables forming the constructs of supply chain resilience (only one variable was removed) were left for further analysis. In the analysis, the eigenvalue of each factor was above one, which accounted for 72.71% of the total variance. This analysis indicated that the model fit the data reasonably well. However, further testing of the model's reliability was conducted.

4.3.3 Reliability Analysis

The quality of a survey can be measured by inspecting its reliability (Paul & Maiti, 2008). The reliability of the data can be checked using

Table 4.4 Outer loadings with reliability indicators

Group	Latent Constructs	Indicators	Outer Loadings
Sustainability of supply chain	Sustainable supply chain—a process view	(PV1)	0.736
		(PV2)	0.770
		(PV3)	0.764
		(PV5)	0.780
		(PV7)	0.720
	Sustainable development practices—external	(SDE2)	0.809
		(SDE3)	0.753
		(SDE5)	0.653
		(SDE8)	0.704
	Sustainable development practices—internal	(SDI8)	0.845
		(SDI9)	0.845
		(SDI12)	0.721
		(SDI13)	0.727
Supply chain resilience	The ability of the company's supply chain to anticipate risks	(AR1)	0.741
		(AR2)	0.670
		(AR4)	0.715
		(AR5)	0.743
	The ability of the company's supply chain to respond to disruption	(RD1)	0.780
		(RD2)	0.749
		(RD3)	0.762
		(RD4)	0.800
	The ability of a company's supply chain to recover from a disruption	(RFD1)	0.812
		(RFD2)	0.792
		(RFD3)	0.837
		(RFD4)	0.795
	The resilience of the company's supply chain to disruption	(RSCD1)	0.823
		(RSCD2)	0.793
		(RSCD3)	0.712
		(RSCD4)	0.811
		(RSCD5)	0.827
		(RSCD6)	0.845

[a] Indicating significance at 1%

Cronbach's alpha. As a rule of thumb, if $\alpha \geq 0.7$, then the solutions are considered risk free, but 0.6 is considered to be acceptable in the case of an exploratory study (Nunnally, 1978; Thun, 2010). Most often, reliability is determined by analyzing the test's internal consistency using Cronbach's Alpha (α). Cronbach's alpha will be high if the variance of the entire scale is much greater than the sum of the variances of the individual items. A high variance of scale items is inadvisable, as it may indicate large measurement errors. The formula for Cronbach's alpha, a measure of reliability, of the test's internal consistency is of the form:

$$\alpha = \frac{k}{k-1} \cdot \left(1 - \frac{\sum_{i=1}^{k} s_i^2}{s_c^2}\right)$$

Where:

α—Cronbach's alpha
k—number of test items
s^2_c—total variance of the overall test results
s^2_i—variance of test items

In addition, in the study of assessing the reliability of the scale, the use of confirmatory factor analysis makes it possible to determine its reliability for both correlated and uncorrelated latent variables and in the situation of correlated and uncorrelated measurement errors. In factor models, the assessment of convergent and discriminant validity is made on the basis of the coefficients of the average variance extracted (AVE) and the values of the squares of correlations between latent variables. The following measures of relevance can be distinguished (Fornell & Larcker, 1981; MacKenzie et al., 2011):

Convergent validity: AVE values are greater than or equal to 0.5—the average variance extracted (AVE) is a measure of the amount of variance that is extracted by a construct relative to the amount of variance caused by measurement error.

$$AVE = \frac{\sum_{i=1}^{k} \lambda_i^2}{\sum_{i=1}^{k} \lambda_i^2 + \sum_{i=1}^{k} Var(e_i)}$$

Where:

k—number of test items
λ_i—factor load of the *i*-th variable
$Var(e_i)$—variance of error of the *i*-th variable

In our study, Cronbach's alpha for all the constructs was greater than 0.8 which is acceptable (George & Mallery, 2016). It can also be read from Table 4.5 that all constructs meet the aforementioned requirement that AVE values should be greater than 0.5, confirming convergent validity. The sustainability constructs were derived from and confirmed by earlier studies: (Das, 2018; Le et al., 2022; Mardani et al., 2020; Tundys & Wiśniewski, 2023). The validity of the resilience of the company's supply chain to disruption construct has been confirmed in earlier studies (Kędzia & Staniec, 2022; Ponomarov, 2012), the validity of three constructs describing SCRES abilities has so far not.

- Discriminant validity: the AVE values are greater than the values of the squares of the correlations between the constructs. This is due to the assumption that discriminant accuracy occurs if a latent variable explains more variation with its own indicators than with other latent variables in the model.

Table 4.5 Values of Cronbach's alpha and AVE coefficients

Latent Constructs	Cronbach's alpha	AVE
Sustainable supply chain—a process view (SSC1)	0.939	0.755
Sustainable development practices—External (SSC2)	0.851	0.588
Sustainable development practices—Internal (SSC3)	0.877	0.637
The ability of the company's supply chain to anticipate risks (RSC1)	0.920	0.747
The ability of the company's supply chain to respond to disruption (RSC2)	0.928	0.765
The ability of a company's supply chain to recover from a disruption (RSC3)	0.928	0.763
The resilience of the company's supply chain to disruption (RSC4)	0.952	0.768

Table 4.6 Values of squares of correlation coefficients (CS) between latent constructs

	SSC1	SSC2	SSC3	RSC1	RSC2	RSC3	RSC4
SSC1	1						
SSC2	0.363	1					
SSC3	0.222	0.131	1				
RSC1	0.587	0.328	0.392	1			
RSC2	0.530	0.287	0.345	0.720	1		
RSC3	0.500	0.223	0.306	0.775	0.713	1	
RSC4	0.500	0.276	0.320	0.704	0.687	0.729	1

Table 4.6 shows the values of the squares of the correlation coefficients between the latent constructs (CS—correlation squares). It should be noted that in the vast majority of cases the AVE values for a given construct are higher than the CS values for individual construct pairs. Higher CS values can be seen between supply chain resilience constructs. Only for the pair RSC1 and RSC3 the value of the square of the correlation coefficient is slightly higher than the AVE value for these constructs (CS = 0.775 > 0.747 (0.763) = AVE).

The use of CFA allowed to determine which of the observable variables (individual questions) most strongly defined the related constructs—exogenous and endogenous latent variables, which resulted in their further reduction. Only those variables that correlated most strongly with a given latent factor were accepted for structural model estimation.

4.3.4 Structural Equation Modeling (SEM)

The created theoretical constructs are now considered to be a linear combination of the observable variables. Structural modeling was further applied to estimate the interrelationships between the latent variables presented. The main objective of the study was how the elements of a sustainable supply chain affect the elements of resilience in the supply chain—the research model is presented in Fig. 4.3.

The model presented here assumes that the elements that make up a sustainable supply chain influence the elements that make up the constructs associated with supply chain resilience. Thus, the study will examine the following specific hypotheses:

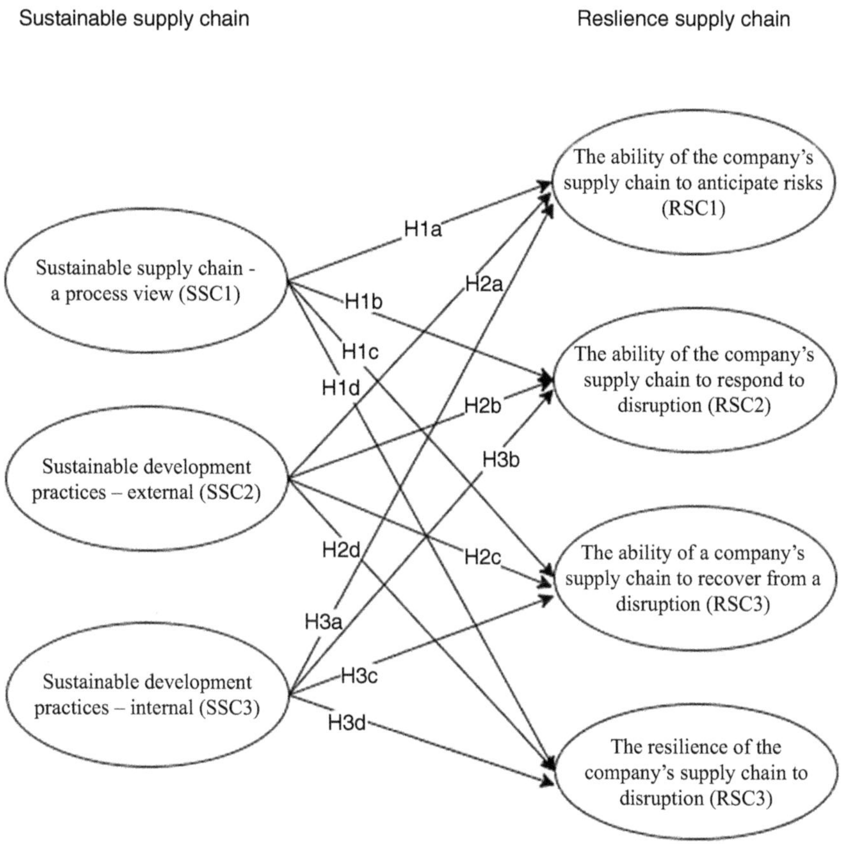

Fig. 4.3 Theoretical research model

- H1a—Sustainable supply chain—a process view (SSC1) affects the ability of the company's supply chain to anticipate risks (RSC1)
- H1b—Sustainable supply chain—a process view (SSC1) affects the ability of the ability of the company's supply chain to respond to disruptions (RSC2)
- H1c—Sustainable supply chain—a process view (SSC1) affects the ability of a company's supply chain to recover from a disruption (RSC3)
- H1d—Sustainable supply chain—a process view (SSC1) affects the resilience of the company's supply chain to disruption (RSC4)

- H2a—Sustainable development practices—external (SSC2) affects the ability of the company's supply chain to anticipate risks (RSC1)
- H2b—Sustainable development practices—external (SSC2) affects the ability of the ability of the company's supply chain to respond to disruptions (RSC2)
- H2c—Sustainable development practices—external (SSC2) affects the ability of a company's supply chain to recover from a disruption (RSC3)
- H2d—Sustainable development practices—external (SSC2) affects the resilience of the company's supply chain to disruption (RSC4)
- H3a—Sustainable development practices—internal (SSC3) affects the ability of the company's supply chain to anticipate risks (RSC1)
- H3b—Sustainable development practices—internal (SSC3) affects the ability of the ability of the company's supply chain to respond to disruptions (RSC2)
- H3c—Sustainable development practices—internal (SSC3) affects the ability of a company's supply chain to recover from a disruption (RSC3)
- H3d—Sustainable development practices—internal (SSC3) affects the resilience of the company's supply chain to disruption (RSC4)

The model parameter estimation conducted showed that almost all of the calculated path coefficients of the structural model were statistically significant, with a *p*-value below 0.01 (Table 4.7).

Table 4.7 shows the parameters of the examined structural model for the selected pathways. A stronger influence occurs where the path coefficient value is greater. For the analyzed constructs, Sustainable supply chain—a process view (SSC1) has the strongest impact on supply chain resilience constructs (0.531 path for RSC1, 0.516 path for RSC2, 0.552 path for RSC3, 0.499 path for RSC4). The Sustainable development practices—internal (SSC3) construct was found to have a smaller effect on RSC constructs (values around 0.3) and the Sustainable development practices—external (SSC2) construct had the smallest effect on RSC constructs (less than 0.2). The process approach (SSC1) has the greatest impact on building supply chain resilience. It's about looking at the supply chain as a sequence of consecutive processes, which yields greater impact than external and internal practices implemented at individual

Table 4.7 Structural parameters of the analyzed structural model

Path	Path coefficient	Statistic t
SSC1->(PV1)	0.842*	61.284
SSC1->(PV2)	0.906*	97.826
SSC1->(PV3)	0.926*	116.492
SSC1->(PV5)	0.826*	55.565
SSC1->(PV7)	0.846*	62.712
SSC2->(SDE2)	0.787*	37.526
SSC2->(SDE3)	0.789*	37.830
SSC2->(SDE5)	0.752*	32.821
SSC2->(SDE8)	0.746*	32.115
SSC3->(SDI8)	0.687*	27.498
SSC3->(SDI9)	0.681*	26.900
SSC3->(SDI12)	0.871*	60.083
SSC3->(SDI13)	0.904*	69.619
RSC1->(AR1)	0.843*	63.088
RSC1->(AR2)	0.877*	79.913
RSC1->(AR4)	0.869*	75.245
RSC1->(AR5)	0.866*	73.556
RSC2->(RD1)	0.871*	76.877
RSC2->(RD2)	0.840*	61.897
RSC2->(RD3)	0.886*	86.409
RSC2->(RD4)	0.904*	101.129
RSC3->(RFD1)	0.867*	74.181
RSC3->(RFD2)	0.882*	83.406
RSC3->(RFD3)	0.855*	68.391
RSC3->(RFD4)	0.888*	87.563
RSC4->(RSCD1)	0.885*	87.930
RSC4->(RSCD2)	0.866*	75.559
RSC4->(RSCD3)	0.849*	67.157
RSC4->(RSCD4)	0.881*	85.428
RSC4->(RSCD5)	0.908*	108.658
RSC4->(RSCD6)	0.872*	79.050
SSC1->RSC1	0.531*	13.895
SSC2->RSC1	0.134*	3.356
SSC3->RSC1	0.328*	9.764
SSC1->RSC2	0.516*	12.681
SSC2->RSC2	0.115*	2.699
SSC3->RSC2	0.302*	8.463
SSC1->RSC3	0.552*	13.001
SSC2->RSC3	0.039	0.872
SSC3->RSC3	0.279*	7.396
SSC1->RSC4	0.499*	12.093
SSC2->RSC4	0.121*	2.796
SSC3->RSC4	0.287*	7.938

Indicating significance at *1%

links in the supply chain and in terms of sustainability only and not in terms of the whole chain. Recent disruptions have shown that they spread through supply chains, disrupting subsequent processes with a domino effect or ripple effect. The results of the study indicate that the implementation of sustainable principles is effective for building resilience if the implementation takes place in subsequent processes of the supply chain simultaneously.

All but one of the pathways proved to be statistically significant (sufficiently large *t*-test value with a concomitant small p-value<0.01). Only the pathway between SSC2 and RSC3 proved to be non-significant. Thus, all hypotheses except hypothesis H2c (Sustainable development practices—external, SSC2) affect the ability of a company's supply chain to recover from a disruption (RSC3) were confirmed. The only unconfirmed hypothesis (H2c) may be due to the fact that researched companies do not engage in sustainable joint activities with suppliers to strengthen the resilience of the entire supply chain, nor do they improve processes with them—they do the improvements themselves, but they do not go beyond their own company. Additionally, they are not yet fully aware of what impact reporting of ESG indicators can have on resilience—this is not yet required by law. While respondents associate sustainable external practices with having the ability of the company's supply chain to anticipate risks or to respond to disruption, they do not see a connection of the impact of sustainable external practices on the ability of a company's supply chain to recover from a disruption. On the basis of such results, it can also be concluded that sustainable external practices may be insufficient to build the resilience of the supply chain in the post-disruption phase.

All the relationships from SEM model are shown in the Fig. 4.4.

4.3.5 Model Evaluation

To evaluate the SEM model, it is suggested that a minimum of four tests of model fit should be satisfied with the acceptability and the compatibility of the model (Kline, 1998; Weitzl et al., 2017; Hair et al., 2021). Table 4.8 shows the main tests that are used to evaluate the structural

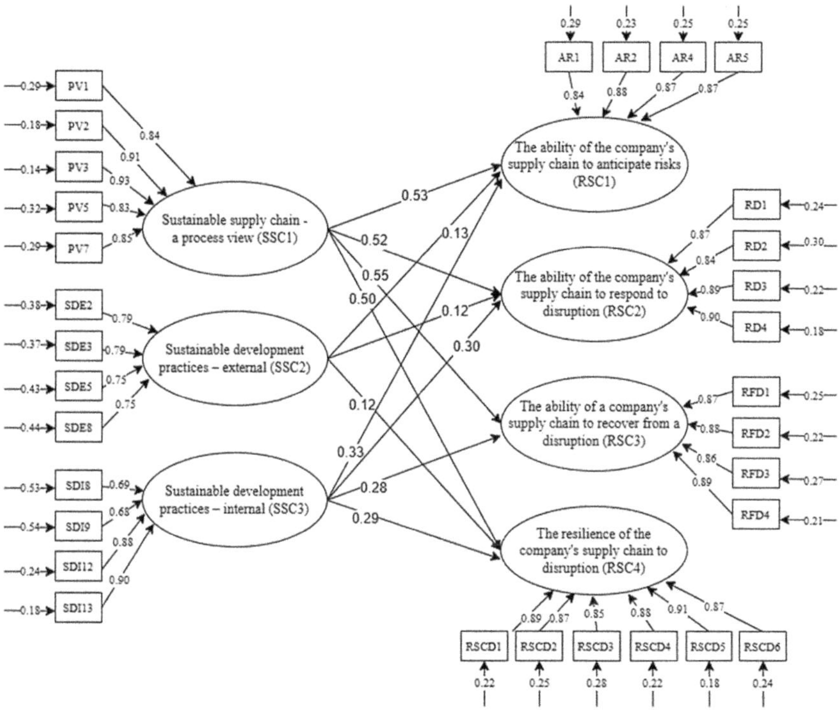

Fig. 4.4 The impact of sustainability supply chain on supply chain resilience—SEM model

Table 4.8 Fit statistics of the measurement model

Fit index	Value	Acceptable value
χ^2/df	3.82	≤ 5
Gamma index of the population	0.937	≥ 0.9
GFI (Goodness of fit index)	0.904	≥ 0.9
AGFI (adjusted goodness of fit index)	0.865	≥ 0.8
RMSEA (root mean square of approximation)	0.076	≤ 0.08
CFI (comparative fit index)	0.904	≥ 0.8

equation model: chi-squared, GFI, AGFI, CFI, Gamma index of the population and RMSEA.

Considering the results from the presented Table 4.8, it can be concluded that the analyzed model has been correctly verified. The ratio of index χ^2 to the number of degrees of freedom was 3.82 (less than 5—Ullman, 2001, Schumacker & Lomax, 2004). The goodness of fit index GFI showed that the model explained 90.4% of the real covariances. On the other hand, the population gamma index was 0.937 and its 90% confidence interval was (0.925, 0.948). These are acceptable measures according to the accepted literature (Segars & Grover, 1993), but the higher the index, the better the measure of fit. Similarly, the root mean square error of approximation (RMSEA) was 0.076—assumed to be below 0.08 (Steiger & Lind, 1980). Furthermore, the normalized Bentler–Bonett index—a CFI of 0.906, was at an appropriate level (CFI>0.8, Bentler & Bonett, 1980).

Given the structural model fit indices and the significance of the model's path coefficients presented earlier, the hypotheses (except for one H2c) can be positively verified. Thus, the elements that make up a sustainable supply chain affect the elements that make up a resilient supply chain.

4.3.6 Structural Equation Modeling (SEM) with Groups (Company Size)

In this subsection, the study of the impact of sustainable supply chain elements on supply chain resilience elements will be repeated but with groupings by company size (Table 4.1). The first analyzed group will be enterprises classified as medium-sized, with 51–250 employees. The second group will be enterprises larger than 250 employees.

The analyzed model will refer to the theoretical model presented earlier in Fig. 4.2. The same hypotheses will be examined taking into account the size of the company. The results of the conducted study can be seen in Table 4.9.

The results by company size (Table 4.9) are markedly different from the results presented earlier for all surveyed companies overall (Table 4.7).

Table 4.9 Structural parameters (only hypothesis) of the analyzed structural models

Path	Path coefficient	Statistic t
Model for medium-sized companies		
SSC1->RSC1	-1.574*	-3.844
SSC2->RSC1	2.527*	5.850
SSC3->RSC1	0.212	1.651
SSC1->RSC2	-2.042*	-4.195
SSC2->RSC2	3.011*	5.908
SSC3->RSC2	0.168	1.101
SSC1->RSC3	-2.508*	-4.428
SSC2->RSC3	0.094	0.534
SSC3->RSC3	3.508*	5.923
SSC1->RSC4	-2.591*	-4.396
SSC2->RSC4	3.671*	5.958
SSC3->RSC4	0.098	0.533
Model for large companies		
SSC1->RSC1	-4.466*	-8.445
SSC2->RSC1	0,493	0,565
SSC3->RSC1	5.299*	12.840
SSC1->RSC2	-5.582*	-9.032
SSC2->RSC2	0.424	0.664
SSC3->RSC2	6.508*	13.877
SSC1->RSC3	5.459*	11.585
SSC2->RSC3	0.506	0.482
SSC3->RSC3	-5.561*	-13.514
SSC1->RSC4	-6.281*	-9.425
SSC2->RSC4	0.418	0.533
SSC3->RSC4	7.235*	14.724

Indicating significance at *1%

In addition to the path that turned out to be statistically insignificant, SSC2-> RSC3 (hypothesis H2c) for medium-sized companies also turned out to be statistically insignificant between SSC3->RSC1, SSC3->RSC2 and SSC3->RSC4. This means less impact of the sustainable development practices—internal aspects on the ability of the company's supply chain to anticipate risks, the ability of the company's supply chain to respond to disruptions, and the resilience of the company's supply chain to disruption. In medium-sized companies, managers are not yet aware of how and why to build resilience of the entire supply chain, and there is no internal pressure in building resilience.

In contrast, for large companies as less relevant in the study came out paths on the impact of sustainable supply chain—a process view on the elements that make up supply chain resilience, so these were paths: SSC2->RSC1, SSC2->RSC2, SSC2->RSC3 and SSC2->RSC4. This may be due to the fact that in large companies' external practices are required but only for individual organizations and not always throughout the supply chain therefore. Consequently, it may hinder building supply chain resilience.

Building resilience in sustainable supply chain has a greater impact when viewed from the perspective of the entire supply chain (looking at the chain as a whole) than sustainability practices from the perspective of just the links in the supply chain. There will be better results in building resilience if all stakeholders of the entire chain are included in the process of building resilience and not just the leader. The validation of the model shows how important a process approach and a holistic view are in building resilience in a sustainable supply chain. A strong awareness of the necessary sustainable supply chain practices and aspects to implement, together with linking them to the requirements of a resilient chain, can result in a positive new business strategy.

This approach certainly requires significant awareness of all supply chain stakeholders. It is puzzling that despite recent global black swan disruptions, knowledge and the need to build resilience in cooperation across the entire supply chain maybe still not obvious possibly because companies lack adequate knowledge management capabilities in the post-disruption phase or they are still in the learning process following crises, the effects of which are still appearing and are difficult to assess. Confirming this conclusion with certainty would require further research.

Building simultaneously sustainable and resilient supply chains is not an easy challenge. It requires a high degree of knowledge, commitment, and awareness among all supply chain stakeholders. SSC 2.0 is based on sustainability factors and enablers, while implementing resilience and risk elimination. The drivers of supply chain sustainability risks need to be clearly and quickly identified in order to mitigate them and continually make the supply chain more resilient to crisis events.

4.3.7 Conclusions and Futures Directions

To know the context of a company's operation in the VUCA (volatility, uncertainty, complexity, and ambiguity) world, it is first necessary to map the structure of its supply chain and supplier-buyer interrelationships. Learning about the flow processes and resources as well as dependencies in the supply chain determines supply chain risk management process. This should be done in a holistic way, i.e. taking into account the supply chain risk (supply risk, demand risk, operational risk) as well as the sustainable supply chain risk (environmental risk, social risk, financial risk), both in the context of internally and externally driven uncertainty.

The problem of resilience of sustainable supply chains is extremely complex. The multifaceted nature of the relationships and determinants affecting risk vulnerability makes it difficult to create universal models to describe and define actions that support the resilience of sustainable supply chains. The new supply chain paradigm of SSC2.0 provides a theoretical framework to identify the various environmental factors that both increase risk and, on the other hand, allow for more effective management of different supply chain strategies.

Understanding the issue of building sustainable and resilient supply chains should be based on comprehensive risk assessment as well as sustainable and resilience practices implementation aimed at risk treatment and monitoring. Thus, SSC 2.0 is able to anticipate threats, adequately respond to them, recover from various crisis, and sustain growth. As research results show, implementing external and internal sustainable practices stimulates strengthening the resilience of supply chains to disruptions in three dimensions: before the disruption, during the disruption and after the disruption. It is a source of important knowledge for business practice on how to transform sustainable supply chains into sustainable and resilient supply chains.

The sustainability risk management supports the resilience of the supply chain to environmental, social, and economic disruptions. Awareness of this relationship should encourage companies to increase their efforts to integrate multidimensional activities in supply chains and improve them toward reducing vulnerability to threats, enhancing adaptation to the turbulent environment and ensuring the business continuity of value adding processes.

The research showed that there are significant differences in the perception and impact of sustainable supply chains on their resilience. Among other things, in medium-sized companies, managers are not yet aware of how and why to build resilience of the entire supply chain, and there is no internal pressure in building resilience. Further lines of research could include analyses disaggregated not only by company size but, for example, by industry or geographic location.

Contemporary global crises caused by threats such as the COVID-19 pandemic and the war in Ukraine bring multidimensional effects, the measurement and evaluation of which goes beyond traditional understanding. These experiences show that resilient relationships with (first and further tiers) suppliers and clients are becoming key to the sustainable development of enterprises. Therefore, building sustainable and resilient supply chains requires going beyond the boundaries of a single company through developing joint efforts that compromise the goals of various parties. In this way, strengthened by sustainable and resilient practices flow processes (from raw material suppliers to end customers) are ready to respond to black swans and effectively mitigate ripple effects.

References

Aaker, D., & Bagozzi, R. (1979). Unobservable variables in Structural Equation Modeling with application in industrial selling. *Journal of Marketing Research, XVI*, 147.

Al-Humaiqani, M. M., & Al-Ghamdi, S. G. (2023). Assessing the built environment's reflectivity, flexibility, resourcefulness, and rapidity resilience qualities against climate change impacts from the perspective of different stakeholders. *Sustainability, 15*(6), 5055.

Ali, A., Mahfouz, A., & Arisha, A. (2017). Analysing supply chain resilience: Integrating the constructs in a concept mapping framework via a systematic literature review. *Supply Chain Management: An International Journal, 22*(1), 16–39.

Allaoui, H., Guo, Y., & Sarkis, J. (2019). Decision support for collaboration planning in sustainable supply chains. *Journal of Cleaner Production, 229*, 761–774.

Ampratwum, G., Osei-Kyei, R., & Tam, V. W. (2022). Exploring the concept of public-private partnership in building critical infrastructure resilience against unexpected events: A systematic review. *International Journal of Critical Infrastructure Protection, 100556*, 1471–4175.

Bag, S., Anand, N., & Pandey, K. K. (2017). Green supply chain management model for sustainable manufacturing practices. In *Green supply chain management for sustainable business practice* (pp. 153–189). IGI Global.

Bentler, P. M. (1990). Comparative fit indexes in structural models. *Psychological Bulletin, 107*(2), 238–246.

Bentler, P. M. (1995). *EQS structural equations program manual.* Multivariate Software.

Bentler, P. M., & Bonett, D. G. (1980). Significance tests and goodness of fit in the analysis of covariance structures. *Psychological Bulletin, 88*, 588–606.

Berr, M., Beloin-Saint-Pierre, D., Hischier, R., Hool, A., & Wäger, P. (2022). SPOTTER: Assessing supply disruption impacts along the supply chain within life cycle sustainability assessment. *Cleaner Logistics and Supply Chain, 4*, 100063.

Bielby, W. T., & Hauser, R. M. (1977). Structural equation models. *Annual Review of Sociology*, 137–161.

Bollen, K. A. (1989). *Structural equations with latent variables.* Wiley.

Brown, T. A., & Moore, M. T. (2012). Confirmatory factor analysis. *Handbook of Structural Equation Modeling, 361*, 379.

Browne, M. W., & Cudeck, R. (1993). Alternative ways of assessing model fit. In K. A. Bollen & J. S. Long (Eds.), *Testing structural equation models* (pp. 136–162). Sage.

Busch, N. E., & Givens, A. D. (2013). Achieving resilience in disaster management: The role of public-private partnerships. *Journal of Strategic Security, 6*(2), 1–19.

Calzolari, T., Genovese, A., & Brint, A. (2022). Circular economy indicators for supply chains: A systematic literature review. *Environmental and Sustainability Indicators, 13*, 100–160.

Carissimi, M. C., Creazza, A., & Colicchia, C. (2023). Crossing the chasm: Investigating the relationship between sustainability and resilience in supply chain management. *Cleaner Logistics and Supply Chain*, 100098.

Chowdhury, R., Heng, K., Shawon, M. S. R., Goh, G., Okonofua, D., Ochoa-Rosales, C., Gonzalez-Jaramillo, V., Bhuiya, A., Reidpath, D., Prathapan, S., Shahzad, S., & Global Dynamic Interventions Strategies for COVID-19 Collaborative Group. (2020). Dynamic interventions to control COVID-19 pandemic: A multivariate prediction modelling study comparing 16 worldwide countries. *European Journal of Epidemiology, 35*, 389–399.

Chowdhury, M. T., Sarkar, A., Paul, S. K., & Moktadir, M. A. (2020). A case study on strategies to deal with the impacts of COVID-19 pandemic in the food and beverage industry. *Operations Management Research*, 1–13.

Cimprich, A., Young, S. B., Helbig, C., Gemechu, E. D., Thorenz, A., Tuma, A., & Sonnemann, G. (2017). Extension of geopolitical supply risk methodology: Characterization model applied to conventional and electric vehicles. *Journal of Cleaner Production, 162*, 754–763.

Dai, J., & Blackhurst, J. (2012). A four-phase AHP–QFD approach for supplier assessment: A sustainability perspective. *International Journal of Production Research, 50*(19), 5474–5490.

Daryanian, N., Kazemi, A., & Adibi, M. A. (2023). A fuzzy robust stochastic model for designing a pharmaceutical supply chain with sustainability and resiliency dimensions. *Applied Soft Computing, 143*, 110357.

Das, D. (2018). The impact of sustainable supply chain management practices on firm performance: Lessons from Indian organizations. *Journal of Cleaner Production, 203*, 179–196.

Das, K., & Posinasetti, N. R. (2015). Addressing environmental concerns in closed loop supply chain design and planning. *International Journal of Production Economics, 163*, 34–47.

Davidson, K., Nguyen, T. M. P., Beilin, R., & Briggs, J. (2019). The emerging addition of resilience as a component of sustainability in urban policy. *Cities, 92*, 1–9.

de Oliveira, U. R., Espindola, L. S., da Silva, I. R., da Silva, I. N., & Rocha, H. M. (2018). A systematic literature review on green supply chain management: Research implications and future perspectives. *Journal of Cleaner Production, 187*, 537–561.

Dey, P. K., Yang, G. L., Malesios, C., De, D., & Evangelinos, K. (2021). Performance management of supply chain sustainability in small and medium-sized enterprises using a combined structural equation modelling and data envelopment analysis. *Computational Economics, 58*, 573–613.

Dillman, D. A., Smyth, J. D., & Christian, L. M. (2014). *Internet, phone, mail, and mixed-mode surveys: The tailored design method*. John Wiley & Sons.

Dolgui, A., & Ivanov, D. (2021). Ripple effect and supply chain disruption management: New trends and research directions. *International Journal of Production Research, 59*(1), 102–109.

Dolgui, A., Ivanov, D., & Sokolov, B. (2018). Ripple effect in the supply chain: An analysis and recent literature. *International Journal of Production Research, 56*(1–2), 414–430.

Elluru, S., Gupta, H., Kaur, H., & Singh, S. P. (2019). Proactive and reactive models for disaster resilient supply chain. *Annals of Operations Research, 283*, 199–224.

Fahimnia, B., Pournader, M., Siemsen, E., Bendoly, E., & Wang, C. (2019). Behavioral operations and supply chain management–a review and literature mapping. *Decision Sciences, 50*(6), 1127–1183.

Fornell, C., & Larcker, D. F. (1981). Evaluating structural equation models with unobservable variables and measurement error. *Journal of Marketing Research, 18*(1), 39–50.

Foroozesh, N., Karimi, B., Mousavi, S. M., & Mojtahedi, M. (2023). A hybrid decision-making method using robust programming and interval-valued fuzzy sets for sustainable-resilient supply chain network design considering circular economy and technology levels. *Journal of Industrial Information Integration, 33*, 100440.

Frederico, G. F. (2023). Rethinking strategic sourcing during disruptions: A resilience-driven process contribution to knowledge on supply chains. *Knowledge and Process Management, 30*(1), 83–86.

George, D., & Mallery, P. (2016). *IBM SPSS statistics 23 step by step: A simple guide and reference*. Routledge.

Golan, M. S., Jernegan, L. H., & Linkov, I. (2020). Trends and applications of resilience analytics in supply chain modeling: Systematic literature review in the context of the COVID-19 pandemic. *Environment Systems and Decisions, 40*(2), 222–243.

Haddadsisakht, A., & Ryan, S. M. (2018). Closed-loop supply chain network design with multiple transportation modes under stochastic demand and uncertain carbon tax. *International Journal of Production Economics, 195*, 118–131.

Hair, J. F., Hult, G. T. M., Ringle, C. M., Sarstedt, M., Danks, N. P., & Ray, S. (2021). *Evaluation of the structural model. In Partial least squares structural equation modeling (PLS-SEM) using R. Classroom Companion: Business*. Springer. https://doi.org/10.1007/978-3-030-80519-7_6

He, L., Wu, Z., Xiang, W., Goh, M., Xu, Z., Song, W., Ming, X., & Wu, X. (2021). A novel Kano-QFD-DEMATEL approach to optimise the risk resilience solution for sustainable supply chain. *International Journal of Production Research, 59*(6), 1714–1735.

Hendiani, S., Liao, H., & Jabbour, C. J. C. (2022). A new sustainability indicator for supply chains: Theoretical and practical contribution towards sustainable operations. *International Journal of Logistics Research and Applications, 25*(4–5), 384–409.

Holgado, M., & Niess, A. (2023). Resilience in global supply chains: Analysis of responses, recovery actions and strategic changes triggered by major disruptions. *Supply Chain Management: An International Journal.*

Hou, G., Wang, Y., & Xin, B. (2019). A coordinated strategy for sustainable supply chain management with product sustainability, environmental effect and social reputation. *Journal of Cleaner Production, 228*, 1143–1156.

Hu, L., & Bentler, P. M. (1999). Cutoff criteria for fit indices in covariance structure analysis: Conventional criteria versus new alternatives. *Structural Equation Modeling, 6*(1), 1–55.

Ivanov, D. (2022). Viable supply chain model: Integrating agility, resilience and sustainability perspectives—Lessons from and thinking beyond the COVID-19 pandemic. *Annals of Operations Research, 319*(1), 1411–1431.

Ivanov, D., Dolgui, A., Blackhurst, J. V., & Choi, T. M. (2023). Toward supply chain viability theory: From lessons learned through COVID-19 pandemic to viable ecosystems. *International Journal of Production Research, 61*(8), 2402–2415.

Izadikhah, M., Azadi, M., Toloo, M., & Hussain, F. K. (2021). Sustainably resilient supply chains evaluation in public transport: A fuzzy chance-constrained two-stage DEA approach. *Applied Soft Computing, 113*, 107879.

Jabbarzadeh, A., Fahimnia, B., & Sabouhi, F. (2018). Resilient and sustainable supply chain design: Sustainability analysis under disruption risks. *International Journal of Production Research, 56*(17), 5945–5968.

Jaggi, C. K., Jain, R., & Verma, M. (2018). Impact of demonetization on supply chain in Indian context. *Supply Chain Management, 12*(1), 1–10.

Jenatabadi, H. S., & Ismail, N. A. (2014). Application of structural equation modelling for estimating airline performance. *Journal of Air Transport Management, 40*, 25–33.

Jöreskog, K. G. (1973). A general method for estimating a linear structural equation system. In A. S. Goldberger & O. D. Duncan (Eds.), *Structural equation models in the social sciences* (pp. 255–284). Seminar Press.

Jöreskog, K. G., & Sörbom, D. (1993). *LISREL VIII: Users' reference guide.* Scientific Software International.

Kaplan, D. (2001). *International Encyclopedia of the Social & Behavioral Sciences*. Elsevier.

Kaur, H., & Singh, S. P. (2019). Sustainable procurement and logistics for disaster resilient supply chain. *Annals of Operations Research, 283*, 309–354.

Kędzia, G., & Staniec, I. (2022). The impact of supplier involvement in product development on supply chain resilience: The mediating role of communication. *International Journal for Quality Research, 16*(4), 973–999.

Khot, S., & Thiagarajan, S. (2019). Resilience and sustainability of supply chain management in the Indian automobile industry. *International Journal of Data and Network Science, 3*(4), 339–348.

Kline R. B. (1998). *Principles and practice of structural equation modeling*. Guilford.

Korol, J. (2005). *Modele równań strukturalnych i sieci neuronowe w modelowaniu rozwoju zrównoważonego*. Akademickie Wydawnictwo Ekonomiczne.

Krzysztofik, M., Fleury, M., During, N., & Scheepens, W. (2021). *Wytyczne do raportowania ESG*. Przewodnik dla spółek notowanych na GPW. https://www.gpw.pl/pub/GPW/ESG/Wytyczne_do_raportowania_ESG.pdf. Accessed 17 June 2023

Larrea-Gallegos, G., Benetto, E., Marvuglia, A., & Gutiérrez, T. N. (2022). Sustainability, resilience and complexity in supply networks: A literature review and a proposal for an integrated agent-based approach. *Sustainable Production and Consumption, 30*, 946–961.

Le, T. T., Kieu, X. H., Behl, A., & Pereira, V. (2022). Building up more sustainable food supply chains: Implications for sustainable development. *Journal of Cleaner Production, 378*, 134650.

López-Castro, L. F., & Solano-Charris, E. L. (2021). Integrating resilience and sustainability criteria in the supply chain network design. A systematic literature review. *Sustainability, 13*(19), 10925.

Ma, M., Wang, N., Mu, W., & Zhang, L. (2022). The instrumentality of public-private partnerships for achieving sustainable development goals. *Sustainability, 14*(21), 13756.

MacKenzie, S. B., Podsakoff, P. M., & Podsakoff, N. P. (2011). Construct measurement and validation procedures in MIS and behavioral research: Integrating new and existing techniques. *MIS Quarterly, 35*(2), 293–334.

Manning, L., Birchmore, I., & Morris, W. (2020). Swans and elephants: A typology to capture the challenges of food supply chain risk assessment. *Trends in Food Science & Technology, 106*, 288–297.

Manurung, H., Yudoko, G., & Okdinawati, L. (2023). A conceptual framework of supply chain resilience towards sustainability through a service-dominant logic perspective. *Heliyon, 9*, e13901.

Marchese, D., Reynolds, E., Bates, M. E., Morgan, H., Clark, S. S., & Linkov, I. (2018). Resilience and sustainability: Similarities and differences in environmental management applications. *Science of the Total Environment, 613*, 1275-1283.

Mardani, A., Kannan, D., Hooker, R. E., Ozkul, S., Alrasheedi, M., & Tirkolaee, E. B. (2020). Evaluation of green and sustainable supply chain management using structural equation modelling: A systematic review of the state of the art literature and recommendations for future research. *Journal of Cleaner Production, 249*, 119383.

McIntosh, A. R., & Misic, B. (2013). Multivariate statistical analyses for neuroimaging data. In S. T. Fiske (Ed.), *Annual review of psychology* (Vol. 64, p. 499).

Mio, C., Fasan, M., & Scarpa, F. (2023). Materiality investor perspectives on utilities' ESG performance. An empirical analysis of ESG factors and cost of equity. *Utilities Policy, 82*, 101555.

Mohammed, A., Zubairu, N., Yazdani, M., Diabat, A., & Li, X. (2023). Resilient supply chain network design without lagging sustainability responsibilities. *Applied Soft Computing, 140*, 110225.

Munir, M., Jajja, M. S. S., & Chatha, K. A. (2022). Capabilities for enhancing supply chain resilience and responsiveness in the COVID-19 pandemic: Exploring the role of improvisation, anticipation, and data analytics capabilities. *International Journal of Operations & Production Management, 42*(10), 1576–1604.

Negri, M., Cagno, E., Colicchia, C., & Sarkis, J. (2021). Integrating sustainability and resilience in the supply chain: A systematic literature review and a research agenda. *Business Strategy and the Environment, 30*(7), 2858–2886.

Netemeyer, R., Bearden, W., & Sharma, S. (2003). *Scaling procedures*. Sage Publications.

Nunnally, J. (1978). *Psychometric theory*. McGraw Hill.

Ocicka, B., Mierzejewska, W., & Brzeziński, J. (2022). Creating supply chain resilience during and post-COVID-19 outbreak: The organizational ambidexterity perspective. *Decision, 49*(1), 129–151.

Ongkowijoyo, G., & Christian, T. F. (2020). Adaptive supply chain management under severe supply chain disruption: Evidence from Indonesia. *Journal of Distribution Science, 18*(11), 91–103.

Paul, S. K., Chowdhury, P., Moktadir, M. A., & Lau, K. H. (2021). Supply chain recovery challenges in the wake of COVID-19 pandemic. *Journal of Business Research, 136*, 316–329.

Paul, P. S., & Maiti, J. (2008). The synergic role of sociotechnical and personal characteristics on work injuries in mines. *Ergonomics, 51*, 737–767.

Paul, S. K., Moktadir, M. A., & Ahsan, K. (2023). Key supply chain strategies for the post-COVID-19 era: Implications for resilience and sustainability. *The International Journal of Logistics Management, 34*(4), 1165–1187.

Paulraj, A., Chen, I. J., & Blome, C. (2017). Motives and performance outcomes of sustainable supply chain management practices: A multi-theoretical perspective. *Journal of Business Ethics, 145*, 239–258.

Perera, H. N., Hurley, J., Fahimnia, B., & Reisi, M. (2019). The human factor in supply chain forecasting: A systematic review. *European Journal of Operational Research, 274*(2), 574–600.

Petljak, K. (2019). Green supply chain management practices in food retailing. *InterEULawEast: Journal for the International and European Law, Economics and Market Integrations, 6*(1), 61–82.

Ponomarov, S. (2012). *Antecedents and consequences of supply chain resilience: A dynamic capabilities perspective*. Doctoral Dissertation, University of Tennessee.

Queiroz, M. M., Ivanov, D., Dolgui, A., & Fosso Wamba, S. (2022). Impacts of epidemic outbreaks on supply chains: Mapping a research agenda amid the COVID-19 pandemic through a structured literature review. *Annals of Operations Research, 319*(1), 1159–1196.

Roostaie, S., Nawari, N., & Kibert, C. J. (2019). Sustainability and resilience: A review of definitions, relationships, and their integration into a combined building assessment framework. *Building and Environment, 154*, 132–144.

Saeed, M. A., & Kersten, W. (2017). Supply chain sustainability performance indicators: A content analysis based on published standards and guidelines. *Logistics Research, 10*(12), 1–19.

Sagan A. (2003a) Analiza rzetelności skal satysfakcji i lojalności. Statsoft. https://media.statsoft.pl/_old_dnn/downloads/rzetelnosc.pdf

Sagan, A. (2003b). Zmienne jakościowe w modelowaniu strukturalnym (w:) Analiza i prognozowanie zjawisk rynkowych o charakterze niemetrycznym (red. E. Gantar). Wydawnictwo Akademii Ekonomicznej w Katowicach, Katowice.

Sazvar, Z., Tafakkori, K., Oladzad, N., & Nayeri, S. (2021). A capacity planning approach for sustainable-resilient supply chain network design under uncertainty: A case study of vaccine supply chain. *Computers & Industrial Engineering, 159*, 107406.

Schumacker, R. E., & Lomax, R. G. (2004). *A beginner's guide to structural equation modeling*. Lawrence Erlbaum Associates.

Segars, A. H., & Grover, V. (1993). Re-examining perceived ease of use and usefulness: A confirmatory factor analysis. *MIS Quarterly, 17*(4), 517–525.

Settembre-Blundo, D., González-Sánchez, R., Medina-Salgado, S., & García-Muiña, F. E. (2021). Flexibility and resilience in corporate decision making: A new sustainability-based risk management system in uncertain times. *Global Journal of Flexible Systems Management, 22*(Suppl 2), 107–132.

Seuring, S., & Müller, M. (2008). From a literature review to a conceptual framework for sustainable supply chain management. *Journal of Cleaner Production, 16*(15), 1699–1710.

Sgarbossa, F., & Russo, I. (2017). A proactive model in sustainable food supply chain: Insight from a case study. *International Journal of Production Economics, 183*, 596–606.

Shashi, Centobelli, P., Cerchione, R., & Ertz, M. (2020). Managing supply chain resilience to pursue business and environmental strategies. *Business Strategy and the Environment, 29*(3), 1215–1246.

Silvestre, B. (2016). Sustainable supply chain management: Current debate and future directions. *Gestão & Produção, 23*, 235–249.

Singh, C. S., Soni, G., & Badhotiya, G. K. (2019). Performance indicators for supply chain resilience: Review and conceptual framework. *Journal of Industrial Engineering International, 15*, 105–117.

Sonnemann, G., Gemechu, E. D., Adibi, N., De Bruille, V., & Bulle, C. (2015). From a critical review to a conceptual framework for integrating the criticality of resources into Life Cycle Sustainability Assessment. *Journal of Cleaner Production, 94*, 20–34.

Sroka, W. (2010). *Wykorzystanie modelu równań strukturalnych do oceny czynników rozwoju przodujących gospodarstw karpackich*. Zeszyty Naukowe SERiA.

Staniec, I. (2018). Modelowanie równań strukturalnych w naukach o zarządzaniu. *Organizacja i Kierowanie, 2*, 181.

Steiger, J. H., & Lind, J. C. (1980). Statistically-based tests for the number of common factors. Paper presented at the Meeting of the Psychometric Society, Iowa City, IA.

Taghipour, A., & Beneteau-Piet, C. (2020). Sustainable supply chain management performance. *International Journal of Innovation, Management and Technology, 11*(6).

The Business Continuity Institute, Business continuity management good practice guidelines, part three, 2007.

Thun, J. (2010). Angles of integration: An empirical analysis of the alignment of Internet-Based information technology and global supply chain integration. *Journal of Supply Chain Management, 46*, 30–44.

Tsai, F. M., Bui, T. D., Tseng, M. L., Ali, M. H., Lim, M. K., & Chiu, A. S. (2021). Sustainable supply chain management trends in world regions: A data-driven analysis. *Resources, Conservation and Recycling, 167*, 105421.

Tseng, M. L., Ha, H. M., Tran, T. P. T., Bui, T. D., Chen, C. C., & Lin, C. W. (2022). Building a data-driven circular supply chain hierarchical structure: Resource recovery implementation drives circular business strategy. *Business Strategy and the Environment, 31*(5), 2082–2106.

Tundys, B. (2020, April). Evaluation of green supply chain-reference models approach. In *DIEM: Dubrovnik international economic meeting* (Vol. 5, No. 1, pp. 129–142). Sveučilište u Dubrovniku.

Tundys, B., & Wiśniewski, T. (2023). Triple bottom line aspects and sustainable supply chain resilience: A structural equation modelling approach. *Frontiers in Environmental Science, 11*, 1161437.

Tundys, B., Rzeczycki, A., & Fernando, Y. (2019). A framework for analysis of the supplier selection in green supply chain. *International Journal of Productivity and Quality Management, 28*(1), 40–67.

Ullman, J. B. (2001). Structural equation modeling. In B. G. Tabachnick & S. Fidell (Eds.), *Using multivariate statistics*. Allyn & Bacon.

Ullman, J. B., & Bentler, P. M. (2012). Structural equation modeling. In *Handbook of psychology* (2nd ed., p. 2).

Vergara, J. I. T., Martínez, J. A. S., & Salais-Fierro, T. E. (2023). Performance measurement of a Resilient-Sustainable Supply Chain through fuzzy multi-criteria techniques. *Computers & Industrial Engineering, 177*, 109059.

Vishwakarma, A., Dangayach, G. S., Meena, M. L., & Gupta, S. (2022). Analysing barriers of sustainable supply chain in apparel & textile sector: A hybrid ISM-MICMAC and DEMATEL approach. *Cleaner Logistics and Supply Chain, 5*, 100073.

Vroegindewey, R., & Hodbod, J. (2018). Resilience of agricultural value chains in developing country contexts: A framework and assessment approach. *Sustainability, 10*(4), 916.

Weitzl, W., Weitzl, W., & Berg. (2017). *Measuring electronic word-of-mouth effectiveness*. Springer Gabler.

Wieteska, G. (2018a). Business Impact Analysis of supply chain disruptions. In *Proceedings of the 8th international conference on management, economics and humanities (978-6-0982-3914-0)* (pp. 110–119). Diamond Scientific Publication.

Wieteska, G. (2018b). The domino effect-disruptions in supply chains. *LogForum, 14*(4), 495–506.

Wieteska, G. (2020). How to measure SCRES? – The perspective of flexibility and redundancy in relationships with suppliers. In A. Michałkiewicz & W. Mierzejewska (Eds.), *Contemporary organisation and management. Challenges and trends* (pp. 173–201). University of Lodz Publishing House.

Wieteska-Rosiak, B. (2017). Kierunki rozwoju gospodarczego miast w perspektywie adaptacji do zmian klimatu. *Studia Ekonomiczne,* (320), 61–74.

Worthington, R. L., & Whittaker, T. A. (2006). Scale development research: A content analysis and recommendations for best practices. *The Counseling Psychologist, 34*, 806–838.

Wright, S. (1921). Correlation and causation. *Journal of Agricultural Research, 20*(7), 557–585.

Wu, T., Zhang, L. G., & Ge, T. (2019). Managing financing risk in capacity investment under green supply chain competition. *Technological Forecasting and Social Change, 143*, 37–44.

Xu, S., Zhang, X., Feng, L., & Yang, W. (2020). Disruption risks in supply chain management: A literature review based on bibliometric analysis. *International Journal of Production Research, 58*(11), 3508–3526.

Yılmaz, Ö. F., Özçelik, G., & Yeni, F. B. (2021). Ensuring sustainability in the reverse supply chain in case of the ripple effect: A two-stage stochastic optimization model. *Journal of Cleaner Production, 282*, 124548.

Zavala-Alcívar, A., Verdecho, M. J., & Alfaro-Saiz, J. J. (2020a). A conceptual framework to manage resilience and increase sustainability in the supply chain. *Sustainability, 12*(16), 6300.

Zavala-Alcívar, A., Verdecho, M. J., & Alfaro-Saiz, J. J. (2020b). Resilient strategies and sustainability in agri-food supply chains in the face of high-risk events. In *Boosting collaborative networks 4.0: 21st IFIP WG 5.5 working conference on virtual enterprises, PRO-VE 2020, Valencia, Spain, November 23–25, 2020, proceedings 21* (pp. 560–570). Springer International Publishing.

Zhang, X., Li, R. Y. M., Sun, Z., Li, X., Samad, S., Comite, U., & Matac, L. M. (2022). Supply chain integration and its impact on operating performance: Evidence from Chinese online companies. *Sustainability, 14*(21), 14330.

Zhu, Q., & Krikke, H. (2020). Managing a sustainable and resilient perishable food supply chain (PFSC) after an outbreak. *Sustainability, 12*(12), 5004.

Index

A

Agility, adaptability and alignment (AAA), 33

C

Closed-loop supply chains (CLSC), vi, 40, 41, 47–48, 53, 59
Confirmatory Factor Analysis (CFA), 148, 153, 157–158, 162
Corporate Social Responsibility (CSR), 30, 36, 44, 45, 52, 56, 57, 59, 61, 156
COVID -19, v–vii, 16–18, 45, 54, 59, 92, 101–113, 144, 172

E

Environmental, social, and governance (ESG), vii, 1–20, 35, 36, 39, 59, 61, 139, 144–146, 166
  resilience in supply chain, 144
  risk factors, 6, 12
  risk in supply chain, 13
EU taxonomy, 1–11, 36, 59

G

Green supply chain, 13, 40, 42–43, 157

K

Key drivers of ESG risks, 4

P

Post-pandemic supply chains, 107

B. Tundys et al., *Sustainable Supply Chains 2.0*,
https://doi.org/10.1007/978-3-031-50337-5

R

Reliability analysis, 158–162
Risk in supply chain, 13
R-strategies, vi, 40, 46–47, 53, 59–61

S

Social and environmental performance in supply chain, 52
Social supply chains, 43–46
Structural equation modeling (SEM), 147–149, 151, 157, 162–170
Supply chain risk management (SCRM), 86, 89, 97, 100, 115, 171
Sustainable development, v–viii, 5, 9, 11, 14, 25–27, 35, 59, 100, 102, 106, 111, 113, 120, 140, 141, 145, 152, 164, 166, 169, 172
Sustainable resilient supply chain, vii, 142, 144–147, 170–172
Sustainable risk, 88, 94–96, 98–101
Sustainable supply chain framework, 36, 44, 55, 61
Sustainable supply chain resilience (SSCR), 139
Sustainable Supply Chain 2.0 (SSC 2.0), vii, 137–172

T

Triple bottom line (3BL), v, vii, 25–34, 36, 39, 40, 48–51, 59, 60, 94, 95, 98, 139

www.ingramcontent.com/pod-product-compliance
Ingram Content Group UK Ltd.
Pitfield, Milton Keynes, MK11 3LW, UK
UKHW020836290926
15470UKWH00004B/1374
* 9 7 8 3 0 3 1 5 0 3 3 6 8 *